Children with Special Needs in the Infants' School

After experience in the Civil Service, industry and the Forces, the author qualified as a teacher in the immediate post-war years of reconstruction and experiment. Her first seven years in the profession were spent teaching both Infant and Junior children in East London.

She was then appointed to the headship of a large Infants' school in another county. During the years as headmistress Miss Webb obtained an advanced qualification in education, and is now a Principal Lecturer in Education, concerned with the training of students for the teaching profession. In addition to her work with children the author has been engaged with adult education for the last twenty years—an interest which is reflected in her discussion of parent-teacher relationship.

Children with Special Needs in the Infants' School

LESLEY WEBB
Principal Lecturer in Education

FONTANA/COLLINS

First published by Colin Smythe 1967
First issued in Fontana Books 1969
Second Impression October 1971
Third Impression October 1972
Fourth Impression November 1974
Fifth Impression April 1977
Sixth Impression March 1979

Made and printed in Great Britain by
William Collins Sons & Co. Ltd, Glasgow

To my mentors, in gratitude

Acknowledgments

The author gratefully acknowledges the help of the following in the writing of this book:

Miss M. H. Bradley, M.A. (Cantab.) who was kind enough to read and comment on the first eight chapters, and whose comments were of great value in constructing the last two; Miss F. J. Howlett, who both allowed herself to be used as the 'sounding-board' of young teachers' needs, and was also of great assistance in the proofreading stage; and Miss G. D. Clark, H.M.I., who gave advice, support and encouragement throughout the whole enterprise, without which the writer might often have lost heart.

Contents

Important Note

Although the essential elements of each case discussed in the following pages are factual, all names and identifying detail have been changed in order to preserve anonymity for the parents and children whose needs have been discussed with the sole intention of helping others. Any resemblance of a case described in this book to one known to the reader is therefore entirely coincidental.

L.W.

Preface

(i)

Most teachers have to deal occasionally, and some often, with difficult children. Whether these children are described as maladjusted, delinquent, backward, underprivileged or simply as naughty they present teachers with problems of discipline, learning and social training which often seem, (and sometimes are), insoluble in the everyday classroom situation. Since there is an immense literature for most of the categories implied above, and much of it very useful to a teacher trying to understand the recalcitrant behaviour of a particular child, it might be asked why yet more should be written.

A justification for such a work as this is that most of the available literature deals with children in a situation other than that of school.[1] In the family circle, in the one-to-one relationship with doctor or therapist, in a special school, in a magistrate's eyes, or as a unit in a large sample used for research, a child is necessarily seen from a viewpoint very different from that of a teacher. Susan Isaacs reminded us long ago that a teacher should not attempt to act as a psychologist; more recently Charlotte Bühler has pointed out how different is the rôle of good teacher from that of good parent. Yet both have also said, and it is surely true, that a teacher who understands something of normal child development, who appreciates the importance of family relationships and patterns and who is familiar with fundamental principles of learning should be able to recognize some children as having special needs, and be able to help them in school.

A teacher is a specialist in her own right. Her special skill is the promotion of learning; and she cannot help a child if he is locked in his own unhappiness, handicapped by dullness, or so socially underprivileged that communication does not exist between them. The teacher must be able to recognize

---

[1] Notable exceptions are Charlotte Bühler's *'Childhood Problems and the Teacher'* (1953) and *'Children in the Nursery School'* by Dorothy May (1963).

these barriers, at least. In many cases she may be able to eliminate them, and proceed to what might be seen by some as her 'proper' job. Certainly, she would be failing to do her own job, and encroaching on the specialist fields of others, if she 'diagnosed' a child as incapable of learning and abandoned him to non-educational and time-wasting inactivity pending his removal elsewhere or his treatment by someone else. The schools' welfare service envisaged by Professor Stott[2] might be an ideal solution – but it is obviously a long way off, and the difficult children of today will probably be grown up with difficult children of their own before the highly trained personnel needed for such a service are available in numbers enough to man it.[3] In the meantime, teachers must cope as well as they can in the classroom, in co-operation with Child Guidance clinics where possible and with other teachers and parents to help children with special needs. By the use of their own expertise *as teachers* they may be able to give a sense of adequacy, achievement and well-being to many children who were previously frightened, truculent or apathetic.

The immediate aims of this book are, therefore, to help teachers to recognize the significance of some sorts of behaviour; to aid them in coming to a decision about possible courses of action in the classroom; to give some indication of the kind of problem it is wise to pass on to other agencies; to suggest ways in which teachers can co-operate with those agencies; and to outline some of the means by which hard-pressed teachers might best cope in the classroom with those children who are receiving no help from other specialists. Even with a fully staffed and much extended Child Guidance service there would always be children in the last category, since without unthinkable powers of coercion some parents would refuse, or utterly deny the need for, psychiatric or other help. For such children the teacher may be the only hope.

Unlike a sociologist, a teacher does not have to look for her sample. It comes to her. Every child of five who is not grossly physically or mentally defective, or of that tiny minority that receives independent education, comes into an

[2] 'Studies of Troublesome Children' D. H. Stott (1966).
[3] See also 'Children and their Primary Schools' chapter 7 for review of services, and recommendations for the future.

ordinary Infants' school. Despite lazy, inadequate, seclusive or migrant parents who may have evaded all the pre-school services for their children, the legal necessity for school attendance brings them to official notice at last. Unlike any other type of school, the Infants' school receives an unsorted group; future university entrants, children who may later need special education, those with minor physical handicaps, the cherished and the neglected, all arrive in the reception class together. The implications of this for the teacher are that she needs a very wide range of educational skills, and must accept a responsibility given to few. She must do more than identify children in special need, difficult as this is, and more than just 'hold' them pending transfer elsewhere. She is concerned with their education in the present, not with 'diagnosis' or 'child-minding'. She must thus try to take appropriate action in the present to prevent trouble in the future; if she does not always succeed, this is understandable – but not to make the attempt is surely irresponsible.

(ii)
Discussion of individual children as a means of presenting principles of approach to those in special need has some advantages as a method. It gives a sense of immediacy and involvement to the reader, and provides concrete examples, of an easily remembered kind, from which to begin discussion and thinking of underlying principles. Moreover, it is commonly found that it is easier to work from the particular to the general than the other way about, and to progress in thinking from the immediate and the concrete to the more remote and abstract. It is possible that as children develop processes of thought in this order, (as Piaget's work has amply demonstrated), so also do adults when faced with unfamiliar material, and for this reason discussion of cases was thought to be a justifiable method for this work.

It is possible, however, that one may never progress from the concrete, the particular, or the purely anecdotal, to consideration of general principles. This is the danger of the case-history method, and one of which the reader must constantly be aware. It would be most unacceptable for any teacher to take any particular 'case' discussed in this book as a direct guide to action with another child. The uniqueness of each individual, in addition to the uniqueness of the mesh of

11

relationships of which he is a part – as contributor and recipient – make it impossible that a course of action found efficacious with one child will transfer to another. It is for the principles of approach that the reader must look in any work dealing with the problems of children. Both reading and observation have a part to play in our understanding of children's needs; without access to the researches, experiences and ideas of others we become narrow and limited – without our own, objective observations and personal involvement we become academic and unrealistic. This whole book is a plea to teachers to both read and look, and by so doing to develop their own ways of helping the children they know well.

Some principles of approach will probably emerge clearly in discussion of individual children, and some are made explicit in the preambles to and the considerations following groups of 'cases'. Those principles which the writer holds in regard to a school's relations with parents and others are further discussed in Chapter 13, and it will be seen that many of the recommendations of the Plowden Committee were already anticipated in the policy of the school from which the 'cases' are drawn – as, no doubt, they were in many others. It may be that some readers will consider that these principles owe more to the psychoanalytic than to other schools of thinking, and this is a bias readily acknowledged. It is not easy to think of the *affective* life of a child without acknowledging the debt to Susan Isaacs, Charlotte Bühler, D.E.M. Gardner, E.R. Boyce and many other workers in the field of child development and education who themselves were, and are, indebted to the ideas that started with Sigmund Freud.

It is hardly necessary, however, for teachers to concern themselves with the more esoteric and detailed theory of psychoanalysis, and this has certainly not formed any part of this book. Fixations at oral or anal phases, development of ego, the function of superego, and the significance of internal processes and forces such as cathexis and libido, as well as detailed discussion of mental illness, are probably the business of doctors, not of teachers. As Margaret Mead says:

'We have certainly not reached a stage in social awareness when ordinarily functioning men and women can afford to carry about with them a knowledge of the cultural psychodynamics that unites them with psychopath and criminal, or those whose inability to bear the strains of the culture has driven them to alcoholism or illness as a defence against them. At the very moment of our acceptance of the fact of our common humanity and our responsibility as citizens to improve a world in which such casualties occur, we must also, at least as the world is organized today, push away such detailed knowledge.'[4]

Teachers will accept their membership of a troubled species, and their responsibility to improve that world in which even children become casualties, and in so doing they may find the *principles* of psychoanalytic thinking about emotional development valuable while they 'push away the detailed knowledge' as Mead so wisely advises. In thinking of children's intellectual, physical or purely social development they will find schools of thought other than the psychoanalytic of first importance. The works of Gesell and Piaget, for example, are complementary; and both these contributions to our understanding of childhood are complementary to the contribution of the Freudians. Similarly, the work of modern sociologists, with their interest in group behaviour, rôle-theory and communication between groups within society has great relevance to the teacher, for no child in her class is there in isolation from his family, his neighbourhood, his social class and the wider society which is responsible for building his school and paying his teacher. The exacting educational philosophy of Professor Peters and his school, also gives the teacher tools, if she will use them, with which to examine and justify her aims, her syllabus and her attitudes to discipline, authority and the everyday needs of children. Because this book specifically deals with children in trouble – and emotional trouble in most cases – one school of thought may seem more often useful than others; but because every individual is an entity, (emotions, intellect, social influences and even physique inextricably combined within to produce the unique 'self'), a teacher cannot afford to ignore any contribution to our understanding of children, and it is hoped that clear indications of useful 'tools' will emerge in discussion and bibliographies.

Finally, it must be stressed that the contribution of the

4 'Male and Female' (Penguin Edition) pp. 389/390.

teacher goes beyond anything she may learn by reading and even by observation. More than most people in their work she gives herself, and this in no sentimental or self-sacrificing sense. She transmits values and attitudes by the very way in which she dresses, speaks and moves. The ways in which she organizes her day and her classroom, provides materials, mounts children's work, tells a story and greets children on arrival convey values to her pupils regardless of any precepts she may offer in addition. Perhaps her greatest contribution as a teacher, however, is her quality of warmth and spontaneity, her ability to accept the short-comings of children with tolerance, and her own with forgiveness – but with determination to reduce them. With the quality of spontaneity added to intelligent reading and careful observation her achievement with children cannot but be acceptable – even if sometimes it is elusive and difficult of definition. Ease and warmth in personal relationships are the basis of success with children in special need, as with 'normal' children; with the spontaneity which is the basis of that ease no teacher need feel that she is less of an 'expert' than anyone else, or that she needs to encroach on the specialist fields of others to gain understanding. The children in her class will regard her as the most important person in the world – beyond their parents – and the one to whom they will look for the support, guidance and sheer warmth they need if they are to become, in their turn, spontaneous and creative individuals.

This book is written about the work of real teachers with real children, about what actually happened, not what ought to or might have happened. None of the staff concerned, including the head teacher, had specialist training of any kind; but with good relationships established between head and staff, staff with each other, and between adults and children, that quality of spontaneity, (which Fromm sees as the opposite of authoritarianism, which Allport equates with creativity, and which so many other writers have seen as both the pre-requisite for and the expression of 'mental health'), was perhaps the key one in the school's contribution to the community it served, and especially in the help given to children with special needs. It is a quality possible of achievement by almost every teacher, and one which every head teacher can foster if she will. Neither specialist skills, small classes, nor ideal material provision can substitute for this warmth and

14

generosity of feeling; and it is partly the function of this work to point out that ordinary teachers in ordinary schools are capable of thinking of and dealing with children in this essentially creative manner.

January, 1967 L.W.

N.B. The Plowden Report, '*Children and Their Primary Schools*,' was published after completion of this book, and only brief reference to it has therefore been possible. Many of its recommendations were anticipated by the work of this school, and others, and it is probably true to say that such work now receives massive support from the Plowden Committee.

L.W.

Introduction

Data and Method

Several kinds of difficulty presented to teachers in the Infants' school have been selected for discussion by means of personal histories. All the children discussed were in the Infants' school stage during the last decade, and almost all were admitted in the normal manner at the age of five years.

The information used was gathered in the course of six years' ordinary record-keeping in one school. It does not lend itself to statistical analysis since so much of it was inevitably descriptive and subjective. Nevertheless, the records were conscientious, thoughtful and regularly-kept; the tests used were of reputable, standardized kind; and factual data, such as date of birth, attendance record etc. necessarily accurate. Although some reduction of this mass of data was obviously possible, and use has been made of simple tabulation and percentages where such devices make for clarity, this work cannot have the rigour of a research project. At the time of making the records they were used for ordinary reference within the school, and it was only later, in discussion with students, that the possible use of such records to other teachers became apparent.

Background to the Study

Locality

The school from which all the 'cases' were drawn was in no way unusual. It is in the south of England, on the edge of a town but within walking-distance of open country. Employment in traditional trades, printing and modern industries were plentiful in the years under discussion. Good living, shopping and leisure facilities make it a popular place in which to live and work – especially for the managerial group and the highly skilled technical men of modern industries.

In the immediate environs of the school a wide range of housing is found – from streets of nineteenth-century cottages and large Edwardian houses still in single-family occupation,

17

to the semi-detached houses of the 'thirties set in pleasant gardens, and modern small estates both council and private. In addition there are several streets of older council houses, some of which are specifically kept for 'problem' families.

Parental Occupations

These ranged from professional (for example, architects, solicitors, university lecturers) and quasi-professional (teachers, lecturers in technical colleges, journalists) to casual labourers and one or two incorrigible 'layabouts' – but by far the largest group was employed in good clerical jobs, such as in the Civil Service or insurance, and in highly skilled trades such as toolmaking, electronics and engineering design. This is an area of high employment, however, and even the unskilled workers are generally well-paid. An analysis of parental occupations between the years 1958 and 1961 gave the following picture:

Professional	2%
Managerial & Quasi-Professional	17%
Skilled Trades & Clerical	46%
Smallholders, Nurserymen etc.	1%
Semi-skilled Workers	25%
Unskilled (but regular) Workers	5%
Unskilled (casual) Workers	3%
Unemployed and/or Unemployable	1%

At any one time there was likely to be wide selection of socio-economic backgrounds represented among the children in the school.

Staff of the School

This was probably more stable during the years under discussion than is all too often the case nowadays. Most members of the teaching and domestic staff were married women, happily settled in the neighbourhood, and most with children of their own. Staff changes in six years were few, and those for reasons of retirement and promotion. Only for one period of two terms was it necessary to have an unqualified person in charge of a class; the effect on the children's work and attitudes was such as to give considerable concern to the rest of the staff as well as to the head – although it is not suggested

18

that all unqualified teachers would prove quite so worrying. The domestic staff was also relatively stable, and formed a warmly-involved and helpful group, as is often the case in Nursery and Infants' schools. Schoolkeeper and secretary remained unchanged throughout the period, and were as familiar to and trusted by the children as teaching and domestic staff. Occasionally non-teaching staff could deal with children in trouble in ways impossible to teachers, and were able to discuss children with sympathy and considerable insight. To give the impression of a consistently harmonious and ideal team would be dishonest. As with all other groups of human beings in fairly close, and sometimes stressful, relationships, there were occasional periods of strain and some personal difficulties that had to be resolved. But they were resolved with goodwill, and the sense of being a team was quickly restored. Obviously, success in handling children with special needs depends to a very great extent on there being a minimum of such emotional needs among the adults who are concerned with them. A recognition and acceptance of adults' needs would also seem to be important both in achieving and maintaining good relationships among members of staff and in making it possible for them to offer the maximum help to children.

Organization
There was nothing very remarkable in the organization of this school. It might with justice have been described as 'child-centred'; but this did not preclude the use of an orthodox timetable for teachers who preferred one, nor of careful plans of work and an overall syllabus. Children moved freely about the school on many occasions, but were 'contained' within a few fixed points of the day and by a very few simple rules. Some teachers were happiest with a fluid timetable and integrated schemes of work; others liked set times for (active) number and language work and a free-choice period at another time of the day. While active, integrated work throughout the day, and vertical grouping, seems most suitable for children in the Infants' school, it is probably better to settle for warmth, interest and appreciation of individual needs within a slightly more 'formal' framework than to bewilder older teachers by imposing methods of organization to which they are not used. A very large measure of freedom of choice, pace of learning

19

and companions was given, even in classes run on more formal lines; in no class was there a ban on conversation, moving about to consult books and use apparatus, or on free and friendly approach to the teacher.

It was possible, during the six years of this study, to keep the reception class fairly small during the Autumn term, and not too unwieldy (i.e. around the thirty to thirty-five level) until Easter. Thereafter, an extra class was set up in a spare classroom to take the children whose birthdays fell between May and July. Termly promotions were, fortunately, not necessary, as the move to the Junior school took place once a year. There were times, of course, when it would have been helpful to a particular child to have been able to keep him for an extra term in the Infants' school, and the once-yearly move made this difficult. On the other hand, there is no doubt that reasonably sized reception classes, and unbroken periods with one teacher make for considerable stability among both children and staff. The practice of keeping one class throughout the children's Infants' school career was preferred by some teachers, and despite the slight administrative difficulty this produced (since not all felt they wished to keep a class so long) it was also a stabilizing experience for most children. Flexibility, in fact, seemed more important than doctrinaire methods – no matter how intrinsically progressive.[1]

Buildings

It should not be supposed that a co-operative staff working according to the organization most suited to them had also the advantage of modern buildings and all the facilities which go with them. The original single-storey buildings had comprised the Infants' and 'big-boys-and-girls' school of what had, effectively, been a village on the outskirts of the town and were built at the end of the last century. A third single-storey building, containing three classrooms, was put up in the 'thirties to take the first influx of children from the new development along a nearby main road. By the immediate post-war years the school was overcrowded, and the three buildings were eventually given over entirely to Infants, while under the reorganization following the 1944 Act children of

1 See *Children and their Primary Schools* ch. 20 for consideration of organization in school.

Junior-school age went to a new building some half a mile away. The legacy of this past included remnants of walls that had once divided Infants from the other parts of the school, an outside lavatory block, an antiquated heating system (including open fires until well into the 'fifties), coke-dumps in the playground, tiny cloakrooms with no hot water until over ten years after the 1944 Act, and windows too high for small children to look out of. But ample space was a legacy, too, with lawns, large asphalt areas, apple-trees and a rough field. Little nooks and corners in old buildings can be used for quiet corners in which to read, or for house-play, or storage; the school bell in an old school building, and the slots and hollows in the soft red brick, made by innumerable sharpenings of slate-pencils, can be a source of interest, and perhaps the beginnings of a feeling for history, for successive generations of six and seven-year-olds.

The following pages are thus to be read with the *ordinariness* of this school in mind. It is possible, when discussing problems in any field, to give the impression that nothing and nobody is normal. The reader must not imagine a school constantly rocked by aggressive outbursts, haunted by withdrawn waifs, at the mercy of pilferers and composed largely of neurotics. Most children in school are happy, adjusted to the demands of relationships and work, and a pleasure to their teachers – and this was true of this particular school. All the more important is it to do what can be done to help those who are not. Finally, as has already been stressed, the causes underlying troubled and troublesome behaviour described in ensuing chapters, and the remedies applied, will not apply exactly to other children. The interactions of personality between child and teacher, as well as the unique nature of both personality structure and environment, must be infinite. The experience of others can never be quite like our own; yet *ways* of thinking can be indicated by a study of cases. *What* to think is the responsibility of the teacher dealing with an individual child. In considering the difficulties and needs of any child it is advisable to bear in mind the 'three rules' of Charlotte Bühler:

Never assume that a problem can be explained by one specified cause. Never believe that explanation can be given without study of the individual situation.

Do not accept descriptions of a child's behaviour as explanation of it. (E.g. to say of a child who is constantly at one's elbow, 'He just wants attention' is to describe, not explain, his behaviour.)[2]

There is hardly a personal or social problem, or any difficulty connected with learning which will not be found in an ordinary Infants' school over a period of a few years, albeit often in embryo. The following pages highlight a few of them.

[2] See 'Childhood Problems and the Teacher', p. 11.

Chapter 1

Identifying Children with Special Needs

In the six years covered by this study 500 children left the Infants' school at the age of seven years, almost all of them for the normal Junior school. Of this number 80 (16%) presented their teachers with unusual problems of both behaviour and learning; unusual, that is, when they were compared with the 84% whose difficulties and misdemeanours were of short duration and resolved by ordinary attention to their learning and social needs. The proportion in some years was higher than in others, and the total at the end of five years' record-keeping was a matter of considerable concern. Discussions with psychiatrists and psychologists at the time and subsequently, however, suggested that the average figure of 16% was a realistic one (possibly even on the low side) in the light of numbers of delinquent, psychiatric and learning-failure cases among older age-groups all over the country. There is no place for complacency, here, when faced by this frighteningly high percentage of difficulty and disturbance even in the Infants' school.[1]

Personality of the Teacher
Identification of these children was made in many ways. Probably the ability of teachers to establish warm relations with children, and to have a permissive attitude towards them was an important factor. Under such circumstances it is possible for children to express their fears and needs more readily than if teachers are afraid of their own feelings, rigid in approach and over-formal in teaching methods. This is not the place to consider the nature of 'maturity' in adults, although such consideration is of first importance for teachers; but it is likely that the teacher who fulfils most of the criteria of maturity also recognizes children's needs most quickly and can accept their most deviant behaviour without a sense of personal affront. It is not necessarily the 'good disciplinarian'

[1] See also *'Education & Mental Health'*, pp. 239-240.

with the class 'under control' who is the mature adult in any of the terms by which that elusive concept is usually defined. Such a teacher may be more at the mercy of his or her own four-year-old's conscience and more afraid of adulthood than is the spontaneous, casual-seeming teacher whose classroom is characterized by eager chatter, movement and easy approach to the adult.

To be 'gentle and undignified' with children, as A.S. Neill has put it, is to have the true dignity of adulthood which seeks neither to impress nor to exploit, but only to help children to grow in adequacy and poise. Recognition of special needs follows naturally from such attitudes.

Record-Keeping.

A second factor in identifying children in need of extra help may seem mundane, but is no less important than personal attitudes: it is simply good record-keeping.[2] Factual particulars of birthdate, address, father's occupation, whether mother is employed and if so where, position in the family, and any special particulars such as a child's need to wear spectacles or a hearing-aid, are normally obtained on school entry, and were for all the children to be discussed. In addition, it is essential for her understanding of individuals that a teacher keeps records of each child's progress in such skills as reading and number-work, and a social record. This last might consist only of a page for each child in a loose-leaved folder, with DATED comments jotted down as they seemed called-for; alternatively, there might be a system of large record-cards with space for details of personal attitudes, social progress, and deviances of any kind, in addition to progress-records in various skills. Forecasts of work expected to be undertaken during the course of a week or a month, and subsequent brief reviews of its actual course and of the responses of some children if these appeared unusual or interesting in the light of a child's previous history, complete what would be a minimum of efficient record-keeping.

Many years ago Susan Isaacs pointed out some of the uses to which well-kept records could be put:

[2] See 'Children and their Primary Schools' chapter 12 esp. paras. 431 to 437.

co-operation between the home and the school;
co-operation between the school and medical services;
value on transfer to another class or school;
value as a supplement to tests and examinations;
value in diagnosis and treatment of maladjustment.

She lays particular stress on the last, and her view is constantly endorsed by psychiatrists in Child Guidance who are all too often given little or no information of value by the schools.

The material of this book was preserved in records of the kinds described, and although used primarily for purposes of educational guidance of individuals had also great value in most of the ways suggested by Isaacs. Another most important use of records is the detection of *patterns* of behaviour, which do not spring to mind when one is noting isolated incidents. It is well worth the teacher's while to look through her records at regular, perhaps half-termly, intervals with a view to identification of significant patterns or syndromes.

Contacts with the Parents

Part of the record for each child will, as has been said above, consist of some factual details about his family. A third aid to recognition of special need is contact with parents. Traditional attitudes of parents towards schools and teachers – subservience encouraged by patronage, distrust engendered by inaccessibility, resentment fostered by lack of explanation, and the whole sterile, miserable and ungenerous concept of 'them' against 'us' – are, where they exist, a major hindrance to successful teaching and effective learning. For children in difficulties they are disastrous. In the Primary schools, at least, the notice forbidding parents to pass a certain point, the insistence on appointments with the head teacher being made in advance and through the secretary, or limitation of times during which a worried parent may talk to the head, block communication with the very parents, and at the very point, where it would be most valuable.[3] To reject the opportunity

[3] See 'Education and the Working Class' ch. 4 – Jackson, B. & Marsden, D.; and article entitled 'Neighbourhood School' in 'New Society', 23rd June, 1966 regarding effects on older children.

that easy communication with parents offers for greater understanding of children in school seems both unintelligent and arrogant. A significant contribution to the identification of children with special needs of all kinds was made by the parents of the children to be discussed later; and more often than not this contribution was made informally and in moments of stress, when a harassed parent had nowhere else to turn.[4]

It might be asked whether such freedom of entry to school were abused. This is impossible of answer. What might seem abuse to one would appear as a touching gesture of confidence to another; a problem that could seem a time-wasting trifle to one head teacher might strike another as of major significance in understanding a child's problems. There are always parents so anxious about their children, or so lacking in confidence in themselves, that they appear frequently at the school. But the very fact that they need to come so often is indicative of a need for help. There are bullies and toadies in every community, and some of them, unfortunately, the parents of children we teach – but it has not been found that they are any more prone to visit a school allowing them free access than to visit those behind the 'keep out' notices. In fact, it is likely that they will be less insistent where there are no barriers for them to resent and nobody ready to take offence or be intimidated or cajoled by their behaviour.

Standardized Tests
Standardized tests may not often reveal a hitherto unrecognized difficulty to a perceptive teacher, but obviously a test-score might do so on occasion. They are probably more commonly used to diagnose errors and compare performance with the 'average' for the age-group after a child has already given his teachers cause for concern. Both tests of intellectual ability and of performance in specific skills (particularly reading) are useful to teachers, although they will use only those in the former category which are designed for use in schools, leaving more exact individual testing of intelligence to educational psychologists trained to apply them. Whether routine application of such tests to all children would benefit teachers is

---

[4] 'Children and their Primary Schools,' ch. 4 *Participation by Parents.*

arguable, although the case for such testing is made by D.H. Stott in his *'Studies of Troublesome Children'* already mentioned above. It is unlikely that such wholesale testing will be possible in the foreseeable future, however, and teachers are likely to continue using reliable standardized tests for their own purposes in their own classrooms. If these are applied strictly according to the author's instructions, and the scores interpreted with intelligence, they give an objective picture of one aspect of a child's development and/or skill, at least. That the test-score is only one facet of a vastly complex whole; that it can never stand alone as a 'judgement' or 'predictor'; that tests should never be used as guides to lesson-content; and that scores should not be revealed to child or parent would seem self-evident propositions. Yet abuse and misunderstanding of the intention of standardized tests are occasionally met in schools.

The only test applied to *every* child in the school over the period of six years being discussed was the simple Word-Recognition Test (R.I) of Schonell. Many other tests were used from time to time on particular children and for specific purposes; and the results of intelligence and personality tests administered by Child Guidance personnel were generously passed to the school and found very helpful.

Agencies outside the school
Health visitors, in their capacity as School Nurses, are an invaluable source of information about children and families. Their professional training includes work in the mental health field; and their professional rectitude ensures that the information they pass on to a headmistress is significant and accurate. They have usually known a child since birth, and may have entry to the home denied to everyone else. At a routine school medical examination the nurse greets almost every mother as an aquaintance of long-standing. It is often by the Health Visitor that a school is alerted to a problem, sometimes even before the child enters; and she can often supply the 'missing piece' in an otherwise insoluble puzzle. It is probable that in some areas there is less liaison between school and health services than ought, ideally, to be the case; it is possible that some nurses, and teachers, take refuge in their own professional skills and ethics to the exclusion of those in another

calling. This is regrettable, but hardly ever irremediable. Contact starts with individuals, and if teachers are prepared to listen with respect, and nurses to trust teachers with confidential information in order to help a particular child, the 'pigeon-holing' of tradition will be broken down where it will do most good – in the Infants' school. Much of the data collected about some of the most intractable cases can come from a devoted and efficient Health Visitor who is prepared to discuss a difficult child or a problem family with the school staff, under conditions of confidence.[5]

Not only the health service, with its 'right of entry' to schools, but the local police force, the N.S.P.C.C. inspector, the probation officer and many others play their part in helping children in need. On occasions they bring the need to the notice of schools; and always they can offer specialist help of kinds beyond the resources of the most interested and skilful teacher. A school needs links with every part of its community; it must not be viewed as a self-contained institution, working in isolation from parents and other social services, but as a valuable and integral part of neighbourhood services. As will be seen in discussion of cases, it is in the best interests of children – the 'normal' as well as the 'needy' – for teachers to have friendly contacts with as many agencies as possible.

Learning Problems

Lastly, but perhaps most obviously, identification of a special need or difficulty comes from learning failure. It is not suggested that every slow-learning child, or every child having difficulty over some steps in a learning process, is in need of prolonged special attention. The ordinary daily task of the teacher is to help children to overcome temporary setbacks and minor failures. But when the failure seems chronic she should look over the child's family records, his relationships and his levels of achievement in other fields, before dismissing his failure as incorrigible or, worse, as attributable to 'laziness'. (This latter is one of those *descriptions* of behaviour against which Bühler warns us, it is never an explanation, for

[5] See *'Report of the Committee on Maladjusted Children'* (1955) H.M.S.O. ch. XVI, paras. 500 to 504 for discussion of the place of the Health Visitor vis-à-vis the educational service. Also *'Children and their Primary Schools'* ch. 7.

no young child in good physical and mental health is likely to be lazy.)

A very high proportion of the children with special personal and social needs were retarded, particularly in reading – 59% of the aggressive children, and all but one of the 9 noted as withdrawn, for example – but it is proposed to give more details of learning failure in discussion of each category of difficulty. Certainly, for the teacher a major identifying factor of children demanding special attention to their personal-social needs is retardation in skills such as reading; and this may be the first intimation of 'trouble' in some cases.

Summary

If a teacher is exercising her full skill, which includes her personal development as far as she can take it, thoughtful and regular record-keeping, warm relations with parents, ability to use and interpret those standardized tests appropriate for her use, maintenance of good relations with other people concerned with the welfare of children, and understanding of the means by which successful learning may be achieved, she will not have to 'look for' children with special needs. They will show themselves to her. She does not need (and neither should she try) to develop the skills of a psychologist – much less those of a psychiatrist – since her attention to the tools of her own trade will serve her far better in the classroom than will the tools of anyone else's. Neither, in becoming aware of the great needs of some children, is there any danger of neglecting the 'normal' majority, for in the exercise of ordinary professional skills the teacher is bound to do justice to ordinary children. Most of the cases of difficulty to be discussed were identified within the school, (which includes those brought to the teacher's notice by Health Visitor or parents), not by psychological or psychiatric examination outside it. Such examination, however, confirmed the gravity of the disturbances in children referred from school to the Child Guidance clinic, and offered explanations beyond a teacher's skill to uncover, as well as suggestions about possibly helpful ways of coping with the children in the classroom. But it was teachers who, by all the means mentioned above, constituted the first 'sieve' through which children passed, and by which many, if not all, were saved from further hurt or continuing failure.

Suggestions for further reading

Allport, G. *Pattern and Growth in Personality* Holt, Rinehart & Winston (1963)

Erikson, E. *Childhood and Society* Hogarth Press (1965)

Fromm, E. *The Art of Loving* George Allen & Unwin (1957)

Fromm, E. *Fear of Freedom* Routledge Paperback (1960)

Gardner, D. & Cass, J. *The Rôle of the Teacher in the Infants' and Nursery School* Pergamon Press (1966)

Isaacs, S. *The Educational Guidance of the School Child* Evans Brothers (1937)

Jersild, A. *When Teachers Face Themselves* Columbia University (1955)

Storr, A. *The Integrity of the Personality* Heinemann (1960)

Suttie, I. *The Origins of Love and Hate* Kegan Paul, Trench, Trubner (1948)

U.N.E.S.C.O. *Education and Mental Health* Geo. G. Harrap & Co. Ltd. (1955)

Winnicott, D. *The Child and the Outside World* Tavistock Publications (1957)

Report of the Committee on Maladjusted Children H.M.S.O. (1955)

Chapter 2

Composition of the Special Groups

Consideration of the kinds of difficulties encountered by teachers showed that there were at least eleven main types of behaviour that either caused disruption of work or worried teachers in other ways. An analysis of all records gave the following picture:

Table I

Type of Difficulty	No.	% of 80 cases	% of 500 leavers
Aggression	20	25	4
Cultural Deprivation	10	12.5	2
Withdrawal	9	10.1	1.8
Severe Anxiety	7	8.75	1.4
Bizarre Behaviour	6	7.5	1.2
Pilfering	5	6.25	1
Sexual Difficulties	5	6.25	1
Marked Immaturity	3	3.75	.6
Conflicting Cultural Expectations	3	3.75	.6
Physical Handicap	2	2.5	.4
Temper Tantrum	2	2.5	.4
Unclassified	8	10	1.6

Aggression is obviously the commonest expression of disturbance, and the largest of 'anti-social' groups. Cultural deprivation as a cause of difficulty in school is perhaps surprisingly common, considering the generally high standard of living in the area; and, despite the fairly common expectation that culturally underprivileged children are prone to indulge in pilfering, the figures give no indication that this is so. The handicap and behavioural difficulties seeming to arise from culturally underprivileged homes were, as will be seen in discussion of the children in this category, more in the area of 'not knowing how' than in delinquent or aggressive patterns. More will be said in the appropriate place of conflicting cultural expectations, but each child in this category had one foreign parent who retained attitudes and codes of behaviour, as well as views on dress, food and household management, which caused some degree of difficulty in children's adjustment to school in this country.

Although the categories in Table I represent the commonest types of behaviour difficulty and expression of need, the children themselves could not be thus neatly categorized in practice. Many of the children whose predominant expression of disturbance was aggressive behaviour were also deeply anxious; children whose main difficulty seemed to arise from their material, linguistic and experiential poverty were likely, also, to have aggressive outbursts on occasions; withdrawal was in some cases accompanied by markedly babyish behaviour – and so on. In each case it is *major* behaviour difficulty which has been used in categorization. In discussion of individual cases it will be seen how very overlapping, and even misleading, categories can be.

Almost all the children represented in Table I had learning as well as personal-social adjustment problems, as has previously been mentioned. It will be more helpful to deal with these in respect of individual cases than in tabulated form, although it should be borne in mind that when reporting a piece of tiresome, bizarre or frightening behaviour in the classroom a teacher almost always relates this information to what she knows of the child's learning. A child in the classroom is a 'whole person', in fact, and the children who make the subject of this book were seen as such in practice.

It is often asked if there are sex-differences in expressions of disturbance. In this 'sample' there certainly do seem to be striking differences between the numbers of boys and girls in most categories. It would be pointless to analyse each, giving percentages by sex, for when a category is represented by only two children the exercise is a waste of time. For larger groups, however, the analysis has been thought worthwhile, and it will be seen from Table II that there are no common behaviour problems at the Infants' school stage in which girls outnumber boys.

18

Table 11   Relation of Special Difficulties to Sex

A. Total no. of children leaving the school	500
No. of boys leaving the school	273 i.e. 54.6%
No. of girls leaving the school	227 i.e. 45.4%

B. No. of children with special difficulties	80
No. of boys with special difficulties	60 i.e. 22% of all boys
No. of girls with special difficulties	20 i.e. 9% of all girls

C. *Ratio* of boys to girls with special difficulties on basis of 80 cases	3 : 1
Ratio of boys to girls with special difficulties on basis of 500 children	$2\frac{1}{2}$: 1

The expectation, according to this sample of 500, would be that while at least one boy in five may present teachers with a behaviour and/or learning problem, less than one girl in ten is likely to do so. Interestingly enough, this roughly 2:1 ratio is also found in reading disability, and M.D. Vernon quotes findings from many investigators confirming the finding. The connection between emotional disorders and learning disability is pointed by Vernon herself, for she refers to frequent aggressive disorders among reading disability cases in boys.[1]

There is obviously much work to be done in connection with sex-differences and the incidence of behavioural disorders of all kinds, including delinquency,[2] and of both physical and mental diseases. Whether the apparent greater vulnerability of the young human male is genetically or culturally determined, and in which disorders the one may be a greater determining factor than the other, has yet to be demonstrated. The teacher of Infants, however, may expect more *obvious* cases of difficulty with boys than with girls – and probably usually does.

[1] *'Backwardness in Reading'* (1957) esp. pp. 110-114.
[2] See Wootton, B. *'Social Science and Social Pathology'* (1959) for consideration of differences in incidence and type of crime according to sex of offender.

She should, nevertheless, be alert to the possibility that just as many girls may be in need of help although their symptoms are, as yet, not so readily seen as such, and may even be complacently accepted as signifying positively 'good' behaviour in some social groups.

A consideration of categories of difficulty shows that in none do girls outnumber boys.

Table III   Analysis of Some Difficulties by Sex

Difficulty	Boys		Girls	
	No.	%	No.	%
Aggression n = 20	16	80	4	20
Cultural Dep. n = 10	6	60	4	40
Withdrawal n = 8	7	87.5	1	12.5
Severe Anxiety n = 7	6	85.7	1	14.3
Sexual Worries n = 5	4	80	1	20
Pilfering n = 5	4	80	1	20
Unclassified n = 8	6	75	2	25

It would be obviously a waste of time to analyse a sample of two, or three, and cases of immaturity, tantrum, conflicting cultural expectations and physical handicap have been omitted for this reason; but except in the case of physical handicap (two girls) and tantrum (one boy, one girl) boys outnumber girls. It might be thought pointless to give percentages on the small numbers in each of the above-tabulated categories; but they constitute ratios easily interpreted and are not claimed as having any statistical significance.

The fairly common assumption that while boys express disturbance or need by aggressive behaviour, girls are more likely to withdraw, show anxiety or have sexual worries is not borne out by the children of this sample. In these three categories the boys outnumber girls by 7:1, 6:1 and 4:1 respectively, while in cases of aggression the ratio (4:1) is as low as any. Only in difficulties arising from cultural deprivation is there a more even distribution between the sexes, as one would expect. But even here it looks as though girls from underprivileged homes cope better with the demands of school, (at least during their early years), than do their brothers. Perhaps their slight advantage in linguistic skills for all the lack of encouragement and example at home, is reinforced by school opportunities; or perhaps the tendency of girls to be less vulnerable to some emotional deprivation might be of significance in this connection. Some research into this apparent ability of girls from socially underprivileged homes to 'socialize' a little more easily than boys in the Infants' school might be very interesting.

Difference in numbers and types of special difficulties according to social background is not easily assessed. The term 'social background' is a vague and inexact one, in any case, and from the teacher's point of view might mean several things according to her own background, the area in which she was working or the nationality of the children with whom she was dealing. Perhaps parental occupation is still the only usable guide, despite all the anomalies of pay, standards of living and attitudes which must be allowed for in using it. An attempt to relate difficulties in school with parental occupation is propably justified, however, if only to demonstrate that 'problem children' arrive in school from many sorts of home, and that neither personal disturbance nor anti-social behaviour and learning difficulty are the prerogative of one social group.

Other difficulties arise when compiling a table of the kind below. The vagueness of some women about their husbands' occupations makes it almost impossible to assign some men to any category at all. What is a 'floor operative' or 'an engineer in the confectionery'? Described as a 'company director' a man might be almost anything from a small shopkeeper to a top-flight expert in aviation; and the teacher makes her judgement as much on the appearance and speech of mother and child as on the description when compiling such records as those used in school.

Further difficulties arise, and result in discrepancies of figures, when the several children of one family are counted as individuals for the purpose of categorizing types of problem, but their father's occupation can, obviously, only be entered once on lists of occupational categories. For all these reasons the following table is presented with reservation, and it would be unwise to regard it as other than an indicator of tendencies.

Table IV Parental Occupation and Difficulties of Children in School

Occupational Group	% in school	% of special cases
I Professional	2	1.25
II Managerial. Quasi-Prof	17	18.75
III Skilled Trades. Clerical	46	25
IV Smallholders, Nurserymen	1	None
V Semi-skilled	25	13.75
VI Unskilled (regular)	5	8.75
VII Unskilled (casual)	3	13.75
VIII Unemployed. Unemployable	1	3.75

It will be seen that from categories I, III and V alike there are fewer children presenting difficulties in school than might reasonably be expected; from the rest a higher proportion than the total numbers in those categories would lead one to expect. Category II parents seem to have a surprisingly large number of children in difficulties; but the discrepancies between the representation of categories VI, VII and VIII in the total sample of 500 and their children's school problems are perhaps not so surprising. If the children having difficulty because of cultural deprivation (poor language skills, timidity, inadequate social training etc.) are omitted the percentage of special cases coming from occupational class VII drops to 3.75 % i.e. there are few cases of aggression, pilfering or other socially disruptive behaviour in this category.

If cultural handicap is omitted, and also those types of difficulty represented by a very small number, the following pattern of difficulty according to social background emerges. Occupational category IV has been omitted, also, as there were no cases of difficulty recorded in six years for children of those few parents who worked smallholdings or were nurserymen.

Table V   Parental Occupation Group and Type of Difficulty of Children

Occ. Group	Aggression n=(20)	Withdrawal (8)	Anxiety (7)	Bizarre (6)	Pilfering (5)	Sexual Worries (5)
I	–	–	–	–	–	1
II	4	2	2	1	–	–
III	3	2				
V	5	3	1	–	–	–
VI	5	–	–	–	2	–
VII	2	1	–	–	1	–
VIII	1	–	–	–	1	–

It will be seen that aggressive behaviour in this sample cuts across the social barriers, but is inclined to be more common as an expression of disturbance among children of the semi-skilled and unskilled workers. This is hardly a surprising finding; but it might be thought rather surprising that children from much poorer homes (in an economic sense, at least) are not as aggressive in school as their more privileged schoolfellows.

Withdrawal also affects children regardless of socio-economic background, but with so small a number of cases it is unlikely that much significance can be attached to figures in the above table. The same can be said of bizarre behaviour – which includes odd movements, curiously garbled speech, apparent hallucinations and irrational interpretations of everyday phenomena – most of which, among the children of this sample, seemed to be the result of brain-damage and/or epilepsy. It is interesting to note, however, that all the recorded cases of this kind were among children from more prosperous and observant families. With one exception pilferers were from less fortunate homes, but considering the relatively large number of underprivileged children in the school it could not be called behaviour typical of this group. Acute anxiety and sexual worries, on the other hand, were rare among the children of economically less privileged parents – perhaps because social and intellectual frustrations were expressed in other ways? – and only one case of either is recorded for any child whose parent(s) are in categories V to VIII. Although there can be no statistical validity for trends discerned in so small a sample of each category, there is obviously a great deal of useful information stored in Infants' school records which, if statistically analysed by experts, might be of immense value in predictive and preventive work, including the indications of socio-economic group for certains kinds of maladjustment or anti-social behaviour.[3]

It would have been interesting and useful to have been able to analyse the eighty cases of special need in terms of intelligence test scores. This is, unfortunately, impossible as reliable scores are available for only just over a third of the group. As has previously been stressed, the records from which this work has been compiled were kept by teachers, and did not normally include the result of an intelligence test. Where such scores are available, as they are for children who presented particularly baffling learning or behaviour problems which failed to yield to teaching skills and good relations in the classroom, they will be given in respect of individuals discussed. In a number of cases they are the test scores recorded by educational psychologists; in others those derived from group or individual tests given by head or class teacher. It is probably appreciated by most teachers at the present time, however, that the whole concept of 'intelligence' is being re-developed, and instruments for its measurement being re-scrutinized in consequence. The inevitable omission of analysis by intelligence test scores may, therefore, be of less moment than would have seemed the case twenty (or even ten) years ago.

[3] For further information about predictive instruments etc. the reader is referred to 'Unraveling Juvenile Delinquency' by S. & E. Glueck (1950); 'The Bristol Social Adjustment Guides' by D. H. Stott & E. G. Sykes (1956); and some material in 'The Home and the School' by J. W. B. Douglas (1964).

Chapter 3

Aggression in Groups

Although many types of behaviour difficult to cope with in the classroom have been categorized under the heading 'aggression' it must be stressed that the term is a generalized one. The assertiveness of a vigorous baby or toddler overcoming obstacles to get what he wants, the rough-and-tumble games of small boys, the chasing and squealing of little girls and verbal abuse shouted by adolescents at each other are all, in a broad sense, aggressive acts. That they are normal and universal few would deny; and to agree this is to imply that there are needs for growth which are served by energetic, combatant behaviour in face of objects, situations and persons. It is now widely recognized that to prevent these means of coming to terms with the self within the environment is not only almost impossible but likely to have serious effects by turning normal striving into apathy or hostility. Teachers of young children, then, will make distinction between what one might call 'needful aggressiveness' and that which is expressive of hostility, hurt and unhappiness. Not every five-year-old who thumps his neighbour at the sand-tray for taking a tool he was using needs psychological treatment. Six-year-olds tend to aggressive acts as they lose their earlier acceptance of adults as all-knowing thought-readers but have not yet gained the confidence in them as guides which is typical of 'sevens' – but, again, few of them are cases for Child Guidance clinics (and those that are probably still behave more like four-year-olds). Her knowledge of developmental stages and needs, gathered from the very different but equally important work of Gesell and Piaget, for example, will probably enable the Infants' teacher to distinguish between what is normal and what is pathological in aggressive behaviour.

It is necessary, too, to appreciate cultural influences. Modern urban societies such as our own practise much larger-scale aggression – sometimes under the guise of 'peace-keeping' – and set a premium on those activities which have a high aggressive content, such as prize-fighting, competitive games and formal military displays. Physical courage is admired, but under modern conditions can easily be displayed only under special circumstances – or enjoyed vicariously through the medium of film. Competitiveness has an extremely high aggressive content, and is yet accepted as most desirable in many schools. Even quite small boys are expected to defend themselves, not to cry if hurt, not to hit little girls (which sanction usually makes nonsense of the two previous requirements), and while constantly shown how important it is to 'win' or 'come top' are also expected to be 'good losers'! It is not surprising that even by the age of five or six many children are confused about what is and what is not allowable aggression – and this the teacher must try to understand.

Further, it is important to appreciate that whether the aggressive behaviour of some children is normal for their age, is due to some emotional disturbance, is a reflection of society's confusion about permissible aggression, or a complex interaction of all three, it is fairly certain that some form of frustration will underlie every case. But to say that frustration gives rise to aggression is descriptive rather than explanatory, and gives a speciously over-simplified 'answer'. It has been said that children must be frustrated in order to grow. To overcome obstacles and to achieve mastery of one's body, thoughts and ever-changing environment is not only the proper task of childhood but the continuing concern of maturity. Elimination of all obstacles, therefore, or setting no limits on a child's behaviour, or doing everything for him, all frustrate the deepest need of all – that of being in command of himself and thus able to maintain equilibrium in his environment.[1]

Beyond a certain point, however, (and this is different for each individual) frustration hinders growth. The younger the child the sooner is his threshold of tolerance reached, and teachers need to be aware of the threshold for each child. He may be able to 'wait a minute' – but he cannot wait ten; he may be able to share the seesaw, but find sharing his toy intolerable; he may well accept 'let me show you' with one tool and fly into a rage if given over-zealous instruction in the use of another. By appreciation of the differences between

---

[1] See for example, 'Childhood Problems and the Teacher' by C. Bühler et al, pp. 15-19 for discussion of mastery, frustration etc. in brief form.

children in this respect, by generous provision of materials and equipment, and by giving opportunity for progressively more experience of waiting, sharing and being shown how, the Infants' teacher may find that she has reduced the incidence of aggression without recourse to other than sound teaching practices.

Finally, in a general consideration of aggression, teachers need to understand their own responses to aggressive acts. Despite an undeniable accent on essentially aggressive behaviour throughout our society, children within it are expected from a very early age to practise a high degree of restraint on their own aggressive impulses, as has already been suggested. If they succeed in this (and the great majority do) guilt about any impulse felt to be aggressive is almost inevitable, and a quite remarkable number of mental devices are developed to ease it. Vicarious enjoyment of aggression; puritanical control of all expressions of feeling; justification of cruelties against certain groups in the name of various 'ideologies'; a reduction of personality to a drab set of conventional responses, lest the quick temper for which one was punished as a child once more flares up; sarcasm, apathy, even some forms of 'extreme' pacifism may well be some of these devices. Even dislike of animals, or irrational fear of fire or thunder, have been found in Child Guidance practice to be fairly common among children with exceptionally strong control over aggressive impulses. It is *not* suggested that all the above 'mental devices' and attitudes arise from too-early control, nor that every individual required to exercise it feels such guilt as to make some easement of this kind necessary. It is important, however, for the teacher of young children to realize that she (as all of us) also had aggressive impulses in childhood, and *may* have retained some attitudes or rationalizations which once helped her to cope with them – but which are not particularly helpful to an adult in relationship with children. Acceptance of the self 'with all faults' is the first and most important step to both eliminating the 'faults' and to success in helping children deal with theirs. Such insight prevents a teacher from punishing a child for shortcomings that are as much her own as the child's, and from that fear of impulsive as well as aggressive behaviour which not only inhibits sound relationship with children, but prevents full use of normal teaching skills.

41

Individual Cases

A. The Leaders of Gangs

The onset of that single-sexed grouping which is typical of
the years between eight or nine and mid-adolescence can be
seen in the Infants' school. Groups are ill-regulated, there are
frequent traces of much earlier behaviour patterns, and children are a long way yet from the close-knit 'secret societies'
of ten to twelve-year-olds. Much of a seven-year-old's gang
activity is an imitation, without full understanding, of the behaviour not only of older children but of television and film
characters. At its best it is providing the social experience essential to development of 'rules' and 'teamwork' and 'loyalty'
in Junior school groups. At its worst it can be a vehicle for
upset and unhappy children 'hitting back' at both other
children and the adult world. It would be foolish to abolish
all gangs in the Infants' school, for many of them are great
fun; equally foolish is it, however, to allow the truly aggressive ones to continue, for much harm, emotional as much as
physical, can be done to younger or less aggressive children by
the occasional 'bad' gang of seven-year-olds. The four following children were leaders of the sort of group it is wise to
break up.

I. Keith

*The eldest child of four; a poor reader, but progressing well
by the end of his Infants' school career; also poor number
skills, and little understanding in this field despite a great deal
of practical work. No intelligence test score available, but
general conversation and responses suggested that he was by
no means as dull as his actual performance in school skills
suggested. Ability to handle shopping and change, organize
a game with 'dinky' cars and illustrate his 'news' near normal.*

Keith's father left home, only temporarily as it turned out,
after a noisy quarrel with the mother. He had always been
fond of his son, who resembled him closely and was everywhere admired for his good looks. After a week of incidents
involving minor hurt and much distress to other children by
Keith and members of his gang his teacher decided to make a
direct reference to the family situation. This is a course only
to be taken by an experienced teacher who has both knowledge
of and affection for the offending child, and who appreciates

42

the possible repercussions of such interpretation. It is also, of course, something of a last resort – but was effective in this case.

While bathing the bruised head of one of Keith's victims, and having required him and the three members of his gang to sit quietly nearby while she did so, she said:

'You're probably worried about your father, but hurting other people won't help, you know.'

Keith immediately burst into tears, and shouted,

'He's coming back! *Tomorrow*! He *said* so!'

Finishing her ministrations, and dismissing the hurt child and the other members of the gang, she suggested to Keith that Ireland was a long way off, and that it might take some time for his father to get back. She helped him to talk about how frightened he had been, and yet what interesting and exciting experiences he had shared with his father before the quarrel. He appreciated, as so many seven-year-olds can, how difficult it is even for adults who are fond of each other to control tempers. And for all the disaster and chaos that such a major familial row represents, he was able to accept the sympathy of another adult, and respond to it by asking if he could help to clear up the classroom. His aggressive outbursts became less and less frequent, and on the return of his father a week or two later disappeared altogether.

The reason for Keith's aggression was thus probably a feeling of fear and helplessness over a parental quarrel and desertion; but that he expressed his hurt in this way may well have been due to both his temperamental qualities and to responses learned since babyhood from an ebullient and often aggressive father with whom he was closely identified. Knowledge of, and a refusal to pass judgement upon, this boy's family was important in the teacher's handling of the aggressive behaviour.

2. Donny
The younger child of two, having a sister some seven years older than himself. Somewhat retarded in reading, but appearing average in all other skills; reading improved towards end of the Infants' school stage. A very anxious-seeming child on entry to the school from another part of the country, but later showing signs of being both humorous and stable.

For Donny there was no such simple interpretation of diffi-

43

culty as had so fortunately been possible with Keith. His father had re-trained for work in light industry after many years as a coal-miner, and was resentful of the necessity both of learning a new job and of moving to the south of England. Despite the improved living conditions and family income Donny's mother, too, was not happy; and his thirteen-year-old sister had threatened to run away from school and go 'back home'. There was obvious repercussions of this family's unhappiness on six-year-old Donny. He had enjoyed his previous school and had done well; he was also an essentially stable child – but to settle down in a new school at the age of six and three months, when one's whole family is upset by a major move, is too much to expect of any child. Within a few weeks Donny was the leader of a little gang, and was terrorizing younger children on the way to and from school.

After several complaints from her neighbours about Donny his mother visited the school. Teachers had also had cause to reprove Donny on several occasions for aggressive behaviour, and he had told his mother enough about this to make her very apprehensive about visiting the school at all. She was hurt, angry, worried about the uncontrollable pugnacity of her hitherto 'normal' little boy, and anxious about her husband's and her daughter's unhappiness. She was also lonely, and knew hardly anybody in the neighbourhood after over three months.

She accepted a cigarette and a cup of tea with apparently astonished relief, and poured out all her worries as though she had not spoken to anyone for years. That her listener turned out to know the very village from which she came was one of those fortunate 'bonuses' which tend to accrue if people talk freely about their families and their past. She was a woman of warmth and intelligence, perhaps needing only this kind of contact to re-establish her confidence in herself, and start on the task of restoring her family's faith in itself. She was willing to follow-up introductions to North-country families in the next street, whose children were in Donny's class (but not, fortunately, among his victims), and to suggest herself that she ought to go and see her daughter's head teacher as she had come to the Infants' school. She realized that until his parents and sister felt more settled Donny was unlikely to improve. What neither she nor the staff of the school anticipated was the almost immediate improvement in his behaviour when he found that his mother had established friendly relations with school. Presumably this eliminated the feeling of total isolation he had previously felt in school, and made at least two of the major parts of his new environment seem related.

It was a pity that Donny could not have spent another term in the school, for his improvement in behaviour was accompanied by improvement in learning, also, and he would almost certainly have been helped by another three months at the school he now knew and enjoyed. The Junior school was yet another change within a year – and one he found it difficult to cope with for several terms.

3. Stanley

An I.Q. of 93 (as measured by a group non-verbal test) and general levels of response which would suggest that this was a fair estimate but reading very retarded indeed until over seven years of age. At the time of his leaving the Infants' school, however, scores on the Neale Analysis of Reading Ability were: Rate:- 6 : 8 Accuracy:- 6 : 10 Comprehension:- 7 : 4; chronological age at the time of testing 7 : 9. Despite his halting pace and his inaccuracies of pronunciation he obviously understood what he was reading as well as is expected of a child only a few months younger than himself. Writing minimal – he did not enjoy this activity – but drawing lively, if immature. Understanding of number-work at least average, and interest shown in practical work of all kinds connected with number concepts. Very restless and chatty throughout all activities, with low powers of concentration but vast enthusiasm for new experiences. An only child of parents rather older than most.

Stanley's parents showered him with expensive presents, an absurd amount of pocket money and extravagant endearments – but often gave the impression that he was rather in the way. He had been born after fifteen years of marriage, and adjustment to a child in the household had probably been difficult. His mother was a big, blowzy woman, fond of jolly nights out with a friend of many years' standing; his father a slight, lined-faced man who tinkered continuously with motorcycles and spent a great deal of time with his racing pigeons – Stanley being welcome to stand and watch these operations, however, if he felt like it. The mother was impulsive and volatile to the point of seeming emotionally unstable, with a loudly-expressed partiality for her son which made her neighbours very wary of complaining about his bad behaviour, and at the same time a ferocity towards him if he upset her which they found equally frightening. Of routine in his life there seemed very little; of indulgence too much; and of restraint or correction in regard to hurting others, using bad language or telling lies about other children none at all.

Yet this child could be confiding and friendly, and responded better than might have been expected to the combination of regular routine and freedom of choice of the Infants' school. Perhaps he found it a relief. His period of 'gang warfare' probably coincided with phases of his mother's temper or his father's preoccupation with a new motor-cycle or an important pigeon race, but this is not a pattern easy to discern. It was possible to divert his energies from aggression to helping staff in school, for he loved to be of use in a messy chore particularly, but his out-of-school terrorizing of small children was less easy to deal with. He impressed his little gang with his strength and physical skills and loved to show-off to them as 'boss' of all the children in the street.

There seemed only one course of action likely to put a stop to these activities, and that was to catch him red-handed in the street and take him straight to his mother. While she refused to listen to complaints from neighbours (and, indeed, frightened them by her blustering) she appeared to regard a headmistress as an authority-figure with whom it was wise to keep on good terms. It is possible that she saw in such persons the characteristics of her own mother (of whom she still stood in awe) and of herself at her most dictatorial. Inaccurate though this picture might be, and dangerous as it can be to 'play into' such a woman's view of authority, there are times when it is the quickest way to deal with a naughty child – and this seemed to be such a time.

Accordingly, Stanley was caught, with his little gang watching in admiration, as he removed a cap from a passing five-year-old, kicked it into a garden, and threatened to twist the child's arm if he told anyone. The gang melted away, Stanley was sent to retrieve the cap, the five-year-old was comforted, and the very sulky offender was escorted home to his mother.

Her threats of punishment for him were so dire that it was difficult to get her to listen to more reasonable suggestions about means of bringing him under control. She agreed, however, to bring him the short distance to school every day for a time, instead of letting him come by himself (which, of course, he was quite capable of doing, and had done ever since he was five), and to meet him from afternoon school as well. Stanley was, as expected, indignant about this, at least at a superficial level. It is possible that to have the full attention of his mother for a few minutes every day, even under such conditions, was not as unwelcome to this child as some might think. Certainly, this course of action required his mother to make at least a symbolic gesture of being responsible for him in view of other people, without, however, subjecting her to any great strain or humiliation. There were no more aggressive acts thereafter, even when his mother ceased to bring him. And the collecting him from school at the end of the day became a regular feature of both their lives, he chatting and laughing about his day in school, she looking down at him fondly and plying him with potato crisps or ice-cream, while they went off shopping or to meet his father.

This is the kind of family situation which can, however, be very difficult to handle. It would have taken very little for this woman to have become aggressive herself about Stanley's treatment at the hands of his teachers; her placatory manner with someone she regarded as being in authority did not constitute a relationship of any real trust or warmth – although such a one did begin to develop after several months of praise from his teachers for Stanley's improved work. She even provided some rather garish decorations for a party at Christmas, which were accepted graciously, and used as intended; but she asked Stanley if he had seen them, and what his teacher had said about them, in a slightly belligerent manner before she was out of earshot of the staff! One might suspect hidden rejection of a child in this sort of family, and perhaps still-unsatisfied childhood needs in both parents. Certainly it is unwise of teachers to do more than deal with such a situation at a 'behavioural' level. Much can be done to 'steady' such a boy as Stanley simply by the ordinary routine and normal restraints of school, as has already been suggested; relations with such parents will not be helped by probing at underlying causes, and need to be as cordial as possible, if at a fairly superficial level, in order to prevent conflict for the child between parents and school.

4. Duncan

A very disturbed and retarded child, with an I.Q. of 80 on one non-verbal test and 85 on another. Scores thought to be an underestimate by the educational psychologist who applied the tests, since Duncan was resentful and suspicious and gave the impression of 'not trying' in the earlier part of both. Probably, however, of below-average ability. Reading did not improve even after two terms of individual remedial work with the head teacher, (with whom he, very slowly, built a satisfactory relationship during this time), and he left for the Junior school as virtually a non-reader. Understanding of number-work sketchy in the extreme, although he liked practical work such as building, weighing and shopping. Recording nowhere near the standard that would be expected in the Junior school.

Duncan was the middle child of a large family, with affectionate but not surprisingly over-pressed parents who could spare him little individual attention. His next-younger brother had been born when he was only eleven months old, and he had some of the characteristics of a maternally deprived child, although in fact his mother was very fond of him. He was remote from adults, but very attached to his younger brother and to the one two years older than himself. He also appeared to have affection for his grandmother, with whom he occasionally stayed for a few days. He was enuretic into his eighth year, and aggressive from the day he entered school – markedly more so when he returned from his grandmother's. As the family lived at some distance from the school he got into various kinds of mischief during the long walk, and on some occasions did not arrrive at all. It was usually possible to keep track of him by asking his older or younger brothers where they had last seen him; and what might have been the beginnings of real truancy was not allowed to develop, at least in his Infants' school years.

Duncan was an extremely handsome, well-built boy, obviously adequately fed and clothed. He was also a good leader, and children older and cleverer than himself were contented to be in his gang. Neither was this always an aggressive one; there were periods of interesting activity, when Duncan would direct the building of a 'camp' from branches left by the hedge-trimmer, or a house from builder's junk. On one occasion he even conceived the idea of digging a cave for a 'den' in the corner of the field, and the gang worked hard at this for several days, giving up only because the ground was baked like concrete after a long, hot summer. It was this ability to organize other children that was exploited to deflect him from aggressive behaviour with his gang. As the leader of a 'litter-squad' he did not allow so much as a match-stick to remain in the school grounds; in stacking chairs or outdoor play equipment, in mopping up and cleaning a cloakroom after a basin had overflowed, or in helping the schoolkeeper to fill coke-hods he was efficient and apparently happy. Such chores also made possible for him constructive contacts with adults, and earned him praise that he obviously appreciated.

Yet school is a place for the learning of certain formal skills, and although a programme of 'chores' can be very helpful to a child of this kind it obviously cannot replace ordinary schooling. For many aggressive children, (who are, nevertheless, capable of leadership), only a short experience of responsibility of this unorthodox kind may bring about such improved relations with adults and other children that learning of formal skills also improves. A sense of adequacy and of 'being wanted' does seem to transfer. But this did not happen in Duncan's case, and his reading and writing remained very poor.

Child Guidance was suggested for him, and the parents were willing to co-operate and anxious to do whatever seemed best for the boy. The clinic was, however, at a distance involving two bus-rides, and with so large a family to look after the mother could not get there. Duncan's father had two jobs, and little time to spare. Efforts to provide babysitters while the boy was taken by his mother to the clinic (and this would have to be a weekly visit, at least, and for some long time) proved abortive. All that teachers can do in such a case is support the parents, enlist the aid of the Health Visitor to talk to the mother about the child's difficulties in an informal manner, and to suggest such extra help as regular visits to a relative with whom the child is happy and from whom he receives the individual attention that he craves. In Duncan's case the grandmother provided help of this sort. Added to the means already mentioned of deflecting aggression, and as much remedial help as is possible with reading, such action probably prevents the child from becoming worse, if it can do no more.

B. *The Inciters of Group Aggression*
Whereas boys of the kinds described above are fairly easy to detect and bring under control, since their aggression is loud, out-going and obvious, some little groups of children involved in chasing, punching, hairpulling and so on may turn out to be 'led from behind', and the ring-leaders less noticeable than the led. Even Duncan, for all his physical strength and organizational powers, was at one time 'manipulated' by a child of the inciting kind.

5. Jimmy
A thin, tense-looking child, of apparently average ability, but somewhat retarded in reading until the term before leaving the Infants' school. An only child of indulgent and inconsistent parents, who seemed nevertheless genuinely fond of him and concerned about his troubles in school. Always on the edge of little flurries of punching or chasing, and frequently accused of hurting smaller children although very rarely actually seen to do so. As there were also occasional incidents of children being pushed or pinched during classroom activities, and the work of others spoilt by him, Jimmy was considered to be a great nuisance by other children of his age and they were not keen to have him as one of a group.

There was opportunity to talk to his mother after a particularly tiresome set of incidents seeming to involve Jimmy, although he denied having any part in most of them, and she agreed that he was not a very happy little boy. Conflicting expectations from his father, who wanted him to be 'tough' in some respects but a biddable baby in others, and great uncertainty on his mother's part as to what were the best courses of action (she seemed to change course almost every day), combined with her monotonous repetition of quite meaningless threats, gave this child no framework or points of reference. His lack of persistence and concentration were probably also due to the inconsistency of his parents, for no steady demands were made upon him and no goals set for him. Incentives were bribes, and rewards were unrelated to achievement.

Counselling these parents was a long, slow business, and it was uncertain whether their increased co-operation in some areas of his upbringing would last beyond the period in which they came to school and took an interest in his work. The attention they both craved, however, was thought to be a legitimate part of Jimmy's 'treatment'. They were likeable but very immature people, the mother with excessive and openly-expressed fears of illness and old age allied with an almost adolescent delight in the latest song 'hits' and exaggerated youthful fashions, and the father enthusiastic and knowledgeable only about football. To talk, as responsible adults, about the upbringing and education of their son fortunately struck them as an interesting experience.

For Jimmy himself the most effective deterrent to aggression proved to be not 'chores' and deflection of energy into organization of classroom equipment etc., (he had too little persistence for this, and other children could not work with him as they could with Duncan, Keith or Stanley), but removal from other children altogether. This is a measure to be taken with extreme care, and under special circumstances. In Jimmy's case it meant that after being a thorough nuisance to other children – either because of his incitement of them, or because of their being hurt or upset by him or his gang – he would be brought with his books, crayons, scissors, or whatever apparatus he was supposed to be using, to the headmistress's room, and there he would do his work. The logicality of this was apparent even to a child of seven. If other children are constantly being disturbed by him, then it is sensible to work where there are no other children to disturb. It must be stressed that this 'treatment' is not to be applied in a punitive sense, since this attitude is likely to give rise to more aggression than it deters. A child is sent to school to be taught, and removal from sources of teaching (as, for example, when a child is put outside a door, or made to sit with nothing to do) is a breach of faith on the part of the teacher. In the quietness of the head's room, and with all the help that a small child needs to do his writing, or other work, Jimmy worked well. Moreover, he developed a good relationship with the head teacher, and in this situation at least was open, confiding and less anxious than he was elsewhere. He was also, for the first time, able to experience the satisfaction of a piece of writing, illustration, number-work or reading

51

carried through to completion and earning praise. This essential piece of learning did seem to transfer to the classroom situation, and he needed only three or four sessions alone with the head teacher before a marked improvement not only in his behaviour but in his learning took place.

6. Greg

A small, lively, seemingly bright boy, with poor performance in all measurable skills. His birthday being in August he left the Infants' school as young as a child can. A quite inexplicable attraction for bigger and older boys in his class, and usually on the fringe of trouble of the kind described in respect of Jimmy. He dared children to do things he would not do himself, boasted of exploits no-one but a gullible seven-year-old would credit, and had a 'bossy' way with younger children that was reminiscent of a four-year-old. Like Jimmy he had poor powers of concentration, persistence and organization of either himself or others. In a constant ferment in the classroom, and aimless, though very physically active out-of-doors.

Greg's parents were both more intelligent and more mature than Jimmy's, but there was inconsistency between them in their handling of the boy. The father was fond and proud of him, smacked him for such things as 'cheek' or spoiling tools, but took no interest in his education, believing this to be the mother's responsibility. The mother was consistently indulgent. What Greg asked-for she gave him, usually without argument. She would watch him with amused affection, and in her eyes he could apparently do no wrong. When faced with his misdemeanours and lack of progress in school she seemed worried momentarily but laughed-off the worry with comments about 'boys being boys' and 'giving him time'. As for his poor performance in formal skills, she attributed this to his relatively short time in the Infants' school, and was sure that he would 'catch up' when he was older. The idea that habits of persistence, and interest in knowing-how, as well as satisfaction in work, can be developed very early, and are essential to later success she found astonishing. Again, a long period of counselling about the meaning and demands of education, carried out informally in chats about Greg's progress, at parents' discussion sessions, and while looking at children's work on 'open' days, made some impression on Greg's mother. But she was not really able to bring herself to support teachers in their efforts to get him to work steadily. When he, like Jimmy, was required to work alone with the head she laughed and commented that if anyone could stop his chatter they deserved a medal. She was not in the least hostile about this action, however, which was something of a gain.

Although Greg's aggression was diminished by firm handling (he disliked being away from other children, and the 'work alone' sanction was more resented initially than it had been in Jimmy's case) and his relations with staff and other children became cordial, his lack of application and his complacence about his work were almost inevitable in view of his mother's attitude and his father's non-involvement in his formal education.

Considerations

Characterized by an experience of parental inconsistency, aggression or rejection (real or imagined), or all three, these boys all had special need for affectionate but *absolutely consistent* handling within an ordered but not rigid school setting. While these are needs for all children, those more certain of their place in the family affections and of the 'rules' of living can probably tolerate better than the boys described above the minor inconsistencies and the small changes in routine to which even the best teachers are liable.

Despite differences of background and of personal qualities, each of these boys found concentration difficult, and tended to give up early rather than persist in a task – even in an interesting and self-chosen one There is a special need, here, for the sort of task, however unorthodox it may seem for performance in school, which will be carried through to completion and give the child an experience of satisfaction – perhaps for the first time in his life, or perhaps, as for Donny, after a period of failure and increasing distrust of his own powers. Only in Donny's case has the family any appreciation of the aims and demands of the Infant stage of education, and thus there is a special need in most such cases for the development of acceptable work-attitudes before the introduction of formal skills. Long-recognized as an essential part

53

of education in the Nursery schools, and accepted as a feature of most Reception classes, such opportunity for the learning of responsibility, job-satisfaction, persistence and concentration is less readily offered to children past the age of six or seven. Yet, if homes and families have not provided such opportunity – and this is not always to be regarded as a 'fault' meriting 'blame' – the schools must accept the necessity for giving a long period for such learning to some children.

The need, in all the cases described, for a bridge to be built between the home and the school, is also more pressing than it is for children whose parents have more understanding of the meaning of education. These latter will tend to build the bridge themselves; in cases like those of Keith, Stanley, Duncan and Jimmy, in particular, it is necessary for the teacher to do the work – at least initially. Unrecognized, and certainly unformulated, one of the great needs of these boys was to have all the adults in their world 'on the same side' and seen to be so. Parents of aggressive children are often themselves aggressive, and may have carried from childhood attitudes of distrust or fear of those in authority – sometimes with good cause, if their own teachers were punitive and remote. It is possible to break this repeating pattern in some cases, and thus help both parents and children to more successful relationships and learning. Certainly, there is likely to be more chance of success when the children are in the Infants' school than after several years of punishment, complaint and resentment in respect of older children have reinforced the parents' (and the children's) belief that every hand is against them.

Suggestions for further reading

Benedict, R. *Patterns of Culture* (1935) Routledge Paperback (1961)

Buhler, C. et al *Childhood Problems and the Teacher* Routledge & Kegan Paul (1953)

Carthy, J. D. & Ebling, F. J. (ed.) *The Natural History of Aggression* Academic Press, London & New York (1964)

Comfort, A. *Authority and Delinquency in the Modern State* Routledge & Kegan Paul (1950)

Dollard, J. et al *Frustration and Aggression* Yale University Press (1939)

Jackson, L. *Aggression and its Interpretation* Methuen (1954)

Lorenz, Konrad *On Aggression* Methuen (1965)

Packard, V. *The Status Seekers* Penguin Books (1957)

Tawney, R. H. *The Acquisitive Society* (1921) Fontana Books (1961)

Chapter 4

Solitary Aggressors

While the aggressive children already discussed are typical of about half the cases of aggression in their ability to gather groups of children around them, and in their possible need for the admiration and support of others, there were many cases where the aggressive behaviour was solitary and the needs of the children concerned either greater than or different from those of the gang leaders or inciters. On the whole, solitary aggressors were younger, including girls, and were thought to be more deeply disturbed than those who led or belonged to gangs. This is, of course, not invariable. Duncan was a deeply disturbed boy, and not every solitary aggressor was so; but this distinction could be made in general consideration of the two groups. Another difference was that while, again not invariably, group aggression at Infants' school age did not lead to destruction of property solitary aggression often did. It is unnecessary to repeat what has already been said about the possible cultural factors in aggressive behaviour, or about the almost inevitable underlying frustration in all aggressive behaviour. Similarly, a teacher's own attitudes are relevant in her dealings with all aggressors. The same general considerations apply to solitary as to group aggression, and must be borne in mind when dealing with it. There do seem, however, to be some differences between these two groups of children which are not attributable to personality, and the following cases, each representative of 'types' of solitary aggression, may serve to underline them.

A. *Aggression Against Property*

7. Paul
A slight fair child, with tremendous energy of the sort associated with the condition known as 'hyperkinesia' – described by Barton Hall in most graphic terms which will be only too familiar to teachers who have had to cope with such a child

in school.[1] *Seemingly bright (although no tests of ability administered), but a little retarded in reading and erratic rather than below average in written work. An imaginative and unusually gifted draughtsman and painter. A lively curiosity about everything attracting his attention, but poor powers of persistence and concentration, and (to quote both his teachers and Barton Hall) 'more trouble than all the rest put together'. High expectations of him from well-educated parents made his erratic progress in school a matter of frequent discussion and exhortation to him. His destructiveness and his constant losing of his own possessions were a source of annoyance to his mother.*

After a tumultuous start to school when he seemed to break everything he touched, including the cherished work or belongings of other children, his mother came to the school. The set of her shoulders as she passed the window, the determination with which she knocked the head teacher's door, and the rapid, but low-voiced flow of her complaints against the school were remarkably akin to the behaviour of her small son. She could not sit still, was convinced that there was a 'conspiracy' (her word) to get Paul a bad name, and, conversely, there never had been such a naughty child since the world began. It took a long time for her to run out of 'steam' – and when she did she burst into tears. Complaints and accusations from other parents had been numerous ever since Paul had begun to walk and could get out of the garden, but were now running at the rate of three or four a week. Torn coats, broken toys, muddied satchels, ruined paintings and shattered models made in school and proudly taken home, had all been brought to her door with indignant protests. Paul had either denied all knowledge of a particular incident or had burst into tears and claimed that other children 'made him be naughty' – an exact reflection, in childish terms, of his mother's view of life and responsibility. It seemed that Paul could not let anything alone, and while there were a few incidents involving his hitting (in one case biting) another child, his main target seemed to be property rather than people.

Many long, 'supportive' sessions were necessary before Paul's mother, an intelligent woman of considerable artistic

[1] *'Psychiatric Examination of the School Child'* (1947) pp. 159-162.

gifts, acknowledged that she had been an over-active child, always in trouble, severely disciplined by her parents and teachers, and resentful of all authority ever since. She told of what a fretful, restless baby Paul had been from birth – the midwife who delivered him had said, 'My goodness! You've got a lively one here!' – and of how her quiet husband had retreated from the demands of his small son, although very fond of him, and proud of his occasional achievements. Once started, this harassed woman seemed unable to stop. She had, she said, a violent temper, and Paul was so exasperating that she often shouted at him, or smacked him; on these occasions he appeared terrified of her, and then she was sorry for what she had said and done. Moreover, such incidents were almost always followed by a piece of quiet, deliberate destruction of someone else's property – 'As though,' she said, 'he was trying to get at me' Occasionally, Paul lost his temper with her, and was open in his destruction of cherished possessions of her own, throwing them down or tearing them up shouting such things as 'You're a horrible old mummy' or 'I hate you'. Not abnormal at three, and understandable in the face of the mother's own fierce behaviour, such outbursts on both sides now that Paul was well over five and at school were obviously a matter of grave concern to this mother. (It is, perhaps, interesting that she never mentioned her husband's reaction to either Paul's aggressive attacks on other children's property, or the scenes between him and his mother.)

The development of a friendly relationship with the head teacher and with Paul's second class teacher helped this intelligent, troubled but not unloving woman a great deal. She showed a genuine interest in child development, learned to praise Paul for his splashy but highly imaginative and lively work with paint and charcoal, and stopped comparing him to his disadvantage with his older sister and with other boys. On the day that she had told him, 'You're a clever little boy, and you're going to be a better painter than Mummy,' he drew a picture in his book of a boy walking along hand-in-hand with his mother and captioned it 'Me and my mummy are frens'. He was then just over six. It would have been a great help to this boy had his father been less remote – but there were signs, before he left the Infants' school (before he was seven, his birthday being in August) that the improvement in Paul's behaviour was beginning to make a favourable impression on his father.

Paul's teacher was herself a volatile and artistically gifted woman, not always patient, but with remarkable insight and great affection for him. She resisted her impulse to grumble at him about his untidy, smudgy writing and his inability to sit properly at a desk – he worked upside-down, or with his feet on another child's chair, or with his own precariously tipped, and was never still for more than a few minutes – and concentrated on the interesting and unusual content of his written work, his lively oral expression, and his excellent painting, drawing and modelling. Despite his over-activity and his poor powers of concentration, praise and encouragement helped him to persist for increasingly longer at a task, and to gain considerable satisfaction from it. His teacher came to realise that it was preferable to let him work in any position, and to allow him to run errands which gave him a chance to rush up and down the climbing frame on his way across the playground than to wage an endless battle, (which no teacher can win), to make him 'sit properly' or 'stop fidgetting'. It is not usually difficult in an Infants' school classroom to let such a child have ample desk room, without, however, isolating him or taking a punitive attitude. It is also reasonable to allow fairly frequent breaks for vigorous motor activity, for work is likely to be more successful if a child is not aching to move about.

A sense of constant failure is commonly found in hyperkinetic children, as Barton Hall points out, because their restless, destructive behaviour exasperates teachers and parents to a point where they are almost unable to praise them for anything. The children, understandably, become more tense, increasingly over-active and, inevitably, more destructive and disruptive – thus earning more censure and becoming even less able to settle down. According to Barton Hall this vicious circle can end in neurosis, delinquency or psychopathic states unless broken early.[2] In Paul's case there was considerable improvement in his work and attitudes after just over a year in school, possibly due to the support given to his mother and

[2] 'Psychiatric Examination of the School Child' p. 162.

59

the steps outlined above taken by his teacher; and the school doctor (who had been concerned about him on school entry) felt that the last resort of giving him tranquillizing drugs was not necessary, and that Child Guidance also seemed uncalled-for.

Temperamental instability, leading to destructive and aggressive acts, is not uncommonly accompanied, according to Barton Hall,[3] by affectionate, sensitive and generous characteristics, and this was certainly true of Paul. An endearing and thoughtful little boy was to be discerned in the middle, as it were, of the fuss and upheaval he could cause. He was, as would be expected, unpopular with other children for a year or more after he came to school, but as he became a little more settled, and a lot more sure of his place in his mother's and the teacher's affections, he made several friends. This, in turn, added to his confidence, and he became more popular in classroom group activities as well as out of school. Ideally, Paul would have stayed in the Infants' school for another month or two, for he was physically small, emotionally somewhat immature, and his progress was just beginning to be really rapid in the last week or two of his last summer term. The exacting conditions of a large class in a streamed and fairly formal Junior school proved stressful to him, but the necessity to make a 'special case' of him in order to retain him for a few more months made such a course untenable. It is unwise to take a course of action which may be constructed by parents, neighbours and the child himself as indicative of failure or 'oddness', and only more flexibility about transfer dates and between separated Infants' and Junior schools in the matter of special needs would avoid unnecessary strain for children such as Paul and others previously discussed.

8. Sean

A tense, tiny child, the illegitimate son of a young mother, said to be mentally unstable, who had him fostered from birth. First fostering broke down after only a few months, and he was in an institution until the age of 19m. when fostered again with the couple who had him until he was nearly seven. This couple took foster children regularly,

[3] Ibid. p. 161.

usually on a short-term basis, and had adopted one of them –
a boy of about Sean's age. Reports of the foster-mother's un-
kindness to Sean were not infrequent, but for several years
the Children's Officer could find no evidence of ill-treatment.

So disturbed did this little boy seem on entrance to school –
he tore, broke, threw or hit almost everything in the classroom,
and yet looked fearful and had fits of anguished weeping for
no apparent reason – that he was referred almost at once for
psychiatric assessment. He was found to have an I.Q. of 110
but to be 'deeply disturbed – possibly pre-psychotic', and the
P.S.W. was very concerned about the coldness and obsessional
cleanliness of the foster-mother. His learning was almost non-
existent, whether this was in the field of social skills or intellectual skills such as command of language, reading or
number-work. He made so little progress, despite help from
the Child Guidance clinic and advice (by Children's Officer
and P.S.W.) to the foster-mother, that he was retained in a
small class where he could have special attention.

In this small group, and with a motherly teacher, who had
brought up four sons of her own, he improved a little. He
was incredibly destructive at first, but in a quiet, almost
detached manner, demolishing toys and materials with a set,
unhappy look on his face and his teeth clenched. If other
children interfered he attacked them with equal ferocity, but
as though they were 'things'. This is a most terrifying
symptom, and one which teachers should be quick to recognize and refer for skilled help. His teacher, with the support
of the head and the advice of the psychiatrist, provided
materials and toys that could be 'destroyed' *legitimately* –
plastic dolls that took to pieces, cars and trains that were in
sections for screwing together, large and small blocks, clay,
etc. – but absolutely forbade the destruction of other objects,
enforcing the sanction by removing him if he disobeyed. In
the playroom of a clinic it may be allowable to permit utter
destruction, although many psychotherapists would not agree
to this; but in school, as in homes and the outside world, it is
not allowable behaviour. Sean had never been allowed to have
anything to take to pieces, and no block-play, water-play or
access to a sand-pit or even the garden soil had been per-
mitted. If one adds these restrictions to the emotional warping
almost inevitable after so miserable a babyhood and subse-

quent experience, it is not surprising that this child simply dismantled everything. The opportunity to do so in the classroom, with a firm and affectionate hand to control his worst excesses, seemed to be of great benefit to him.

After a few weeks of near silent absorption in toys of the kind described, and with 'messy' materials, Sean began to talk a little to his teacher. He wanted to know what was in her shopping bag, after she had done some shopping on the way to school or at lunch-time, and she let him help her sort things out. This he appeared never to have done, and examined everything with interest. If he started to pull packets open, or to poke his fingers through wrappers, however, he received the little tap that his teacher had almost certainly dealt out to her own boys when they were small; and this he accepted happily, just asking about the next package. After his teacher had hidden a small packet of sweets at the bottom of her basket, to be found by Sean, but shared with the rest of the class, he began to show pleasure by smiling every time she came in with the shopping. He smiled very little, as a rule, and this was the kind of incident which encouraged him to do so.

He also developed a great interest in doll-play, and was often to be seen trailing round the classroom and adjacent hall and playground with an armful of dolls and Teddy-bears. These he would put to bed on the floor, or in the house-corner, wash, dress and then gather up again. He was nearing six at the time that this play started, and his aggressive behaviour with objects and with children was slightly diminished. He resembled, in movement, in chubbiness, in his conversation and in his monologues with the dolls a very much younger child – but a rather happier one, than previously. The tenseness in his face and a stiffness about his gait also seemed to diminish at about this time. Staff, and some parents who were fairly often in the school, were asked not to comment on the nature of his play except in a friendly and approving manner, for odd though it might seem for a boy of six it was the most positive and constructive activity in which he had yet indulged. It may have been that he was treating the dolls as he himself wished to be treated by a real or imagined mother, for his tenderness in handling them and his soft crooning to them were in arresting contrast to his destructive and aggressive behaviour, and could not but be counted as progress.

His foster-mother found the changes in him unbearable, however. He had been silent and biddable at home, submissive to her except for very rare moments of tearful violence, and always clean. Now he was noisier, occasionally defiant, and wanted to play with water and dig in the garden. Despite explanation and support this foster-mother was unable to accept the changes as improvements, and punished him severely for the most ordinary behaviour. Neighbours again told of how they heard him screaming, and the Children's Officer made arrangements for him to be removed. Whether this was wise it is hard to say. At the time it seemed the only possible course – but Sean cried bitterly on being told that he was going to live somewhere else, and clung to his foster-mother. He was not moved suddenly, but given time to visit the small residential school where he was to be placed, and assured that he would be able to visit his foster-parents quite often. Nevertheless, he was a withdrawn and haunted-looking waif when he left for his 'new home', and it is argu-able that although he was not well treated by his foster-mother he had for her the only permanent attachment of his short life. In his placement in a small unit with particularly skilled and devoted people trained to help deeply disturbed children his need for highly specialised treatment was officially recognized at last; but it is unfortunate that such children as Sean cannot more often be permanently fostered (even if per-mission for adoption is withheld) from birth, or at least brought up from birth in a small 'family unit' children's home. Sean had experienced three changes of 'mother' before he was two years old, and the work of Bowlby and others has surely demonstrated – even if some of the *detail* in evidence is questionable – that the ability to form normal relationships, and behave normally with objects, is likely to be severely im-paired by such experience. His greatly impaired learning, which put him beyond the skill of any teacher in an ordinary school to help, would also have been attributed by Bowlby, Gesell and Armatruda, and many others, to the disastrous early experience. That a teacher could co-operate with psy-chiatrist and psychiatric social worker to the extent of helping him even so little in the learning of some social skills is, how-ever, a considerable contribution.

B. *Aggression Against Persons*

9. Tim

*Started in the Infants' school at the age of seven, having been
in a unit for deeply disturbed children for the previous two
years. This was a residential unit, and Tim had received very
good teaching in the school attached to it. I.Q. 93, and
although learning of formal skills retarded could read and
write at about the standard of an average six-year-old on entry
to the Infants' school. This was a considerable achievement,
for he was still a deeply disturbed child, and his venture into
normal school was something of an experiment. Continued to
live at the residential unit, and to receive the encouragement
and support of teacher and house-mother there, so that
eventually entry into Junior School and discharge to an
ordinary Children's Home was 'cushioned'.*

His early history was a confused and tragic one, as disastrous as Sean's, but somewhat different in its effects. His
mother had rejected him, left her husband, lived with other
men, by whom she had had children she did not reject, and
had Tim back home for short periods before once more
'dumping' him on the local authority under one pretext or
another. She made the empty, cruel promises of so many inadequate and chaotic women of her kind – to have him home
when she married again, or moved to a new house, or at
Christmas. She promised to visit him, and did not turn up;
promised him presents which did not arrive; told him she
really loved him best of all, and in the next breath that he
was so wicked that she had had to get rid of him. He had
been in various 'homes' almost all his life, until he was so
disturbed that he had been found a place in the unit already
mentioned. Here he improved remarkably with the affectionate, consistent and permissive handling he had never previously known, and with psychotherapy. Unlike Sean, he remained capable of forming relationships, despite his understandable distrust of people, and by the time he was ready to
try himself out in a 'normal' school was superficially a jolly,
friendly little boy.

But his adjustment was still 'fragile', and very small things
upset it. When upset, perhaps by someone borrowing his pencil,
or by a small change in routine, he would fly into terrifying
rages and destroy whatever came to hand, moving on to attack

any adult or child he fancied had caused the 'trouble'. He was a square-faced fair boy, of a placid appearance, but in these rages his face would go deep red and contort quite frighteningly. He was well-built and strong, and capable of hurting other children badly, so was immediately removed at the onset of a rage. Restrained from physical assault, he discharged his fear and anger in a stream of appalling language – another reason for expeditious removal from other children! Having been warned beforehand of his hyper-vulnerability, the head placed him in the small class mentioned before in connection with Sean, with the same teacher. She was fond of him from the start, for in many ways he was a boisterous boy of the kind she understood well, and was far more 'reachable' (and teachable) than Sean. She was unshocked by his occasional bad language, although she left him in no doubt that it was unacceptable, and had the foresight to prevent many incidents that would have upset him. (She kept to an invariable routine, for example; she was meticulously fair in the 'shares' of material or the sweets from her bag; she was careful to remember when it was his turn to do little chores – since failure to provide this sort of security for so deeply hurt a child re-awakens fears of being rejected, 'left out' and thought 'bad'.) Gradually, and perhaps because he had already had experience of consistent treatment from his previous teacher and his house-mother, he became loyal and co-operative with this teacher. He had many of the characteristics of the ordinary seven to eight-year-old, despite his immaturity in some aspects of his behaviour, and liked to be responsible for carrying her books, putting away her materials and hanging up her keys. He was friendly with the head teacher, too, and 'dropped in' for a chat like a little old man several times a day. Perhaps he needed to make sure that people did not disappear, and that they had time for him. Sometimes his visit to the head teacher simply consisted of putting his head round the door and pulling a face, or giving a friendly wave of the hand; but there was nothing offensive in these gestures, and they were a *positive* attempt to make and maintain good relationships of a kind not observed in Duncan, Sean or even Paul.

In dealing with Tim's most frightening outbreaks of aggression the first requirement was, as has been said, to remove him from the source of his anxiety. To this end there was an understanding that his teacher would bring him to the head and would then either stay in the quietness of the head's room and calm him down while the head took over the class, or that he would be left with the head teacher until he was 'better'. Sometimes the one course seemed more fruitful, sometimes the other. But whichever course was followed there was only one effective way to calm him and that was to hold him, physically, very close to the adult – preferably with his back to her, for he could kick hard as well as flail about with fists. This is a wise way to deal with a toddler in a tantrum, and when he was in a 'state' Tim was, to all intents and purposes, back in his fourth year. The attacks became less frequent probably as Tim became more sure of his place in the school, and he played well with other boys for prolonged periods. In the same way as Duncan, he appealed to other boys, perhaps because of his physical maturity and his cheerfulness when engaged in activities he enjoyed.

This was a case where the school played the supporting rôle to the therapist, with teachers willing to abide by psychiatric advice yet able to offer, as a therapist cannot, plentiful contacts with other children in a normal setting. Such cases are, perhaps, not common; but where a residential unit for children as disturbed as Tim is set up in the district the Infants' school may have a part to play in bridging the gap between residential treatment and ordinary schooling. It is a prerequisite for success, in such cases, that there is very close liaison between everybody concerned with the child. Competing for his affection, or regarding one's own function as the 'key' one, whether one is house-mother, therapist or teacher, is not only unprofessional – it can be disastrous for the child.

10. Padraic
A very tense boy, alternating between extreme aggression and extreme anxiety. Third child of young parents, with two slightly older sisters who alternately fussed over and bullied him. Said by the Child Guidance clinic to be of average intelligence, but very retarded in all language skills and number-work, and seeming incapable of sustained effort in creative work or play of any kind.

Padraic's mother was a devout Roman Catholic, who felt guilty at sending him to a non-Catholic school, and did so only because of the pressure on places and the long distance from the Roman Catholic school. She worried about him constantly, exhorting him to be good, kind and gentle 'to please Our Lady', and reminding him of the punishment awaiting naughty boys. His father, less devout but a regular communicant, told him to 'hit back' at people, and assured him that 'the Lord loves a brave fighter'. To this confusion for the child was added conflict between his own apparent inclination to enjoy the opportunities of school and his uneasiness, derived from his mother, at being there.

Nevertheless, Padraic's mother was co-operative with the school, partly because Padraic was taught by a Roman Catholic teacher, to whom reference has been made in connection with Sean and Tim. The inability of this boy to settle down, his extremely violent attacks on other children, and his retarded learning concerned his mother deeply, and she agreed to the school doctor's suggestion that he be seen at the Child Guidance clinic. She was co-operative up to the point at which suggestions by the psychiatrist conflicted with her religious beliefs – as was to be expected. But her priest gave qualified approval to the boy's being treated at the clinic, (he believed that all the troubles would clear up when Padraic was older and attended the Roman Catholic School), and she attended regularly.

The father treated the whole affair as a piece of woman's nonsense, but was not openly antagonistic. He was an orderly at a local hospital, where he walked about with his white coat open in the manner of a doctor, with something looking very like a stethoscope sticking out of the breast pocket, and patronized the psychiatrist when he visited the clinic. His lordly manner and his affected knowledge of all things medical (including psychiatric) set up in his son the same sort of conflict between loyalties to father and therapist as he suffered between Church and school. The psychiatrist acknowledged the great difficulty of treating a child under such circumstances, and enlisted the aid of the priest, a move which proved very helpful.

In school Padraic was supported in the small class referred to above, and allowed considerable freedom to run about outside with a ball and large toys. He was also allowed much 'messy' play with water, sand and clay, which he seemed to need more than most children; and he was particularly soothed and helped to some persistence in activities by play with 'small world' toys such as farm animals, Noah's Ark set, a family of tiny dolls, etc. He could be heard muttering about their being 'killed', 'smacked', 'sent to prison' and so on as he played. It is not for the teacher to interpret such play to the child – only to provide opportunity for it and restrain the child from actual (as opposed to symbolic) destruction of the material. Padraic's therapist, however, noted that his play with similar toys at the clinic became more purposeful and his conversation about it more significant after he had had opportunity to engage in it at school for several weeks. It was likely that he was able to 'carry over' his therapy between weekly sessions at the clinic in this activity at school.

He left the Infants' school for the Roman Catholic school a term earlier than expected, and was still in treatment, and improving in behaviour at the time. His aggressive outbursts were less frequent and vicious, his anxiety much diminished, and the night-terrors from which he had suffered into his seventh year had almost ceased. But his learning was still retarded, and it was hoped that this would receive special consideration from the very sympathetic head of his new school. In such a case as Padraic's, with conflicting loyalties and expectations between not only the parents but between Church and school, and father and therapist, it is difficult for the teacher to help. As Padraic's case has shown, however, tolerance, willingness to accept help from unfamiliar quarters, sympathy with the mother's own conflicts, and the exercise of sound infant method, can probably effect some improvement in the child.

11. Martin

A small, dark, intelligent boy, of great physical energy, and unusual belligerence. The second child of four, with an older sister and two younger brothers. Father had had what was probably meningitis in boyhood, and had been erratic, aggressive, and irresponsible in regard to employment ever since. He assaulted his wife, beat his children, drank too much, had a period of drug-taking and was often in fights. Indulged the children on occasions, and Martin, in particular, admired him. The mother was stable, (if understandably anxious), hardworking and a woman of considerable sense and humour. After some particularly unpleasant assaults this woman divorced her husband, and when Martin entered school at five had been coping alone with the four children for nearly a year.

Martin fought several children in his first day or two at school, for no reason that could be discovered, and continued to defend by violence tools or materials he was using even after he must have realized that there were plenty to go round. He seemed to resent women, and called his teacher names such as 'old pig' and 'silly daft woman' when she restrained him from hitting another child. He may have blamed his mother for his father's leaving the family, as well as resenting her firm handling of him – she was determined that this strong-willed little boy was not 'going the way of his father'. These attitudes he appeared to transfer to his teacher. She knew the mother well, however, having taught the older sister, and was understanding of Martin's confused and angry feelings.

Restraint and removal from the scene of his aggression, the provision of much outdoor play, and consistent refusal to be bullied by him, helped Martin to employ his energy and express his hurt in more acceptable manner; but one of the needs of this boy was to have a man to admire and talk to, and it was here that the schoolkeeper was invaluable. Physically vigorous and with motor skills developed beyond the average, Martin was what the schoolkeeper called 'a little cracker' with a football, even before he was six. Small-sized, but real footballs were part of the equipment in the school, and Martin helped the schoolkeeper to keep them inflated, properly laced and maintained, as well as being shown how to control a ball with head, hands and feet. The two of them were often to be seen having a few minutes' kick-about before and after school, as well as in school time. Martin, as Duncan, liked to chat to the schoolkeeper in his shed, examine his tools and equipment, and go down to the boilerhouse with him. This relationship was one of the most helpful that could have been established, for the schoolkeeper also knew and liked Martin's mother, and was on excellent terms with the teaching staff and head; thus he provided a very necessary model of how men treat women.

In his longing to be 'manly' Martin was more mature than most of the aggressive boys so far considered. He was also more persistent in his work, and more concerned with success in formal skills. He learned to read just after he was six, and was delighted with his skill. Encouraged by his mother, he was going to the public library before he was seven. His written work was lively in content, if untidy, and his illustrations for it as vigorous as himself. His normal delight in mastery of school work was an important factor in helping him to express his hurt and deflect his energy. His teachers realized this, and he was given as much opportunity as possible to exercise his skills, and distracted to them rather than punished for aggressive outbursts. He was removed from the scene of fights early in his school life, of course, and given quiet tasks to perform while he 'cooled off' – but, later, preventive action was more possible, and more effective.

It is possible for the staff of an Infants' school to play a very important part in supporting deserted and divorced mothers. Although Martin's mother was sensible and stable, she felt, in common with almost every woman in a similar position, vulnerable and inadequate on occasions. A woman without a husband, whether widowed, divorced or deserted, obviously lacks emotional support, adult companionship within the home, and financial security if her children are still young enough to preclude her from doing a well-paid, full-time job. She lacks status in the eyes of friends and neighbours, however sympathetic they may be – and she is exposed to dubious and often very tiresome attentions from men who consider her 'fair game' for anything but marriage. The ordinary courtesy, consideration and time offered by an understanding school staff is at least an aid to self-respect. Dealings with the National Assistance Board if necessary, information about holidays for the children, help available for school uniform, and pre-school facilities for younger children can all be matters for informal and discreet discussion with a woman who knows, trusts and likes head and staff of the school to which her children go. The school is in a better position to give this sort of help than most other agencies, for it is not the source of money, demands no details of income, lays down no conditions, and does not supervise the mother's life in any particular. It can be 'neutral ground', in fact, on which the mother can be simply herself. Martin's needs were served in part by just such help offered to, and warmly accepted by, his mother.

12. Clifford

The second child of two, with a sister only a year or little more older than himself. An intelligent, well-educated family, materially prosperous, and deeply concerned with the well-being of the children. An I.Q. on three tests, at intervals of 97, 90 and 95 – but a reading performance at the age of 7 : 5 much higher than these consistently 'low average' ratings would have suggested, viz: Rate: 9y. 1m. Accuracy: 9y. 4m. Comprehension: 10y. 4m. (Neale Analysis). Number-work (Schonell tests of arithmetical skills only) very little below average for chronological age, and of a standard rather higher than intelligence scores led teachers to expect. In practical work he was slapdash, and showed little interest.

Clifford had outbursts of aggression against other children mainly in response to name-calling or verbal teasing. He lisped a little, and spluttered when angry, which tended to incite more teasing than ever. His teacher reproved children who teased others rather more obviously than she reproved children like Clifford who responded to it by attack. It is just not possible for small children to tolerate teasing (which is often only a form of aggression), and far from helping them to develop 'thick skins' or to laugh at themselves it either drives them into withdrawal or into behaviour of Clifford's kind. (It is doubtful, in any case, whether the insensitivity to the feelings of others implicit in the suggestion that one should develop 'a thick skin' is what we are aiming for in our social education of children; and what adult, other than one mentally unbalanced, is *really* amused by his own shortcomings?) The first need for Clifford was to feel that his slight speech defect was of no great importance, and this was achieved by the 'tone' set by the teacher of the Reception class.

Clifford continued to be prone to aggressive behaviour when thwarted in quite minor ways, however, and resembled a very angry three-year-old when he was in such a state, even at the age of six. He would go very red, his eyes would fill with tears, and he would lower his head and charge, with fists and feet flailing wildly. He had to be restrained in the manner described as efficacious with Tim, and would usually end up sobbing, again like a much younger child, on somebody's knee while his victim was comforted by somebody else. Fortunately, these outbursts were fairly rare, and disappeared altogether by his last term in the Infants' school. They did seem in-

71

dicative of some disturbance, however, and his mother came to school at least twice a term to talk about his progress and behaviour since she, too, was worried.

Meeting Clifford's mother helped teachers to understand a little about her son. She was a cultured but shy woman, obviously of an anxious temperament, but with a great deal of warmth and considerable humour once she could relax. She had a noticeable, but by no means incapacitating lisp, and spoke very quickly when worried. She explained that Clifford had had several very frightening attacks of asthma when a baby and toddler, and that this was a family complaint. He had also been an active, impatient baby, had talked and walked early, and had always been prone to sudden fears and excitements. In fact, he fulfilled most of the criteria listed by Barton Hall[4] as being characteristic of the asthmatic child – including the over-mothering by an intelligent woman understandably afraid of his catching colds, playing with anything likely to bring on an attack of asthma, or getting over-excited. Her realization of the need to 'let him go' and become independent conflicted with her anxiety about the troubles he got into when he was away from her. It was not very difficult to help this essentially sensible and affectionate mother, for she really only needed confirmation of her own view that Clifford's furies and regressive behaviour were not symptomatic of gross disturbance, or any grave abnormality. That he was still something of a 'baby' she admitted, but did not fall into the error of becoming 'tough', remote or cool with him in the expectation that this would help him to grow up.

Active outdoor activities, encouragement and praise for his performance in formal skills, the preventive action already described, friendly support for his mother, and the non-competitive atmosphere of the Infants' school seemed to help this boy in controlling his emotions, and to reduce the generalized anxiety to which asthmatic children are almost always prone. Speech therapy was thought to be unnecessary in Clifford's case, but might well be of use in similar ones.

[4] 'Psychiatric Examination of the School Child' pp. 130-132.

13. Joanna

A solid, vigorous little girl, tall for her age, the middle child of three, with a sister four years older than herself and a brother three years younger. The family had been in Australia until a year before Joanna's birth, and were contemplating emigration to New Zealand while Joanna was in the Infants' school. Intelligence test scores from tests taken both in school and at the Child Guidance clinic showed Joanna to be of high-average intelligence, and her reading was not retarded.

So aggressive and spiteful was this child during her third term in the school that she was shunned by quite a number of children who had formerly been happy to play with her. She chased children, pulled hair, locked younger children in the lavatories or in cupboards, hit anyone who tried to join her in games with her skipping rope or ball, and was noisy in the extreme. When restrained or reproved by teachers she flounced and sulked, but was just as naughty again as soon as she had opportunity. It is possible that the onset of this behaviour coincided with the parents' talking about emigration, but there were obviously other 'roots' to it. Unlike most aggressive boys, she did not easily deflect her aggression into energetic performance of chores, or seem to get much release from 'messy' play or even from the legitimately destructive play that had helped Sean. In fact, she tended to despise such games, being in some ways a mature little girl, interested (if in anything at all) in the sort of sophisticated motor skills popular with eight to nine-year-olds. As Martin with a football, so was Joanna with a skipping rope or on the climbing frame; she was a highly skilful performer, with excellent motor co-ordination and considerable grace. Perhaps her admiration for her older sister provided an incentive for development of such skills. She was allowed considerable scope for the physical activity she loved, and encouraged to dance and move to music, receiving praise for her undoubtedly good performance. After such a session she would be 'peaceful' for a short period – but it became obvious that she was going to need more help than this.

Her unpopularity with her classmates, combined with her gregarious nature, (for she was always seeking their company), was causing more resentment, and consequently more aggressive behaviour; and she was being increasingly spiteful to her little brother. Her mother came to the school to discuss Joanna's difficulties, and to ask for help with her, and was very willing to have her referred for Child Guidance. Perhaps because her mother was relieved to have her worry taken seriously, and to have opportunity to talk about the family in general, Joanna herself improved greatly in attitude and behaviour within a few days. When she was seen at the clinic the mother had also had a visit from the psychiatric social worker and had benefited greatly from this, having been able to talk freely about the child's early history, her jealousy of her little brother, and her outbursts of anger when rejected as a playmate by her older sister and her friends. It emerged, also, that Joanna had several stays in hospital in her third year (described by the psychiatrist as traumatic in each case), and that the mother felt guilty about this. This mother had begun to feel that she was to blame for difficulties with both daughters, and badly needed the advice and support of teachers, psychiatrist and social worker. There was, in fact, little evidence that the mother was 'to blame', but the father's restlessness and somewhat immature personality may have contributed to the slight insecurity felt by his wife and children.

Once the mother felt supported, and the father had also been advised, there was thought to be no need for immediate therapy for Joanna, and she had two apparently successful sessions with the psychiatrist before being referred for review in another three months. The P.S.W. meanwhile visited the mother, and the school continued to help both. At her referral interview she had improved so much that it was not thought necessary to treat her – but the psychiatrist felt that this child was still 'at risk', and proposed to see her at termly intervals for a year or two. There were probably confusions and disturbances in Joanna that were not uncovered in this time, nor explicable in terms of the information obtained from the mother or the school. But to stabilize her, to promote successful learning, and thus to give her a sense of adequacy and achievement, was a viable course of action that might well aid her in dealing with other worries.

Considerations

It would be tedious, and is unnecessary to repeat all that has already been said at the end of the previous chapter about the many ways in which teachers can deal with aggressive behaviour by their classroom routine and provision, their contacts with parents, their readiness to use unorthodox 'remedies' and their skill in deflecting aggressive behaviour into acceptable channels. All this is fundamental to their dealings with 'solitary' aggressors also.

There is, however, one noticeable manner in which children such as (for example) Sean and Padraic differ from gang-leaders such as Duncan and Stanley: they cannot relate with other children at all. It is true that forming a gang to rush round the playground terrorizing other children constitutes unacceptable social behaviour – *but it is truly social*. However inadequately they may do so, the group aggressors lead, follow and even occasionally co-operate with other children. At Infants' school age this must be counted as gain. For children like Sean, on the other hand, relationships of any kind are either impossible or much more rudimentary than those formed by even so disturbed a boy as Duncan; and it may be that from the point of view of social-emotional development they are at the stage of two-year-olds and must be 'brought up' from that stage rather than thought of as naughty five or six-year-olds. Sean's being allowed to look through his teacher's shopping and then to share sweets with other children is an example of the kind of 'strategy' which may help a child to make a normal relationship.

The children discussed in this chapter were probably all more deeply disturbed than those in the previous chapter – with the possible exception of Duncan. This may be true of most 'solitary' aggressors when compared with those who form gangs, but it would be unwise to make this assumption on the basis of so small a sample as that from which these cases were drawn. It is likely, however, that teachers dealing with children of the kind described above will often feel that the failure to form satisfactory relationships, which is common to all of them, constitutes good reason for calling upon outside help. Certainly, in the cases of Tim, Sean, Padraic and Joanna the help of the Child Guidance team was essential, for no teacher could be expected to unravel and deal successfully with the emotional immaturities, confusions and damage of such children. Yet it should also have become apparent in discussion of their cases that the social milieu of school and relationship with an adult in the classroom were probably important ingredients in the healing and socializing process.

Suggestions for Further Reading

Barton Hall, M. *Psychiatric Examination of the School Child*
    Edward Arnold & Co. (1947)

Bettleheim, B. *Truants from Life* The Free Press, Illinois
    (1955)

Jackson, L. & Todd, K.M. *Child Treatment and the Therapy
    of Play* Methuen & Co. Ltd. 2nd Ed. (1948)

Lowenfeld, M. *Play in Childhood* Gollancz (1935)

Chapter 5

Withdrawn Children

The term 'withdrawn' perhaps needs some definition, for it is now widely used to describe many conditions. To some psychiatrists it covers the extreme isolation of some types of schizophrenia, while for many teachers it may be a legitimate description of the temporary shyness exhibited by a small child faced by a new situation or strange persons. For the purposes of this book it is used simply as a *description* of behaviour, and applied to children who withdraw themselves from contact with both adults and other children. That this withdrawal may be due to many causes ranging from serious mental states to the temporary shyness already mentioned will, it is hoped, emerge from a discussion of cases.

Although the ability to make satisfactory relationships was impaired in the cases of aggressive behaviour already discussed, these aggressive children performed overt actions of such a kind as to bring them into contact, if only physically, with teachers and children. Despite the depth of disturbance in some of these children they responded to hurt and fear by attacks on life, and had not entirely given up the struggle to establish themselves as persons within their circle. This was true even of the grossly disturbed Sean; but it will be remembered that he had, in fact, shown withdrawal symptoms within the home, and that these were regarded by everyone but his foster-mother as being more worrying than his aggressive and destructive behaviour.

A really withdrawn child can be said to have given up the attempt to relate with other human beings, or to come to terms with his physical environment; and this is true, if only temporarily, of the very shy as well as of the deeply disturbed child. It should be said at this point that *extreme and chronic shyness* should never be accepted as normal. No normal child, however temperamentally gentle and timid in the face of new persons or situations, resists for long the overtures of an understanding teacher or the interest of other children. To help normal children to overcome this understandable caution on

77

their first entry into school is part of the everyday job of the teacher, and one that is universally accepted as such. Continuing refusal or apparent inability to make contacts with others and to experiment with the apparatus and materials of a normally well-equipped classroom, however, should not be dismissed as due to 'shyness'. This is to describe, not to explain; and explanation is certainly needed if such withdrawal persists for longer than a week or so.

Where the aggressor has, by definition, put up a fight in the face of his hurt, fear and uncertainty the withdrawn child has capitulated. To the imperceptive teacher he may be less of a problem than his aggressive classmate; but to the perceptive he is a frightening prospect. It is a truism, but one that bears repeating, that it is at the quiet child that the teacher must look very carefully. If she reads through her records and finds she has written nothing about him for several weeks; if she remembers that he has never asked her a question, or chatted about his doings at home; if she cannot recall seeing him at play with others – then he is in need of her special observation and attention. Even if his work is satisfactory (and it very rarely is) it is not normal for a child – or an adult, for that matter – to lead a life among but not communicating with his fellows. Normal children like to be on their own sometimes, and it is very necessary to their full development in feeling and intellect that this need be met in school by the provision of quiet places in which to work, or just to sit, and appreciation by the teacher that assimilation of experience, construction of imaginative projects, and simple desire to sit and watch are legitimate parts of learning. This temporary withdrawal in order to rest, absorb or grow is, however, of a very different order from that of the child who never joins in, and teachers who know and care about individuals will be in no doubt as to the difference.

The children whose cases are discussed in this chapter were all a source of anxiety to their teachers and/or parents because of the 'total' nature of their withdrawal. Ordinarily shy new entrants and the normal assimilative or contemplative periods common to most children – and particularly to seven-year-olds – will not be discussed; but it is hoped that such normal withdrawal will be noted, allowed-for and used as some sort of yardstick by which to measure the more serious and prolonged withdrawal of children with special needs.

14. James

Almost impossible to test for intelligence, due to his muteness and negative attitudes, but believed to be only a little below average. Attainments virtually nil; and, on the rare occasions on which heard, speech incoherent and babyish. Recognized early in his school career as being in a very grave emotional state, and referred through the school doctor to the Child Guidance clinic. Described by the psychiatrist as 'grossly disturbed and severely inhibited'.

James' mother had been killed in a motor accident when he was three and his brother only a few months old. The father, who had been driving, blamed himself for the accident, but apparently without just cause. The family belonged to an extreme and bizarre religious sect, with mystic notions about the significance of blood. For this reason James' father kept the blood-stained coat in which his wife had been killed, and showed it to his two small sons from time to time. Other rules of the sect forbade both the keeping of birthdays or Christmas and the provision of most of the pleasures of childhood. To such a grim background for James was added the damage of having four changes of mother-substitute before his father married again when he was five. By the time he entered school he was a round, rosy child who looked much younger than five, and was completely withdrawn. He made no response at all to what went on in the classroom; if moved gently to a position from which he could see something interesting, he stayed there until moved elsewhere. If spoken to he sometimes shook his head, and on one or two occasions said 'No'. Even if tools or materials were put into his hands he would merely move them languidly before letting them fall. Sometimes when looking towards the water-tank he showed signs of some interest, but then only by a more intent stare and a faint smile. Attempts to get him to play with water failed. In fact, he gave the impression of not daring to move. Only in his walking across the playground on leaving, or returning to, his father, and in the meticulously careful way in which he hung up his outdoor clothes did he show any measure of self-determination.

Attempts to discuss him with his father were ineffectual in all but persuading him to agree to James's referral to the clinic. It was impossible to 'get past' the rigidity of this man's religious beliefs, young as he was, and his agreement to James having psychiatric treatment was made only on the understanding that it would involve 'no pills, medicines or bloodletting' and would be helpful in getting the boy to learn. The P.S.W. found the young stepmother, although a member of the sect, more reachable, and it was with her that most of the discussions at the clinic took place. Nevertheless, little progress was made in several months by either clinic or school, and James might have retreated even further into his own strange world had it not been for a minor accident.

He bumped into the corner of the building as he came into school, suffering one of those tiny abrasions to the scalp which, in small children, bleed very profusely. The head teacher bathed and plastered his head in her own room, and while she was doing so James began to talk. He rambled on, incoherently but excitedly, about a big girl called Mavis who had a bad cut, about the colour of blood, about the size of the cut, (his own was minute, and he was assured of this), about how Mavis cried and 'the daddy' cried. It seemed very likely that he was talking about the death of his mother; but the head teacher made no interpretation to him, just chatting to him in a general way, and letting him look at and play with some toys in the room while he brought his unwonted spate of communication to an end. The psychiatrist, however, was informed immediately of this incident, and on James' next visit to the clinic used the word 'Mavis' as James moved the small toys lethargically about, in his usual uncommunicative manner. Later, this doctor said that the word had acted like dynamite on a dam. James' memories of his mother, his fear about her death, his terror and loneliness with mother-substitutes all came to the surface in both words and most revealing play. The accuracy of his memories was a telling reminder of how much a small child registers of what goes on around him.

From this point some improvement in James' social responses was noticeable. He smiled at his teacher occasionally, painted pictures of fire-engines, ambulances and aeroplanes in a big, splashy, immature manner, and even accepted tools or materials from other children on a few occassions. Once or twice he spoke to his teacher. But with his therapist he was much more positive, playing fiercely with toys, smearing clay on walls, shouting and talking excitedly all the time. It was decided that this very disturbed and retarded little boy should go to a boarding-school for maladjusted children when he was seven, for he was by no means ready for the demands of the normal Junior school. His father agreed to this rather reluctantly, but was encouraged to give consent by his second wife, who was finding that James' younger brother was a very difficult child, and was also expecting a child of her own.

The function of the school in a case like this is a very delicate one. Nothing can, or should, be said about the extreme religious views of parents; teachers cannot undo the damage done by severe maternal deprivation; even the long-term help of the clinic may result in only partial success. The main concern of teachers dealing with so severely disturbed a child as James should be twofold: to keep the child aware of their presence and of where he is, no matter how unresponsive he may appear, and to seek skilled help as early as possible — thereafter, of course, co-operating as fully as possible with the clinic team. Two years of patient work by teachers and therapist were probably responsible for James' readiness to go to a special school as a fairly responsive, if still badly damaged, child instead of as a mute 'lump' and once there to make good progress.

15. Dennis

A stout, sullen-looking boy, believed to be of normal intelligence, although not tested, but retarded in formal skills. Monosyllabic in response to adults, and not noted as having spoken to another child in the first six weeks of his school life. Entered the school at the age of six, having been abroad with his family (father in the services), but with no record of attendance at Forces' school. Wandered out of school on several occasions, apparently being on the way home.

So odd and remote did this boy seem that attempts were made to find something about his background very soon after he came to the school. Dennis's mother did not appear either to bring him to school, to meet him, or at medical examination; a younger brother and sister were found wandering, in their indoor slippers, a long way from home and were returned to their house by neighbours who, however, could not persuade the mother to open the door for the children until they had gone away. The Health Visitor was concerned that she could not get into the house, for she could hear a baby

81

crying almost constantly, and the two toddlers seemed to be left to their own devices while Dennis was at school. The father's reply to a note asking if he would call and discuss his son's failure to settle down at school stated that he was too busy at the moment.

A persistent Health Visitor did eventually gain entry to the home. She found Dennis's mother to be a well-educated; pleasant but desperately anxious woman, apparently pregnant again although the baby was only six months old. The nurse's opinion was that the woman was in a very poor physical and mental state – a view which was shared by the head teacher, who accompanied the Health Visitor on her second visit. A firmly-worded letter to the father eventually prevailed-upon him to come to the school. His hearty, confident, hectoring tone made communication difficult. He offered to thrash Dennis, put a lock on the gate to stop his toddlers wandering, and to 'push the wife along' to the clinic, and only the most severe comments on the state of his wife caused him to promise that he would call in a doctor. In the event, it was as well that he did so, for when the doctor called the next day he found Dennis's mother to be in a very serious state in regard to her pregnancy, as well as in a most unstable mental condition, and he put her into hospital immediately.

Dennis continued to live at home and be cared-for by his father while the younger children went to relatives. The boy was patently relieved to talk of his mother being ill, and did not (perhaps for obvious reasons) wander out of school during the time she was away. Her mental condition was found to be very serious, and it appeared that she had had a bad breakdown following the birth of the now seven-month old baby. Dennis had lived for many months with a mother suffering from delusions of persecution which made her terrified of going outside the door; she had talked to him of the dangers lurking outside, and had cried when he set off for school every day. It is not surprising that this little boy had been unable to respond to the overtures of teachers and other children. To him they must have been utterly suspect, for no young child doubts the word of his mother, and is, of course, quite incapable of judging her mental state and thus having an objective picture of the situation. He did what all children are likely to do in this situation – threw in his lot with the mentally ill mother, and rejected the sane outside world. Treatment at the clinic would have been of great use to this boy, it was felt; but while the mother was away it was not possible to start on such a course, even had the father agreed to it.

His teacher helped him by letting him talk, by giving him plentiful opportunity to play-out his bewilderment, and by persuading him to take an interest in reading in order that he would be able to write to his mother, and to read to her when she came home. He was making reasonable progress, and plans had been made to refer him to the clinic for extra support, when the family moved to a neighbouring town. Here, on the mother's return from hospital, neither Dennis nor the next-youngest child who was now five attended school for four months. Only the comments of the Health Visitor that there seemed to be two children of school-age who were always at home brought the matter to the attention of the local education authority. Dennis's records, passed on from his first school, had apparently escaped notice at the office.

Such a situation as this child found himself in is not as rare as one might wish it were. A seclusive mother can, by definition, go unnoticed for a very long time; and her effect upon her children is invariably serious. The conflict of the child between the phantasies of his sick mother and the realities of the outside world is almost unimaginable. Yet, as will be seen in discussion of another case (that of Adrian, p. 86) modern views on mental illness and its treatment meant that, much more often than in previous years, a gravely sick parent is at home with the children for long periods before admission to and often immediately after discharge from hospital. The right of the adult to be treated compassionately, and at home, may conflict with the right of the children to be brought up in sense and sanity, and in this situation teachers have difficult decisions and a hard task to face. Perhaps, when seemingly impaled upon the horns of this peculiarly unpleasant dilemma, teachers may decide that their own responsibility is for the child, and take what steps they may to ensure that he gets maximum support from all the agencies possible. To do this is not to be lacking in compassion for the sick adult; but mental illness in a parent is a dreadful and dangerous burden for a child, and it is with his future that teachers must be concerned.

16. George

*Entered school at the age of six-and-a-half from a village
school in the same county, his parents having been killed in
a car accident only a month previously. A tall, gangling boy,
with signs of what had been a cheerful disposition still apparent. Performance in formal skills almost nil, perhaps not surprisingly, but thought to be of near-average intelligence by his
previous head teacher.*

George had been a generally cheerful child before the
death of his parents, but with occasional periods of slight
anxiety. He had had the reputation among his classmates of
being a bit of a clown, and had been very popular. The circumstances of the parents' deaths, the manner of its being
broken to George and his brother – by a policewoman in the
middle of the night – and the almost immediate refusal of
relatives to take any responsibility for the boys after the
funeral, made it unlikely that George would recover easily,
soon or completely from the shock. Traumatic as loss of
parents must always be, it is possible for children who were
previously well-loved and who are immediately cared-for by
understanding relatives to make remarkably rapid recovery.
If they can talk openly, and with pride and affection, of their
parents, even such total bereavement may do less lasting
damage than many adults might think possible.

In the case of George and his older brother, however, none
of these conditions were met. The head of their previous
school reported that these boys had been a source of irritation
to their parents, who had sometimes threatened to put them in
a 'Home', and that the marriage itself had been unstable since
George's (apparently unlooked-for) birth. The boys had, possibly, considerable guilt-feelings about their parents' deaths,
were unwanted by uncles and aunts, had no one with whom
to talk of the matter, and had lost home, most possessions
and their dog – taken by neighbours – in one blow. Greater
desolation can hardly be imagined.

Both boys were put into a small and friendly local authority
children's home, and George was put into the small class
when he came to school. He played alone at first, but with
the toys normally found interesting by a boy of his age, such
as construction sets, trains and building materials. He seemed
quite incapable of reading or of settling down to any effort
such as writing or drawing, and was not pressed to do so. At

regular intervals of about an hour, he retreated under the teacher's desk and went to sleep, usually for about ten minutes. It was not thought wise to waken him until enquiries had been made about his health; but when the school doctor pronounced him to be a physically very fit child it was realized that he was, quite literally, retreating. The doctor felt that he was still in a state of deep shock, and asked to see him again in another three months with a view to seeking psychiatric help if the boy had not been able to come to terms, on his own, with the new life he now had to lead.

In the meantime, the teacher took him about with her while she did small chores, let him join other boys in sorting out her shopping or tidying her cupboard, and while offering him ample opportunities to experiment with all sorts of materials, did not prevent him from sleeping at intervals. These became longer, and the sleep less heavy and shorter as the term moved on – but George was still withdrawing in this very literal way on occasions by the time he left for the Junior school. So cheerful and settled did he seem, however, both in the children's home and with his teacher, and so strong was his attachment to his brother and (in school) to Tim, that it was not thought necessary to call upon psychiatric help. Nevertheless, it was felt that his adjustment was still 'fragile', and in view of his continued learning retardation also, he was to be seen by the school doctor at shorter intervals than is usually the case.

It is not often that a teacher will have to cope with a child suffering such total bereavement and rejection by the relatives – but when she does her liaison with the child's previous school and with the warden or house-parents of the children's home are obviously important. So is the medical examination of a child who sleeps in this manner, for this habit may stem from physical causes as well as from emotional upheaval, and thorough physical examination is advisable as soon as possible. In George's case psychiatric treatment had not been thought necessary, at least during his Infants' school life, but it might be a most helpful course in other cases. It is difficult to see how such complete collapse of a child's whole world can be represented to him in such a manner as to help him to accept it and pick up the threads of attachment and learning from where they were broken. An understanding teacher may do much to help, especially if the child can be retained in her group for a long period; but most teachers will feel that help of a therapist is as welcome as it may be necessary.

17. Adrian

A tiny, dark, neat boy, seeming very anxious indeed, and speaking to no one at all during the first month in school. Later tests by the Educational Psychologist showed him to be of superior intelligence; and when he was heard to speak it was in a patently cultured accent and with great sense. Somewhat retarded in reading, writing etc. by the age of six-and-a-half. Not observed to play with other children for many months, and to retreat against the wall if they came too close to him while he was in the playground.

Adrian was obviously from what is usually described as 'a good home', and was an attractive-looking little boy. He came and went like a mouse, however, and watched classroom activities with apparent apprehension. His own activities were confined for the first term in school to producing minute, jewel-like pictures in wax-crayon, which he tucked carefully into his satchel, and showed to no one. He resisted invitations to paint or take part in other activities with a shake of the head, and could not be persuaded to so much as look at his teacher. In musical activities he was a spectator, but not an indifferent one. He smiled when certain pieces of music were played on the record-player, and gave a quick little nod of his head when his teacher told him the names of these. His classmates who had shown some shyness on entering school were lively, talkative members of the class after a very short time, and it was felt that Adrian's inability or refusal to join in or to talk to anyone was not a result of 'newness'. After a few weeks in school his routine medical examination was due, and it was hoped that some clue to his withdrawal might emerge at this time.

The usual letter to the parent giving notice of the medical examination, and incorporating an acceptance slip to be returned to school, elicited no reply of any kind from Adrian's mother. A further letter was sent, by post since it was possible that Adrian had forgotten to deliver the first, but no answer to this was received. As the boy's teacher was very concerned by his continuing withdrawal, and the school doctor was due to arrive within a day or two, a third, and personal, letter was sent to Adrian's mother, and the Health Visitor notified of the curious lack of response to the first two notes. She was not able to give much information about the home, for the family had been attended by another Health Visitor when Adrian was a baby, but she knew the road as a very prosperous one, and the particular house as well-cared-for and set in large gardens. She was baffled, on calling, to find a well-spoken, white-haired woman washing a large car in the driveway who insisted that no little boy lived there. She agreed that her name was the same as Adrian's but continued to deny his existence. Asked his address, Adrian whispered the number at which the Health Visitor had called. The head teacher remembered that it was Adrian's father who had brought him to school on both his pre-entry visits and on the first day of term, and it looked as though there might be some mystery about the mother.

This turned out to be the case. A day or two after the medical examination, at which, of course, Adrian had not been examined since neither parent was present, his very worried father appeared at school to explain why no one had responded to letters, and why the Health Visitor had received a denial of Adrian's existence. The mother had had several severe mental breakdowns, but had been pronounced well enough to return home some months previously – and had, in fact, coped well and normally with the everyday business of running a house and looking after Adrian. Encouraged by this, and with the assurances of her doctors that she was in no danger of breakdown in the forseeable future, the boy's father had gone abroad on business for six weeks, making arrangements with a son at university and other relatives to recall him if his wife seemed to be unable to cope. That they had not done so was due to one of those series of coincidences that no one can guard against; and the father had returned to find a gravely sick wife, a terrified Adrian, and torn-up letters all over the garden.

This father wished to have psychiatric help for Adrian as soon as possible, for years of experience of mental illness had given him considerable insight into the state of mind induced in children by parental illness of this kind. He explained that he had sent his second son away to an understanding boarding-school at the age of nine, when his wife had first become ill, and planned to send Adrian to join him as soon as possible –

certainly, as soon as he was seven and could be received into the kindergarten department of his brother's school. He had hoped that his wife might have a few years of freedom from her illness in which, as he said, 'to enjoy Adrian'; but despite previous optimistic medical forecasts this now seemed unlikely. So co-operative and kindly a parent makes the task of the school much easier than it might otherwise be, and Adrian was sent for treatment at the Child Guidance clinic within a week or two. Thereafter, he improved in his relationships with his teacher, and after another term was playing with two other rather quiet, but normal, friendly boys.

As has already been said in discussion of Dennis (p. 81), the presence of a mentally ill parent constitutes a heavy burden for a small child. In much the same manner as Dennis, Adrian had cast in his lot with his mother, although very frightened of her as Dennis was not, and had found the effort to relate the sane world of school with the phantasy world of his mother quite beyond him. Even the few weeks of exposure to a severe phase of his mother's illness had made a deep impression on him, and it took his therapist and his father several months to get even this very intelligent little boy to accept that his mother was ill, and that he could discuss her with other people if her talk or behaviour worried him. The father's compassion and understanding in regard to his wife were obviously a great help to Adrian, for he was not called upon to ignore, despise or endure his mother's odd state, only to identify with his father in being sorry that she was so ill, and in helping her to 'get better' by having treatment in hospital. It is possibly not madness that children fear so much as the necessity to pretend that it does not exist – a necessity which may lead them to withdrawal, to ape the sick parent, or to a serious denial of all knowledge which results in learning-failure at all levels. It is not, however, for the teacher to discuss the mental illness of a parent with the child, unless (and this must be a rare occurrence) under the guidance and instruction of the child's therapist and other parent. There was no need for Adrian's teacher to do more than acknowledge that she knew his mother was ill and hoped she would soon be better; beyond this, her function was to involve him in the normal, enjoyable experiences of learning and relationship with other children, and in a pleasant, 'sane' relationship with herself.

18. Mary

A large, dark, sullen-looking child, the eldest of four children at the age of five, and with twin baby sisters, in addition, by the age of seven. Intelligence thought to be somewhat below average, although failure to attend sessions with the Educational Psychologist precluded testing in the Infants' school. Retarded in reading, with a reading age of 5:7 at the chronological age of 7:2 on Schonell test R.I. – no score at all on other reading tests administered.

From her earliest days in school Mary was a source of worry to her teachers. She would sit under her desk, or in a corner, twisting any piece of cloth that came to hand, shredding a piece of paper, pulling her own hair, or rocking backwards and forwards. Sometimes she combined two of these activities, and occasionally accompanied them with quiet crooning sounds. She bore, in fact, many of the stigmata of the severely disturbed, possibly psychotic, child, and was shunned by other children even when the teacher drew her out from her corner and invited her to watch activities in the classroom.

The school doctor was very concerned about her, and questioned her mother closely about her past history. Mary's mother was a tired-looking woman of not very great intelligence, who did not seem able or willing to remember any feverish illness or unusual incident that might have led the doctor to think the child had some brain-damage. She maintained, in fact, that Mary had been 'all right' until she started school – a contention she gave up later in Mary's school career – and was likely to be 'all right' again once she had settled down. She wearily rejected any suggestions made about referral to a specialist or a visit to her own doctor with the child.

The teacher persisted in offering Mary a variety of materials, often putting these under the table where Mary was crouched or into her hands. She talked to her, took her by the hand, and occasionally placed the child on her knee while she was telling a story. No response came for many weeks, but by the end of her first term in school Mary was nodding or shaking her head, and by the end of her first year was making brief, gruff answers to some questions, and was coming out from under tables to croon over dolls or crayon rather aimlessly in the main part of the room. The rocking had almost ceased, and the pulling of her own hair was very rare, but these seemed small gains in a year, and another effort was made to persuade the mother to accept referral to the Child Guidance clinic. By this time, however, Mary's mother was pregnant with the twins, and could hardly have been expected to accept the suggestion. The Health Visitor reported that the woman was wearily resentful of this pregnancy, especially having been told that she seemed to be carrying twins, but had resisted all suggestions that, after the babies were born, she should attend the Family Planning clinic. Only the most determined and brisk attitude of the Health Visitor caused her even so much as to drag herself down to the ante-natal clinic, and to make arrangements for her confinement. For Mary she had little time, although she was not unaffectionate.

At the beginning of her second, and last, year in the Infants' school Mary had a new teacher who continued with the work of the first, and added more materials to those the child by now accepted to play with. This had to be done carefully and gradually; a few new crayons were put in the grubby little tin she insisted on using, or a new doll was laid beside the one she had 'adopted', or a doll's bath was put on a table where she was sitting. Often she ignored or threw down such additions initially, accepting them later if she thought no one was watching. Her experience was thus slightly widened, and it looked as if something might be done to help Mary, even without the obviously desirable services of the Child Guidance clinic.

It was at this point, however, that there occurred one of those series of events that can wreck a school's best endeavours with a child in special need. Mary's teacher left, and others were absent by reason of illness, necessitating not only the ordinary disruptions in routine and relationships but the appointment of an unqualified teacher to Mary's class. Despite the support of experienced staff, the removal of small groups for reading and writing activities in the head's room at regular intervals, and much advice and guidance, the new teacher was apprehensive and uncertain in her approach to the children. The class deteriorated in both behaviour and performance of formal skills, and Mary reverted to sitting under a table and rocking. Attempts to put her in another class were futile, for she returned immediately to the room she knew, despite her distrust of her new teacher. This teacher's mixed attitudes of fear and annoyance in her dealings with Mary were understandable, for the child was at her most difficult; but they elicited even more difficult behaviour – and on one occasion Mary bit her teacher on the leg as she passed the table under which the child was sitting. Mary's resentment at the loss of her 'own' teacher was at least indicative of her ability to make relationships of a kind, but obviously such behaviour could not go unchecked. Mary's mother was once more sent for, and although now in an advanced state of pregnancy, was more helpful than she had previously been.

She acknowledged that Mary had been 'funny' ever since the birth of the third child when she was three, had shown signs of bitter jealousy of all her younger siblings, and was resentful of her mother's pregnancy and the prospect of yet more babies in the house. She had started bed-wetting, also – a circumstance her already overburdened mother viewed with dismay. It was this 'final straw', however, which provided the lever needed for so long: Mary's mother agreed to the child's being referred for psychiatric examination. Any course which would save the extra work of washing bed-linen and nightclothes every day was welcome to the harassed, tired and baffled woman. How she was to get Mary to the clinic was a problem the head teacher and the Health Visitor thought they might hammer out together later. In the meantime, the Health Visitor arranged for the provision of a patent apparatus to control the enuresis; and the visit of the P.S.W. gave much-needed emotional support to the mother.

Mary was the victim not only of teacher shortage and staff absence, but of shortage of Child Guidance personnel also, and could not be accepted for treatment at the clinic for several months. The return from absence of a teacher she knew and liked was a help to her in the meantime, and with much patient encouragement she once more emerged from her hiding places and was restored to some appearance of normality. She even took a fleeting interest in books on occasion, and had begun to read a little by the end of the summer term – but only to one teacher, and only 'if she felt like it'. Attempts to retain her in the Infants' school were not successful. She was, in any case, well past her seventh birthday by the end of the summer term, and a large child for her age; but it was the reluctance of her mother to agree to the retention, and the sudden interest of the father shown by his refusal to entertain the idea of retention that were the main reasons for her being sent to the Junior school in the ordinary manner. As has already been mentioned, to retain a child beyond the usual age of transfer can underline the child's oddness or difficulty and make parents feel at a disadvantage in their relations with other parents. It was not in Mary's best interests to have acrimonious discussions with her rather aggressive father on the subject, and the suggestion was dropped.

Mary was in no state, emotionally or academically, to cope with the demands of the Junior school, moderate as these were likely to be. Despite her tiny skill at reading and her occasional gruff answers to the one or two people she had learned to trust, she was a patently odd child, and regarded by other children as such. In the class to which she had belonged in the Infants' school, and with the support of adults for the children who otherwise have been frightened or contemptuous of her, she had had a niche which it would be unreasonable to expect her to have made in a class of older children with another teacher. Mary was passed on as a 'problem', a victim partly of her family's situation and attitudes, and partly of the shortcomings of professional services in both school and clinic; shortcomings which were due to circumstances beyond the control of either, but which will be sadly familiar to both.

Considerations

The five children discussed represent between them the kind of problems presented to the teacher by withdrawal, and the kinds of background which may be found on looking closely into their cases. Unlike the aggressive children, they give no clue to their troubles – only by their withdrawal do they indicate the depth of their hurt. While the aggressive child, even if deeply disturbed may give his teacher clues to his trouble in the form of conversation, painting, writing, or in his play, the withdrawn child, by definition, does none of these things, and it is therefore all the more difficult for the teacher to know where to start.

The importance of the school medical examination has been stressed in regard to cases of withdrawal. Not only the terrible emotional experiences outlined in the case above, but partial deafness, brain-damage or other physical conditions may cause a child to withdraw from his fellows, and such conditions may have gone unnoticed within the closed circle of home. In the case of traumatic experiences such as those described the importance of early psychiatric help and advice for child, parents and teachers cannot be too often pleaded. In the case of James it undoubtedly saved him from very much graver trouble than that he was already in by the time he was five; and in Adrian's case it was essential to his acceptance of his mother's state.

The two cases of mental illness of parents were typical of many in the course of the years in which these records were kept, and although the children with mentally ill parents did not all respond by withdrawal, (acute anxiety and bizarre behaviour were other responses), the possibility of such illness when a child is withdrawn should not be ignored. It is here that a teacher is faced with not only practical difficulties, (since a seclusive mother, for example, simply goes unnoticed, and many cases of mental illness are 'hushed up' out of a sense of shame), but with ethical problems as well. It is the right of individuals to privacy in regard to their family affairs; and yet to sacrifice the future of a child to the principle of adult privacy is surely unallowable to those concerned with the education of the young. To keep mentally ill persons 'locked away' for months or years on end, as was once the practice, is neither morally defensible nor now legally allowable; yet their presence within the family, especially where there are young children, can be disastrous to the children. It is proper that teachers keep accurate and honest records of children's progress and difficulties but many teachers have felt it improper to put on record for the use of the child's later teachers such information as was available in the cases of James, Dennis and Adrian with respect to their parents. More than in most other categories of need discussed in this book the problems lying behind withdrawn children involve teachers in professional, practical and ethical decisions of a different nature.

It is apparent from the cases discussed, however, that in most cases of withdrawal a major emotional upheaval will be found to have taken place in the child's life. This is not always a matter of parental death, as in the case of James and George, or of parental insanity, as in the cases of

Dennis and Adrian. Mary seemed to have suffered some severe upset around the time of the birth of a younger sister, and the nature of this had yet to be ascertained when she left the Infants' school. It is in the best interests of children's relationships and learning that teachers know of such happenings in regard to withdrawn children, for only through such knowledge can they take steps to help the child.

The means by which children can be helped by teachers have been outlined: early referral to the school doctor; psychiatric treatment as early as possible, if this can be obtained; the co-operation of the Health Visitor in cases such as those of Dennis, Adrian and Mary; and in the classroom the constant keeping in touch – often literally – with the child, the refusal to be discouraged or made impatient by the weeks or even months of little response, the adding to materials already accepted and the continuous effort to help 'normal' children to accept without sneer or fear the silent child in their midst. A perceptive teacher will notice such clues as James' sudden talk of 'Mavis', or Adrian's response to music, and make appropriate use of such knowledge. Alone of all the adults who have come into contact with him the withdrawn child's teacher can initiate the building of the bridge back to relationship, for she sees him every day, and has at her disposal not only her professional skills but access to specialized help and, above all, a company of normal children to whom she can help him relate.

Suggestions for Further Reading

Freeman, H. E. and Simmons, O. G. *The Mental Patient Comes Home* Wiley (1963)

Kaplan, L. *Mental Health and Human Relations in Education* Harper & Row (1959)

Mills, E. *Living with Mental Illness: A Study in East London* Routledge (1962)

Rutter, M. *Children of Sick Parents: an environmental and psychiatric study* Oxford U.P. (1966)

Smith, W. C. *The Stepchild* Univ. of Chicago Press (1953)

Chapter 6

Anxious Children

While many of the aggressive and withdrawn children already discussed might have been categorized as suffering from anxiety – indeed, withdrawal could be said to be anxiety carried to its extreme – the children who will be discussed in this chapter were not markedly aggressive or so withdrawn as to cause this to be their distinguishing feature in a classroom. Anxiety for the purposes of this work is defined as that state of tension, uneasiness and discomfort that springs from no external source of danger, but is internal or subjective. Each school of psychology has produced its own theory of anxiety, and some of these are summarized and discussed by Jersild in the *'Manual of Child Psychology'* (2nd ed. 1954) edited by Carmichael, in a paper which may be found both interesting and relevant by teachers of young children.

Whether one accepts the view of Freud that anxiety has its roots in early fears of losing the loved object; or of Horney that it arises from attempts to control a complicated environment by adoption of devices which are only partially successful; or of Sullivan that children become 'selves' by interaction with adults, and therefore find themselves very vulnerable to disapproval, it is surely beyond question that this 'emotion' of anxiety is one of the most wasteful and sapping of all affective responses. Unlike the emotion of fear, it is not discharged by attack upon or flight from a clearly discerned danger. Because its roots are deep and complex it is often not recognized at all, the anxious child or adult simply working at 'half-power', with a general feeling of uneasiness and inadequacy which he can neither explain nor of which, in many cases, he is consciously aware. Anxiety might even be thought of as an 'anti-emotion', since the mental energy dissipated on defences, unconscious fears and conflicts, efforts to keep the self going at all and the pointless physical movements often associated with an anxious state, cannot be expended on positive emotions such as love, delight, pleasure in creative activity – or even goal-directed anger. The anxious

95

child cannot make full use of his emotional, mental or physical powers, and is therefore a problem to his teachers and needs special help.

Anxious children in school may vary greatly, according to individual temperament, the roots of the anxiety and the kind of environment provided by the home and by the school itself – but they are all inadequate in relationship and find less satisfaction than they should in work and in play. Most of them have physical habits which betray their generalized fear and inadequacy; they chew their nails or their pencils, twist their forelocks, suck the points of plaits or collars, jerk knees or heads, and tend to edge away from physical contact. Some of them work with a quite obsessional application, as if to prove that they are 'good' and acceptable; but most work below their potential, and only suffer increase of anxiety if reproved. Almost all of them cope, somehow, with their schooling during the early years, but are less and less successful as they grow older. It is important for teachers to avoid adding to children's anxiety by unrealistic demands in school.

'The school,' writes Jersild in the paper mentioned above, 'dispenses failure on a colossal scale. Moreover, much of this failure is due to questionable standards which require that all children go through certain academic exercises that have little if any meaning to them. It is perhaps only on the assumption that there is a large amount of hostility towards children in our society (as suggested by Alcock's study)[1] that we can explain the fact that our society tolerates the kind of self-derogating treatment to which so many children are constantly being subjected in the name of education.'

It is certainly the function of the Infants' school to give children experience of success in their work, and a sense of adequacy within themselves, in order that no anxiety may develop from their early experience of school. Those children already anxious on entry may have their anxiety mitigated, or even eliminated, by the good Infants' teacher making full use of all her resources.

19. Perry
One of the first children to come to the notice of a new teacher on her taking up her appointment at the school,

[1] Made in 1948, with an English sample.

*reported as having been a deeply anxious boy for the previous
five terms that he had been in the school. Very tall for a boy
of seven, with a quick, twitching movement of the head.
Thought to be of at least average intelligence, although not
tested; but very retarded in reading at first testing (reaching
age of 5:7 on Schonell test R.1 at chronological age 7:1), but
making great improvement after individual help (reading age
7:2 on same test at chronological age 7:6). Other work poor to
average, and persistence lacking.*

Perry's mother had died at his birth, but he had been
brought up at home by his maternal grandmother and in the
company of his two older sisters and his father until the latter
married again when Perry was four. His grandmother had then
left the home, and Perry was reported as having been very
upset at the time. His stepmother disliked young children,
although she had been a teacher, and made no secret of
this to Perry. She regarded him as 'stupid and backward', and
severely corrected him for his slight lisp. When he was seven
she said that she was determined to 'get some sense into him',
and would spare no efforts to ensure that he worked hard at
school and 'did t e family credit'. Perry had to go through a
reading primer   ery night at home, from the age of five
– with remarkably little result as far as reading performance
was concerned. When the stepmother told the head teacher of
this she was asked to desist; but she was contemptuous of
'soft' methods, and said she would continue to teach him, and
that he was just bone idle. Only the response that if she were
going to teach him to read at home he would be allowed to
have his play in school finally drew from her the reluctant
undertaking to stop the nightly, fruitless and seemingly miserable 'reading' sessions.

The father seemed more gentle and understanding than
the stepmother, but he, understandably, was unwilling to
argue with his wife over the boy, and tended to let things
drift. Perry's shirt collars were chewed to rags – another bone
of contention with his stepmother – and he stammered badly,
went pale, and showed the whites of his eyes like a frightened
horse if spoken-to directly by an adult in school. He cried
easily if only slightly hurt, played with other boys but dared
not get himself grubby, and moved with a shifty, shuffling
gait as though not wanting to be observed. He worried about
everything, from a change of classroom to a heavy rainstorm,

and was unable to commit himself to more than tiny immature pictures in the corner of his paper, tiny writing and minute plasticine models.

Perry was, however, an affectionate boy by nature, and responded quickly to a new young teacher, and to a head-mistress who had persuaded his stepmother to abandon the reading-lessons. He was given little jobs to do before school, allowed to take his time in speaking (and not corrected or made 'to start again'), and given individual reading help in the quietness of the head's room. Here, he blossomed after a few sessions, becoming an animated and charming boy, de-lighted by his success. It was agreed that his reading progress would be kept a secret until he could take home a library book and read it to his stepmother. Despite her opinion and treatment of him, he still tried to please her – a response which is probably common in anxious children who have had some experience of satisfactory relationship at some time in their lives, and who are constantly placating even aggressive adults in the fading, but hardly-relinquished, hope that they can establish such another.

The contact of the stepmother with the school was at first antagonistic, as has been suggested, but with Perry's im-provement his stepmother was able to accept him more willingly, and prepared to discuss him more kindly. It is true that there is something aggravating about a stammering, shuffling, collar-sucking child, who jerks his head aside and shows the whites of his eyes when approached – at least to a vigorous, determined woman who is not enamoured of small boys in the first place. That she has been at least partly to blame for the deep anxiety of the child his stepmother could hardly be expected to accept; but the more she nagged him, the more inept, nervous and unprepossessing he became, and this is a vicious circle the teacher may sometimes be able to break. Perry's stepmother was not a warm woman, and it was not likely that he would make with her the kind of relation-ship he had with his grandmother (who was the only 'mother' he had known). His teachers' helping him to feel efficient, liked and useful in school, however, probably made it possible for his stepmother to take a slightly more constructive view of him. The cessation of stammering and collar-sucking, and his friendly, if still shy, approach to people by the time he left the school meant that he entered the Junior school as an unnoticeably 'ordinary' little boy.

20. Jonathan

A thin, tense-looking, fearful child, of superior intelligence and advanced in reading skill. Other skills poorly developed, and seeming of little interest to the boy. He enjoyed painting, however, and produced some startling powerful and colourful work.

Jonathan, like Perry, shuffled or 'drifted', chewed his collar ends, was jumpy if spoken to, and always seemed worried about something. He spoke clearly and well, nevertheless, and was an interesting child to talk to, once he could feel confident enough to have conversation. His chronic forgetfulness was a matter of real concern to his teacher, however. He was capable of setting off for the hall to fetch a book and forgetting where he was going; he forgot his satchel, his cap, his blazer and his gloves in turn, and on one occasion walked all the way home without his shoes on, having forgotten to replace them after taking off his soft slippers. He would forget to deliver notes, and it was not long before his teachers sent any communications to his parents by post, for a note could be left in Jonathan's satchel for weeks. So pronounced and obviously genuine was this forgetfulness that it was mentioned to his mother.

This woman was a highly intelligent, attractive woman, appearing very fond of Jonathan and his older brother, but terrified, on her own admission, of her husband. She acknowledged him to be a moody and difficult person, and attributed Jonathan's anxiety and forgetfulness to his having to cope with conflicting demands at home. She had considerable insight into the family problem, but said there was nothing she could do to save Jonathan and his brother from her husband's black moods and violent rages. He had recently had an eight-foot wall built round the garden, and had forbidden the boys to go outside it, for example; when the older boy had gone out on his bicycle his father had thrashed him in the street. Certainly, on the one occasion he came to school he behaved in a boorish and overbearing manner.

Jonathan's desire to please both parents, and his fear of his father seemed to be a very great strain. The school doctor

99

found the boy tense and underweight, took a serious view of the extreme forgetfulness, and asked his mother if she were prepared to accept pyschiatric examination for him. She felt that this might be helpful, but doubted whether the father would accept such a recommendation. The doctor offered to see the father, and managed to do so; but the mother's forecast of her husband's reaction proved accurate. He took the view that the school, the doctor and the boy's mother were trying to say that the boy was 'soft in the head', and absolutely declined to give consent to further examination of any kind. Jonathan's teacher did what she could to help him to relax – and the introduction of a fluid day at about this time, praise for his undoubtedly good performance in activities involving reading, and simple 'drills' to help him to remember more important matters, seemed to help him to become less tense. Despite his improvement, however, he remained an anxious child to the end of his Infants' school years.

His mother's suicide, several years later, was tragic indication of the emotional 'climate' of this family, and a measure of how greatly help had been needed. Obviously, there is little the school can do in cases of this kind, but support for the mother is certainly possible up to a point, and efforts to gain the co-operation of the father might, in a similar case, meet with more success than in Jonathan's. Patience with the child, and recognition that forgetfulness of the kind described is a symptom of tension, (it is to be remembered how very much Jonathan had to forget), and should not be punished, at least make life in school a chance to relax and perhaps even to gather strength for the stress of home. To have even five hours a day for five days a week in which demands are rational and conflict non-existent is surely better than to face trouble continuously. This is not to suggest that teachers should criticize or antagonize the parents. Even an implication of this kind can only serve to make a child more anxious; and teachers will not wish to 'judge' unhappy parents, in any case. Support and understanding for the child, and for the parents if this is possible and acceptable to them, does not involve a holier-than-thou attitude. In Jonathan's case referral for psychiatric help would almost certainly have resulted in a recognition of his mother's grave state of mind – and possibly the averting of tragedy. Such a case is a shocking reminder to teachers that persistence in the attempt to get help for a child may not be the wasted effort it sometimes seems to be; for if a child is eventually seen by a psychiatrist the parents will be seen, too, and help may be more timely for others than it was for Jonathan and his mother.

21. Gareth

A boy with a nervous twitch of the head, a retiring manner, and most apprehensive expression. Rarely observed to smile or laugh, but played with other children in a normal manner. Although well-cared-for and well-dressed always looked somewhat unkempt, with shirt-tails not tucked in trousers, or tie round the back of neck, socks wrinkled round ankles, and so on. Pulled nervously at clothes if spoken to by an adult, and twisted legs tightly round a chair-leg while working. Very poor performance in formal skills, especially in reading. Accent cultured, but speech hurried and sometimes babyish. Cried easily and was timid in trying new skills.

This pleasant, but apparently very anxious boy spent a reasonably normal first year in school, and although always a little shy made friendly relationships with both his teacher and a few other quiet children. It was felt that he was not in such a state as to warrant discussion with the parents, but his behaviour and progress were carefully watched. The birth of his baby brother when Gareth was four may have upset him temporarily, although he did not show signs of overt or hidden jealousy and seemed genuinely fond of the baby by the time he himself was five.

His progress by the end of his first year was not as great as his teacher had hoped, and his anxiety seemed markedly increased. Despite many opportunities to do so, his parents had visited the school rarely – his mother had attended for Gareth's medical examination in his first term, and had been seen at the back of the hall during the Christmas entertainment; neither parent had come on open days or to parents' discussion sessions. This was an unusual circumstance in such a neighbourhood for parents seemingly well-educated themselves. Although the circumstance was puzzling, however, there seemed no valid reason for making enquiries into this apparent indifference to the boy's progress during his first year in school; and it was not until reading tests and other observations made Gareth's lack of progress very plain at the beginning of his second (and last) year in the school that it was decided that some discussion with the parents should take place.

Before anything could be done about this Gareth's mother arrived in a state of considerable distress to see the head teacher.

She flung herself down on a chair in the head's room, lit a cigarette, and said, without any preamble, 'My God! I can't stand any more of this. I've got to talk to somebody.' She was an elegant, attractive woman, extremely well-spoken, but at this stage nearly as incoherent as a child. Over cups of tea and to a patient listener, she poured out the miserable story of the last year. Her marriage was on the verge of collapse, and the Marriage Guidance counsellor had failed to effect even rational discussion between husband and wife, much less real understanding. The husband was accused by his wife of gross immaturity, and of being 'in his mother's pocket'. It appeared that his mother had recently taken to spending all day and the evening in the house on the pretext that her daughter-in-law could not cope with the children. The husband regarded this with complacence, even pleasure. On the other hand, Gareth's mother freely admitted that she had had a rather meaningless flirtation with her husband's business partner two or three years before, and that this had probably given her mother-in-law the excuse she had been seeking to 'take over' her son's marriage.

All that it was possible to do at this juncture was to calm the woman, and give assurance that she could come and talk about the matter again later, if she wished. It was obviously of no use discussing Gareth, except in passing, for his mother seemed only too aware of the damage the parental estrangement was doing, yet was still attempting to deny it – and to be given reassurance that her denial was justified. This could not be done. She admitted that the boy had heard arguments between his parents about their respective unfitness to have the children, threats of removing them from the home, appeals to his grandmother by his father, and bitter reproaches by his mother. It was hardly surprising that his anxiety had increased; but time is needed to consider family situations of this kind, and information from 'the other side' gathered as well, if this is possible, before fruitful discussion of the child's problem can be started.

On the next day, and because his mother had told him that

his wife had been to the school, the father arrived – also in a state of tension and self-pity. His story was the mirror-image of his wife's – thus, incidentally, removing any doubts there might have been about the wife's story being a phantasy, which is a possibility not to be overlooked in such cases – and it was apparent that he viewed his mother with unusual awe, and felt his wife was being unreasonable in resenting her presence. He repeated several times that his mother was 'a marvellous person' and knew just what to do about the children. He seemed much less concerned about his wife's flirtation with his partner than he was about her failure to get on with her mother-in-law. In regard to Gareth he had only one major concern, and that a somewhat unrealistic one: whether the boy would be 'forward enough' to go to his own old public school at the age of thirteen. Like his wife, he seemed too absorbed with his personal anxieties to be able to discuss the boy's present anxiety and lack of progress in a constructive manner.

Further talks with both parents, an attempt to confront them with each other, efforts to get them to consent to psychiatric help for Gareth and advice for themselves were abortive. Each admitted that their poor relationship was probably responsible for the boy's lack of progress in school, but neither seemed prepared to give an inch to the other in order to help their older son. Both parents appeared to regard the head teacher as his or her own confessor; and it looked as if they were, in fact, playing-in to each other and using this third party as an excuse for further hurtful behaviour. This was a situation that obviously could not be allowed to go on.

The responsibility of teachers is to the children they teach, and much as they may wish to help parents (and can often do so, in fact), there may be occasions when they must help the child in spite of the parents. With the permission of the parents, it was agreed that Gareth should be allowed to talk of his troubles, if he would, to the head teacher. This is an unusual course, and one not to be undertaken lightly or unless absolutely no other course seems possible. The advice of the psychiatrist in charge of the Child Guidance clinic was sought in regard to the boy's situation – but neither his name, nor details likely to identify the family were given –and this advice followed.

103

In the course of helping the head teacher, playing in his classroom, and so on, he built up such a relationship with her that he was able to mention his worries. From this point, and always in privacy, his doubts and fears were made explicit. He thought he had forfeited his mother's affection because he had been 'wicked' (his grandmother's word), and that his mother had had his baby brother to 'replace' him. He loved his father, but was terrified that he would send the mother away. He longed to please his mother, but to do so seemed to bring down upon him the displeasure of his grandmother, of whom he was very frightened. And he was bewildered by the accusations of 'wickedness' brought by each parent about the other – for he loved both, and both protested love of him. Only truthful answers to such poorly-formulated but crucial questions must be given – but this is not easy. Over a period of some months, however, Gareth seemed to accept that adults, even when angry with each other, are not necessarily 'wicked' in the irredeemable way in which small children think of wickedness; that parents do not hate their children because they quarrel with each other; that his mother had had the baby not as a replacement for him, but just because mothers like to have more than one child, as a rule; that both his father and his mother loved him, but were too angry and upset to be fair about each other. With the confused ideas of relationships common to young children, he also believed that he could 'become' his grandmother's little boy, and the prospect appeared to terrify him. He was assured that, no matter what happened, this was absolutely impossible, that he remained his mother's son, as his father was the grandmother's. Even so simple an explanation of relationships as this can be a comfort to a child in so confused a family situation; and Gareth made many enquiries, normal for his age, but rather more pointed than is usual, about the relationship of teachers to their parents, husbands and own children to clarify his ideas. He needed a terminology, as all children do, in order to discuss his family, and this was given him, casually, over a period. A child who hears a married woman refer to her husband as 'my daddy', or his own father talk of 'mummy' for both his mother and his wife, and whose grandmother refuses to be addressed as 'granny' or 'grandma', is likely to be confused, in any case; for Gareth such confusion may have been particularly dangerous, since it seemed to have robbed him of his own identity as 'son' and 'grandson'.

His anxiety diminished somewhat by his last term in the school, and his work began to improve, although still poor for a boy of nearly seven. His parents had continued their deadly battle with each other, but the affair seemed to be moving to the resolution of divorce by the time Gareth left for the Junior school; and they were at least talking with some sense of the arrangements that could be made for the children. Neither was able to accept full adult responsibility for his or her actions, however, and while there seemed considerable justification for the wife's accusations of immaturity in her husband, she herself was hardly more adult in her attitudes. Continued help for Gareth would be necessary if his school performance were to improve to a point at which he would be 'average', but it was doubtful if this could be given in the Junior school. Staff shortage made provision of remedial work almost impossible; and large classes, arranged at that time in three streams, made it likely that Gareth would be put in a C-stream, and stay there. Parental refusal to accept psychiatric help lessened the possibility of advice for his teachers from the school's psychological service. In a case like this the Infants' school can do very little. Gareth had only too good reasons for anxiety, and those beyond the resources of the school to eliminate. Yet the appeal made by these parents is not the sort to ignore or dismiss; and their inability to accept help is no cause for denying to the child what little help he can be given.

22. Cory

A thin, dark, tense child, prone to nail-biting, a nervous twitch of the face, a ducking movement if touched or handed anything, and bed-wetting until the age of six-plus. Of average intelligence on group tests in school, but with a reading-age 10m. below his chronological age at the beginning of his last term in the Infants' school. The youngest child of three, and expected to equal or surpass the very superior performance of his elder sisters.

Cory was not a source of great worry to his teachers in his first year, although very tense and over-anxious about keeping clean. He was inhibited in such activities as painting, clay-modelling, sand-play and water-play by this anxiety not to get his clothes dirty. Provision of enveloping overalls helped him a little, but he was inclined to worry about even their getting splashed or stained, despite his teacher's constant reassurance that this did not matter. By the end of his first year, however, he was pursuing most of the normal activities with considerable pleasure. He continued to come to school in immaculate white shirts, bowties and dark suits – an unusual dress for boys in the neighbourhood, most of whom wore coloured shirts and loose sweaters or blazers. His parents were very concerned about his progress, and visited the school on every possible occasion, as well as making a special visit once each term to ask about his work. While such interest and co-operation were welcome, it was felt that for them Cory was something of a symbol; they were inclined to talk mostly of his future, rarely of his present except in relation to what they hoped it would lead to. Neither parent, although well-educated, had been to university, yet each expressed determination that Cory should go. This was not an uncommon ambition in the area, for most of the skilled men of the electronics and other modern industries were well aware of the value of higher education in obtaining 'top jobs' in their own fields. Cory, in fact, was a typical, if rather extreme, example of children who are probably made anxious by well-meant but perhaps too-early and too-firmly expressed parental ambition.

Frequent talks to the mother about the aims and a long-term result of modern Infant methods appeared to make a favourable impression; she was inclined to relief at the thought that her son was not stupid, lazy, or 'odd' because he enjoyed the many lively activities of school, and she came to some appreciation of how very much a child learns by what is apparently 'play'. Cory's father was not convinced, however. He took the view that the boy was lazy, and needed to be made to work, and that the methods of the school were fanciful. This was a view widely held by fathers, in particular, and yielded only slowly to four or five years of explanation, discussion, exhibitions in the school, and personal contact. Cory's father was not aggressive or obstructive, but he remained unconvinced, and continued to question his son about his daily achievements in school. By the end of the boy's first year the somewhat difficult situation had arisen in which a mother previously in agreement with her husband about the upbringing, including the education, of her son, was now inclined to side with the school against the husband. This is not a situation that is in the best interests of the child, and it occurred to the staff and head that they had unwittingly helped the development of the inconsistency between parental demands on the child.

Fortunately, the parents' solidarity in always coming to the school together, and conducting their argument in a non-acrimonious manner with class-teacher and head made retrieval of this situation possible. It was agreed that it did Cory no good to have extra reading lessons from his father at home, for example – but that as he was somewhat retarded he would be given extra help in school. Further compromise was made about his number-work, his father suggesting that he taught him some 'proper arithmetic' in connection with measuring, counting etc. while father and son did carpentry or serviced the car, the school supplying experiment with weights, measures, spatial relations and so on in the course of what the father described as 'play'. Such activities as painting, modelling and cutting were accepted by the father with a shrug, but with the admission that Cory seemed to enjoy them.

From this point, and perhaps because he was told openly of the discussions and their outcome, Cory ceased to be enuretic, bit his nails less often, and lost most of the nervous physical habits that had characterized him previously. He was still an anxious child, but the anxiety of his parents (expressed in their ambition as well as in general behaviour) suggested that he might also be prone, by reason of temperament and family attitudes, to anxiety in the face of ordinary work-demands. Most seven-year-olds show considerable concern about their standards and performance in relation to that of others, and it was too early when he left the Infants' school to say how much of his anxiety would diminish in the ordinary course of development.

This is a case representative of many, and in which the school itself is part of the pattern. When the deeply-held convictions of teachers about the aims of education in the Infants' school seem opposed to those of parents, the first consideration must be the well-being of the child. This is not to sacrifice principles – for the essential principle of modern education of young children is that the whole good of the child is being fostered. This involves his ability to relate well with both parents and teachers, as well as to develop the skills (such as that of reading) which will please them all. If parents set such a high premium on formal skills that the child feels inadequate and anxious because he has not achieved them in school, it does not help him to be told, even by implication, that his parents are 'wrong' and that the school is 'right' to offer him opportunities which seem to his parents like 'play'.

Such a situation presents the thoughtful teacher with yet another dilemma – but one which, with generosity towards the parents, and always with the interests of the child in mind, it is possible to resolve. By allowing free discussion, by putting the work of the school on show with full explanation of its intent and origins, and by making it possible for the child to fulfil the expectations of the parents while at the same time enjoying the work of the school, much of the kind of anxiety instanced by Cory might be reduced. This is not to say that these are tasks easy of accomplishment. Many parents are not so able to talk and compromise as were Cory's; in some cases there will be underlying tensions between the parents that are expressed superficially by antagonism to 'outside authority'; and the process of co-operating with parents may go on for years before, among the parents in a neighbourhood, understanding of and confidence in the school are widespread.

23. Eleanor

A small, shy, but affectionate child, with no nervous habits of the kind instanced in previous cases, but a need to go often to the lavatory, a tendency to cry if work did not seem to her to 'come right', and having severe nightmares. Of superior intelligence, (tested by the Educational Psychologist) but retarded in reading, writing and number of skills until her last term in the Infants' school.

This gentle and retiring child made friends with one or two girls early in her school life, and was confiding with her teacher. From the beginning she set herself very high standards, and showed great anxiety if she did not attain them, often sitting persistently at a task long after her teacher was quite satisfied with it and other children were engaged

108

in some quite different activity. It was thought at first that parental demands must be exacting, but this turned out not to be the case.

Eleanor's parents had married late, but very happily, and were cultured, gentle people. They were extremely devoted to their two children, (Eleanor also seemed fond of her younger brother), and not only by temperament but by conviction were both permissive and consistent in their dealings with the children. There seemed no reason for Eleanor's unusual anxiety about her school performance, nor for her nightmares, and the school doctor suggested that this anxiety might be a temperamental trait which would nevertheless be less of a burden to the child as she grew older and more accustomed to the demands and routine of school. Certainly, all her symptoms diminished throughout her first year, and she seemed a fairly happy little girl.

She retained her teacher into her second and last year of her Infants' school career, and it looked as though, now she was six, her earlier anxiety had almost disappeared. Quite suddenly, however, there was a regression to her earlier state. She cried frequently over her work and even over paintings and models, she needed to pass water at increasingly shorter intervals, and her mother came worriedly to school to say that the nightmares were now a nightly occurrence. No clues to this state seemed to be discoverable, and the mother asked if Eleanor could be referred to the Child Guidance clinic. This was arranged almost immediately, for the clinic was now fully staffed, and there was no waiting-list. In play with her therapist Eleanor almost immediately revealed the source of her trouble: she was extremely jealous of her brother, despite her very normal and affectionate behaviour towards him, and was very afraid that she was going to hurt him. She had been only eighteen months old when he was born, and had once sat on him on a sofa when he was very small. Her naturally affectionate disposition, together with the increased understanding of a child of five and six which disposed her, at an everyday level, to be very fond of him, were at odds with her 'baby self', and the conflict was more than she could cope with. This seemed to be a straightforward case, and the therapist was confident that Eleanor could be helped effectively and soon. It was suggested that the practical step of accepting the brother in school a little earlier than had been planned might also help her, since she would then not have to think of him as being at home with her mother while she was in school.

After consultation with the mother and the therapist, it was decided that, in this case, the step would be a worthwhile one, and Joel was admitted to the reception class at the age of four-and-a-half. In some cases this might be an unwise course, for the older child might be given the impression that he or she was omnipotent and had only to demand removal of a younger sibling from the mother to have the deed done. Much depends on the maturity and understanding of the parents, as well as of the older child in such a case. In Eleanor's case the action was taken in conjunction with therapy, and the result was excellent. She was able to be a 'big sister' to Joel in a quite legitimate manner, and at the same time to acknowledge him as a schoolmate, having shared experiences with her away from the home. Together with continued help from the therapist and some remedial work in reading with her teacher the action seemed wholly effective. Eleanor was able to discontinue her visits to the clinic after about four months, and there was a complete disappearance of all her symptoms.

Only a few weeks before the end of the summer term, however, her realization that she would be going to the Junior school, (an event which she, in common with almost every other child, regarded with pleasant anticipation as marking another stage in being 'grown up'), together with Joel's comment that next year he would be taught by Eleanor's teacher, were probably contributory to a renewal of anxiety symptoms. They were not severe, and she had only one nightmare before saying to her mother,

'Take me to the clinic tomorrow, Mummy! Please take me. They know what to say to me there!'

Her mother was touched and impressed by Eleanor's faith, and by her ability to formulate her need, and telephoned the clinic at once. She was asked to bring Eleanor along the next morning. Only two visits to her therapist were needed to restore the child to adjustment, but she was told that she was always to ask her mother if she felt she needed to talk to the therapist again, and assured that there would always be somebody there to help her. To this she said,

'And you could help Mummy and Daddy and Joel, too, couldn't you? If they wanted you to, you could.' This unusually generous readiness to share the therapeutic situation was measure of this child's security with both parents and clinic. Most children tend to regard the clinic as their personal refuge, and parents have to be helped not to be resentful or to feel 'shut out'. It must be remembered, however, that the good intelligence and the very affectionate attitude of Eleanor's parents, together with her own intelligence and disposition, made such mature generosity of attitude possible for her. All the other anxious children so far discussed had to cope with some sort of marked parental inconsistency, lack or un-happiness which was a factor in their anxiety. Eleanor is an example of a child whose anxieties stemmed from completely personal roots, and who, although outside help was needed, was yet able to include her parents in her treatment. In a case like this the function of the school in supporting parents, child and clinic can be a satisfyingly effective one.

Considerations

In three of the cases discussed, those of Perry, Jonathan and Gareth, the marital problems of the parents seemed to be at the root of the children's anxiety. In the case of Perry there were, of course, the factors of deprivation and the attitude of a step-parent to be considered; nevertheless, his father's failure to come to terms with the conflicting needs of his son and the behaviour of his second wife could be described as a 'marital problem' of a kind. The difficulties con-fronting teachers of children whose parents are 'at odds' with each other and/or with the child have been outlined. It is possible, in many cases, to persuade parents to accept help in their own troubles from Marriage Guidance counsellors, their own doctor, or their minister or priest. Such help was effective in cases not discussed here – but, on the whole, these were not such seriously disrupted or unhappy relationships as those of Jonathan's and Gareth's parents. Sometimes the school is the only agency that can even approach the prob-lem, ineffective as the advice of teachers may be in such situ-ations. An important part of the school's function, however, is to support the child as best it can, and to put on record enough of the details of the case (especially in regard to dates) to give guidance to a child's later teachers in their dealings with him. At the very least this might save a child the embarrassment of having to explain that his parents were dead, divorced or not his own at an age when such explanations would seem most difficult; at most, such a record might influence greatly the treatment given later by a therapist or the attitude taken by a magistrate, as well as the course of remedial teaching.

Children not very unlike Cory will be found in many schools, and enough has been said in discussion of his case to indicate what a school can, and should, do about this widespread and possibly increasing 'academic anxiety'. It is essential that children, and their parents, do not take as their criterion of personal acceptability such things as reading early, coming 'top', going to certain sorts of schools or being in the A-stream. Most children do not read at the age of five; only one child in a class can possibly come 'top', and the great majority will not, while the practice of grading classes and schools like eggs exists, be in the elite. To suggest to children, however, that they are less than adequate as human beings on these counts is as anti-educative as it is nonsensical. In the Infants' school children can learn to accept the superior skills or advantages of another child as easily as they accept that some have red hair; to give them the impression that there is something lacking in themselves because they have a less or a different kind of ability is to induce anxiety – for there is absolutely nothing the young child can do about such a 'lack'. The modern Infants' school should be, as most are, the exception to Jersild's indictment that schools dispense failure on a colossal scale. By supporting the child and starting on a non-patronizing programme of explanations to parents such schools can start to reduce anxiety and improve educational processes in one move.

Of the third ground for anxiety, as instanced in Eleanor, little need be said. For a child having such deep-rooted fear or jealousy as a prime cause of anxiety much may be done, even in cases where parents are less co-operative or insightful than were Eleanor's. The support of Child Guidance personnel for a parent baffled by the child's behaviour is often an insight-giving and an educative process, and one that is much more often appreciated than resented or rejected. The ordinary processes of referral, and the continuing understanding and professional help of teachers while the child is in treatment are within the resources of every school.

112

Suggestions for Further Reading

Freud, S. *The Problem of Anxiety* N.Y. – Norton (1936)

Horney, K. *Our Inner Conflicts* N.Y. – Norton (1945)

Jersild, A. T., Markey, F. V. and Jersild, C. L. *Children's Fears, Dreams, Likes, Dislikes, Pleasant and Unpleasant Memories* Child Dev. Monograph No. 12 (1933)

Jersild, A. T. and Holmes, F. B. *Children's Fears* Child Dev. Monograph No. 20 (1935)

Chapter 7

The Pilferers

There is an enormous literature on delinquency, much of which deals with the problem of thieving. For the teacher who wishes to understand more of the roots of this age-old social problem the works listed at the end of this chapter may prove enlightening, and it is not proposed to analyse the theories of such anti-social behaviour in this work. It is, however, wise for the teacher of Infants' school children to bear several basic propositions in mind when dealing with the infant pilferer.

First, there is the obvious one that young children have a very vague concept of possession; it is only at the age of about three, for instance, that they begin to use the pronouns 'my' and 'yours', and for a year or two after this they will be uncertain of the exact significance of them. In connection with this natural difficulty in appreciating what 'belongs' to themselves and others, children from normally good homes are allowed considerable freedom in the home to look at, share and use materials and objects; at the same time being given guidance in what must not be used because they are the possession of parents or siblings and the owners' rights over such objects are paramount. In some situations the possessions of the child himself are also respected, and he learns by first-hand experience of this kind the limits of ownership and the protective sanctions that guard it. It is not in the interests of his eventual 'morality' that a young child be made to share everything with brothers and sisters, nor expected to give up his toys for his parents to play with. From this he is more likely to learn either that anybody can use, take or spoil anything, or an extreme possessiveness that might eventually cause him to become a selfish, mean and tiresome adult. In a normally good home respect for other people's possessions, and expectation of respect from them for one's own are learned in the ordinary course of living with possessions.

Secondly, a teacher will usually realize that there are

114

homes in which this code does not apply. Poverty may make the possession of any goods virtually impossible; the parents will have minimal household utensils, the children few or no toys and small treasures. In cases like this it is difficult to see how the ordinary rules of behaviour towards property can possibly be learned. In some poverty-stricken homes the lack will be made good – up to a point – by petty thieving of coveted articles, by the father from his place of employment, by the mother from stalls or shops, by older siblings from school or the market, and this behaviour accepted as not worthy of comment, much less of censure. Poverty as a first cause of stealing is not by any means as common as used to be thought; but the inadequacy and fecklessness that, in a prosperous society, makes some people incapable of earning a reasonable living may be a cause for indifference towards 'pinching and nicking'. The inability to foresee the results of one's actions, which is a concomitant of poor intelligence, is usually a factor here, also.

A third consideration is that of the psychological implications of stealing. The child from a socially 'good' home may steal from his mother – particularly money or sweets – on the birth of a new baby, removal of house, the presence of a relative seen as a rival in the mother's affections, after a minor or major quarrel between the parents, or simply on first being sent to school. It hardly needs the arguments and cases of psychoanalysis to demonstrate that such a child is likely to be taking, in symbolic form, the love he feels (justifiably or not) that he is being denied. Objective study of her pilferers over a number of years will demonstrate to the Infants' teacher that their response was made in almost every case to a real or imagined withdrawal of parental affection. It should not be forgotten that a child from a poor home, of the kind outlined in the paragraph above, will be just as prone to respond to lack of love in this way as the more privileged child, and that not all pilferers from 'bad' homes are pilfering as a means of getting possessions they crave, or as a natural family habit – although both these factors may well be in operation also.

Fourthly, teachers should be able to distinguish between different kinds of need by straightforward observation of the type of 'crime'. Who does he steal from? What does he steal? What does he do with his plunder? These are the first questions to ask. Only when they are answered is it possible to formulate answers, and these will always be tentative. It is as foolish to treat all young pilferers alike as it is to attribute all adult anxiety to the same cause; this is to treat the symptom as the cause, to describe rather than to explain, and to evade the teacher's responsibility for promoting social as well as intellectual adequacy in every child.

Lastly, in this general consideration of pilferers, it is important for teachers to appreciate that ours is an acquisitive society. As has already been pointed out in connection with society's views on aggression, there are confusing anomalies in regard to stealing for the young child to encompass. In a society which puts so high a premium on protection of property that the stealing of money is much more severely punished than physical violence against a child, (a sentence of thirty years for robbing a bullion train, three months for breaking the arms of a two-year-old child, for example), and in which the 'perks' of most jobs involve a greater or lesser degree of dishonesty, the young child is likely to be baffled by the 'rules'. Father brings home two cans of 'buckshee' paint from work; but the son gets thrashed for taking sixpence from his mother's purse. In another social strata father takes for granted that his complex attempts to evade income tax are acceptable to his friends; but is overwhelmed by shame when his daughter is found to be cheating at an examination. It is against a background of such anomalies that a teacher must view some, at least, of the pilfering that may occur in her class of young children. Further, it is few people who could say, with absolute truth, that as children themselves they did not steal – and that as adults they have never (for example) pocketed excessive change without comment, ridden two stops further than they had paid-for on a bus, or had a sort of immoral sympathy for a clever jewel-thief who relieved some outrageously wealthy person of her diamonds. To take a long, cold look at our own shortcomings in a society which has ceased to regard acquisitiveness as the mortal sin it was in the eyes of mediaeval churchmen, (and, indeed, has made it a virtue), is to understand some of the roots of theft in children. This is not a full explanation, even in a minority of cases; but it is an inescapable background to all. Pilferers in the Infants' school will not be helped to socially acceptable behaviour by sanctimonious strictures about declining moral standards and their own unworthiness. The world outside gives them a quite different picture of their elders.

24. Brian

The third boy in a family of (eventually) seven. Two older brothers already left the Infants' school with reputations as pilferers when a new head teacher took over the problem presented by Brian. Regarded as an incorrigible thief by the age of seven. A sullen, silent boy, with a cringing appearance when reproved and no ascertainable skills of a formal kind. Intelligence as measured by a non-verbal test in school showed him to be of low-average ability, and not dull or very dull as had been thought. Punished severely during his first six terms in school for his pilfering, he eyed all adults with suspicion and dislike.

Brian's father was a skilled tradesman, but a gambler, who rarely brought home his pay-packet intact. He was largely indifferent to his children, but occasionally thrashed them if they became a nuisance to him. The mother was an illiterate countrywoman, far from stupid, but lazy and with no liking for her sons. She indulged her daughters, but was like her husband, usually indifferent to what the children did or were. Most of their doings went unnoticed and unpunished. The children's early attempts to attract the parents' attention by normal devices, and by taking home paintings and so on from school appeared to have failed. The parents regarded school as a sort of reformatory, inimical to them and to the boys, but occasionally used it as a threat if the boys' behaviour impinged upon their own concerns.

Brian took almost anything that came to hand, and did various things with his loot. He ate the sweets he stole, spent the money on more sweets, wore stolen gloves, and carried about in his pockets the small toys he took from other children's desks or satchels. He did not share any of these things, apparently having a straightforward need to own what was normal for other children to have. Since the parents seemed unlikely to come to the school about him, the head teacher went to the home. The mother was subservient, vague, specious and distrustful, but did yield to the overture so far as to offer her visitor a cup of tea. After some fairly sensible discussion of Brian's trouble she undertook to give him some sweets occasionally, and to refrain from using school as a

117

threat. Several subsequent visits, with no object other than to keep contact, and to try to overcome the 'them against us' attitude of the parents achieved very little – but Brian was markedly more friendly with the head teacher after they had taken place.

In school, punishment for his pilfering was discontinued. Nearly two years of it had done no good; and, in any case, what kind of punishment could be inflicted that he had not had in greater measure from his parents? Withdrawal of love, the occasional heavy thrashing when he came to his father's notice, and the lack of possessions make nonsense of normal sanctions for such a child. Keeping him in after school was pointless, for it bore no relation to the 'crime' in the first place, and in the second was meaningless to a child who had nothing particular to go home for. As a positive measure, however, the cessation of punishment had considerable impact. He was also allowed to visit the head teacher's room when he liked, to tidy his teacher's desk, and to forage in cupboards to his heart's content. The staff were apprehensive at first, but as the weeks went by and Brian took nothing from any of these places they added their own gestures to those of the others. Classroom doors, previously locked during the lunch-hour, were left unlocked; the schoolkeeper let Brian into his shed to do odd jobs; the secretary allowed him to look in her office, which was also a store. And still there was no pilfering.

His teacher, who rather surprised herself by her attachment to this hitherto unattractive and unreachable boy, took to giving him a sixpence on Fridays as 'pay' for the extra work he did for her, thus ensuring that he had 'something to jingle' as other children had; the schoolkeeper gave him a biscuit occasionally, the cook an extra bottle of milk, the head teacher toffees from her tin. Brian, in fact, was given symbolic affection and trust by a whole group of adults. Even had he reverted to pilfering it was agreed that this policy should be continued – but in fact, he did not steal again while in the Infants' school. His mother accepted this as flaccidly as she had accepted the pilfering, and had to be constantly supported in order to get her to take any interest in him at all. His father also seemed indifferent to what was happening, but at least appeared to find the boy less of a nuisance.

Brian's great-aunt, a humorous East Ender, seemed to be

the only person who registered any interest or pleasure in the reform. She was fond of all the boys, and worried about their bad habits and their parents' indifference. On one occasion, early in his 'treatment', when Brian had taken home a packet of sweets given him by his teacher, she brought Brian and the sweets back to school, being under the impression he had stolen them. This was a somewhat upsetting indictment, for Brian was indignant, sullen and tearful by turns, but the woman's real concern and his affection for her nephew made it possible to resolve the misunderstanding without real harm being done. Had she lived she might have been the stabilizing influence Brian needed, for she had been appalled on moving to live near her nephew to find the family situation so out of control and feckless. Too late, as she felt, to do much about the older boys, she had taken Brian in hand almost at once, and was very willing to co-operate with his teachers. In the manner of many of her generation, she had a great respect for education, and urged Brian to do his best at school. Her death, soon after he left the Infant's school, shocked and embittered him – and by the age of eleven he still spoke of her with longing and affection.

Brian followed-up his reform in the matter of pilfering with fierce attachment to his teacher, and a determination to learn to read. At this task he persevered, and had just begun to make sense of print when he was due to leave the school. This teacher also set briskly about the business of giving Brian some pride in himself in other directions. On the basis of her very real affection for him, she was able to get him to accept and use a new tie, a cap and blazer given by an interested parent, and handkerchiefs. She taught him to clean his shoes (which job he enjoyed so much that he ended by cleaning other people's as well), and to comb his hair properly. More remarkably still, she taught him the manners of a very different class – to raise his cap when he met teachers in the morning, to open doors for others, to be courteous in making requests – without spoiling a very sound relationship. At the family-service meals in school he sat near her, chatting away and behaving at table as though he had been brought up in her own home. At first amused, and then astonished, the rest of the staff ended by having deep admiration for this piece of social re-training – especially as it was done incidentally to the efficient teaching of a class of forty. It was a constant reminder that once a vicious circle is broken a virtuous one can be set up, for Brian now received the ordinary praise and the ordinary rewards of being 'good' and became better still.

The administrative rigidities that it is hoped will soon cease to bedevil Primary education made it impossible to retain Brian in the Infants' school until such time as his reading was of average standard for a child of his age, and his reform in the matter of pilfering firmly established as permanent. He wished to stay, although he knew he would be the oldest boy in the school if he did so, and his teacher was prepared to retain him and continue her work with him. But he was not physically or mentally handicapped, he was not receiving psychiatric treatment, and his parents had made no request for his retention although this course had been suggested to them. He was within three months of his eighth birthday at the end of the summer term, in any case, and the head teacher of the Junior school was reluctant to accede to a course which would involve Brian's being nearly nine on eventual arrival in the Junior school.

Perhaps Brian's was a case in which some flexibility in transfer from Infant to Junior stage would have been particularly useful, for he made little success of his first year at the Junior school, in any case, and by his second year there was in constant trouble of all kinds. It is obviously impossible to say whether retention in the Infants' school would have prevented this kind of career in the Junior school; it may not have done. There were indications in his case, however, which suggested that Brian's improved adjustment, behaviour and learning *might* have been confirmed by a continuation of the relationship with his Infants' school teacher for another year.

25. Tessie

The older sister of Martin (p. 68) and therefore with the same difficulties of background. A minute, thin-faced child of considerable humour and charm, but often appearing tense, and having nightmares after the father left home permanently. Anxiety decreased, but pilfering constant during first two terms in the Infants' school. Intelligence believed to be at least average, but performance in reading very poor indeed – eventually found to be due, in part at least, to a very un-

*usual visual defect. Lively interest in and vigorous pursuit of
other activities from first entering the school.*

Tessie stole like a magpie for many months after the final
break-up of her parents' marriage, and at first this was assumed to be due to her feeling that her father had rejected
her. Some features of her pilfering were, however, atypical of
such 'affection-stealing'. She stole bright objects and sweets,
always sharing them with other children, and it looked as
though the need for acceptance by other children was as
great as the need for affection at home. Tessie's teacher was
warm and understanding with her, and her mother (as has
been explained earlier in discussion of Martin) very co-
operative with the school. There was very little money to spare
in this family for sweets and toys, but the mother agreed to
let Tessie have a copper or two every week to spend on
sweets, and the teacher gave her sweets to share with the
rest of the class. The pilfering diminished, but did not entirely
stop. The head teacher was in the habit of giving little oddments to the children at frequent intervals – foreign stamps,
pretty buttons, a handful of conkers, beads from a discarded
necklace and attractive containers, for example – and every
child in the schoo. was a recipient of some trifle of this kind
in the course of a year. Tessie was particularly appreciative of
such oddments, and soon learned to ask if she could have this
or that article when it was finished-with. There was nothing
unpleasantly acquisitive or worrying in these requests; she
loved pretty things, especially if she could count them, swap
them and compare them with the possessions of other children,
and in view of the shocking experiences she had endured
with her father it was felt that she was making very obvious
compensation for herself. That she was freely given these little
oddments which were in themselves pretty and shareable,
seemed to help her a great deal. The more she was given, the
less she pilfered, and for several months the giving was un-
stinted.

When the pilfering had ceased altogether, and Tessie was
nearly six, her requests for pretty 'bits' diminished. It looked
as though she were now satisfied that affection from her
mother was forthcoming, despite the family upheaval, and
that she was loved and trusted in school. Certainly, she was a
popular child, and generous in her treatment of children as
she had been in her bestowing of material possessions. That

children liked her regardless of whether she had anything practical to give them probably took her longer to learn; young children have only 'things' by which to symbolize the affection for others which adults have learned to put into words, gesture or simply kindly manners.

'I'll give you a sweet if you'll play with me' or 'You can have a go on my bike if you come home with me' or 'will you let me have a go of your skipping-rope?' are not, among young children, the blatant pleas and bribes their equivalents would be among adults. They are crude, early experiments in starting relationships with persons as unsophisticated as oneself.

If relationships in the home are unsatisfactory, and hence arouse not only fears of being unwanted in the child but give poor models of relationship, it is difficult for a child to grow beyond the stage at which affection and attention is seen as something that can be bought. Such situations as that experienced by Tessie distort attempts to relate with others not only because of the generally accepted lack of security but also because of the lack of *example*. When Tessie said,

'My daddy didn't never give my mummy any money', and, later, 'He buyed me some sweets once', she was probably expressing her own view of one of the main constituents of relationship: giving. Her own excessive giving, even when she had to steal the things to give, may have been both attempts to clarify for herself the basis of relationship and to behave to others as she wished her father to behave to her.

Discussion with her mother was most fruitful. It was agreed that Tessie should have a special time to herself with her mother, after the younger children were in bed, and that her urge to give and to help should be channelled into as many helpful ways as possible, without overloading her with responsibility. The mother's own anxiety about the child's pilfering also had to be allayed, and here her good relationships with the class-teacher and the head were of great value. Advice and help from the school doctor about Tessie's eyesight also relieved her of the suspicion that the child was incorrigibly backward – although it was a year or two before the effects of this defect and the family upheaval made it possible for Tessie to learn to read. The child's own temperamental qualities of gaiety, affection and desire to work hard were certainly an important part of the satisfactory outcome, as were the mother's stability and affection; but the school's rôle in such a case is essential in helping both parent and child to make full use of these assets.

26. Grenville

A small, lively, bold boy of average intelligence, according to group-tests of intelligence applied in school, and only a little retarded in formal skills. Lacking in persistence for most tasks, but capable of enthusiastic and lively work in creative and experimental work. Mostly interested in vigorous outdoor activities, at which he was skilled beyond the average. No pilfering reported during his first eighteen months in school, during which time he was a happy, popular child, described as a 'firework' by his teachers, but by no means troublesome.

Grenville was the son of parents who had moved from the East End of London, a cheerful, intelligent couple fond of their four children, of whom Grenville was the youngest, and including them casually in the full life of the family. The children were allowed to roam freely, but were under the rough, but apparently fairly consistent, discipline of being required to come home for meals and bed at reasonable hours, and to maintain conventional standards of cleanliness, honesty and presentable work at school. The father left contact with the school to his wife, but was friendly and co-operative on the occasions on which the headmistress visited the home.

With such a background it was difficult to see why Grenville suddenly started pilfering in school. He was six-and-a-half at the time, had had no recent upheaval at home or in school which might have accounted for such behaviour; and was not known to have stolen from home or in the neighbourhood. He stole small sums of money left on teachers' desks while collection of dinner-money was in progress, but was not realized as being the culprit for several days. Particular care was to be taken, thereafter, to have no money lying about in the school, and the incident might have passed without knowledge of the culprit had the school not been broken-into on the following weekend. The 'crime' was so patently not that of an expert that the police suggested it had been committed by a small child. A window which had failed to catch when closed had been opened, the room entered, and four half-crowns taken from an unlocked desk. (The teacher was mortified by this circumstance, and declared herself unlikely to be guilty of the same omission again.) The room concerned was Grenville's, from which the small sums of money had previously been missing; but there were thirty-six other children in this class, and there had been nothing to connect any particular child with the incident. Small finger-marks on the window-frame, and the scuffing of small, rubber-soled shoes on the sill pointed to its being a child of Infants' school age, and possibly in Grenville's class, but this was all.

A major 'witch-hunt' in such a case is usually as fruitless as it is distasteful. Young children are bewildered and frightened by it, eductional time is wasted, and relationships within a class or school can be severely strained or disrupted. Moreover, searchings, lectures and the threat of punishment for the culprit when found are unlikely to encourage him to come forward, are largely incomprehensible to most children, and may (at worst) result in some quite innocent child bursting into tears and confessing to the 'crime' simply to end the tension. It seemed possible only to keep an eye open for children seeming anxious, or having some family problem of recent occurrence, who might have committed the act. But Grenville himself solved the puzzle. On the morning after the break-in was discovered he brought a large box of sweets to school, which he shared with his friends, and was also heard by the head teacher to ask if anyone wanted a smoke. Watching from her window to see what would happen, she saw Grenville pull a packet of cigarettes from his pocket, and indicate that he was going behind the modern classroom block.

He was followed, and a little orgy was found to be in progress. Watched by two of his friends, who were coughing and screwing-up streaming eyes as they smoked half a cigarette each, Grenville was smoking a whole one with obvious ease, blowing the smoke through his nostrils, and flicking the ash like a villain in a Western film. He had obviously had a lot of practice. The boys were taken to the head teacher's room, and the two followers dismissed after a stern reproval and request that they would not do such a thing again, (at least until they were grown up). Grenville, left alone with the head, looked less confident than he had previously, and yielded at once to firm, but non-punitive questioning. He had indeed broken into the school and taken the money; and he had taken previous small change also. Asked where the rest of the money was, he said,

'I'll show you. But it's hid round the corner.'

He led the head teacher out of the playground, down the road, and behind a chapel. There, buried in the hedge in a matchbox, were the remaining two half-crowns. Although very chastened by now, Grenville had the dramatic flair characteristic of his family, and had probably seen himself as a cunning and uncatchable robber.

Discussion with the mother elicited that she had smelled smoke in his bedroom, but thought her husband had been in there; had been worried about Grenville's poor appetite in the last few weeks; and had noticed him going off with a group of older boys on several occasions. Both she and the father were firm with Grenville, and co-operative with the school in this matter, and his father agreed not to thrash the boy 'this time', but was not prepared to say that he would not do so if there was a recurrence of stealing. He was very prepared to take the other steps thought necessary, the first of which was the ending of Grenville's real addiction to nicotine. The family doctor was helpful in this respect, although Grenville's mother said he laughed at first, and that she herself had felt very foolish at taking a six-and-a-half-year-old to the doctor to be cured of smoking. The second step was to get assurance from his mother that she would both give him some extra attention (in the manner agreed with Tessie's mother) and would ensure that he had regular, small amounts of pocket-money instead of the casual, irregular and much larger sums he had previously been given. As a third step, some control over his keeping company with much older boys seemed to be necessary, and this his mother undertook to attempt.

All seemed to be well, until a week or two later Grenville entered another school in the locality with a group of young boys and was caught by a policeman. There was no question of breaking and entering, for the school was open, pending a meeting on the Saturday afternoon, and the absence of the schoolkeeper in another part of the building was an invitation to these children to go inside. Grenville, who had been operating the stage curtains in the school hall with great interest and delight, swung them back and went into one of his comic song-and-dance acts just as the policeman appeared at the door. The rest of the children, having seen him coming, had disappeared, and Grenville was left to explain his presence. He was taken home by the constable, who was more amused than angry, but did not reveal this to Grenville, and his mother came to the Infants' school on Monday to ask what could be done with him.

'It serves him right, the little devil,' she said, 'but I wouldn't 'arf 'ave liked to 'ave seen 'is face when that copper come into the 'all just as 'e went into 'is routine!'

The incident was not in itself very serious, but as Grenville had already broken into his own school, and might readily get the idea that this was a simple thing to do, some action seemed called-for.

It was in Grenville's case, among others, that the co-operation of the police was so helpful. A talk with the inspector, who was known to most of the school staff, resulted in an agreed plan with the parents. Grenville was to be taken, in his best suit and after a haircut to underline the seriousness of the occasion, to the police station. There was to be no threat at all, for the police were rightly unwilling to be used as 'bogies' but Grenville was to be told the truth – that he was too young for his naught y behaviour to bring him to court, but that the police inspector wanted to have a serious talk to him. Accordingly, escorted by both his father and his mother, Grenville went to the police station. With his hat, cane and gloves laid on the table, and the constable who had caught the boy in the school standing to attention behind him, the inspector gave Grenville a kind but firm (and short) talking-to. Grenville seemed to be very impressed by this ceremonious and symbolic stand of 'the law', and by the unbroken ranks presented by the adults in his world. While being neither humiliated nor severely punished, he was helped to see that his naughtiness was neither clever nor brave, but only likely to end in uncomfortable situations for himself. A child of this age does not reason; it is not suggested that the causal connections between crime, due processes of law, and punishment would be appreciated, nor that such treatment as described would be wholly or lastingly effective in Grenville's (or any other) case. Nevertheless, in conjunction with the other steps taken, it symbolized the strength and the consistency of those to whom he looked for guidance. For so lively and energetic but not deeply disturbed a child, always testing the limits to which he was allowed to go, the adults must not only make clear what the limits are – they must be seen by the child to agree on them.

Considerations

Three different backgrounds to pilfering have been outlined in this chapter, and three different approaches to the problem described as arising from the special needs of children having very different problems to cope with. It will be seen that the presence of both parents is no guarantee that a child will feel wanted and cared-for; that the absence of one may be, to a certain extent, compensated-for by the concern and understanding of the other; and that from a warm and ordinary home a child may still go out to steal. It should be obvious, also, from discussion of these three cases, that although the fundamental approach to the pilferer in the Infants' school will not change from one case to another, the needs of children are so different as to demand a different interpretation of fundamentals. Each of the children discussed needed affection – but so do all children, and to say that the pilferer needs this is to go only half-way (although admittedly in the right direction) to solving his problem. Brian needed to be trusted, and to have a relationship in which affection was combined with demands on his self-respect and practical help to his attainment of it. Tessie needed to give, as well as to be given-to, and to be allowed to talk about her absent father; not only affection for her, but continued support for her mother was an essential in this case. Grenville could not have been cured entirely by affection, either; parental co-operation with the school, the advice of a doctor, and the help of the police were all of value in his case.

In none of these cases, nor in any others, is it very likely that conventional punishment would have been of any use, even if it had been thinkable in the Infants' school. For Brian it has been tried and found not only useless but an aggravation of his trouble; for Tessie it would have been the grossest violation of an affectionate and trusting nature; and only the adult of most limited and humourless mentality could suppose that the lively Grenville could have been helped to stop smoking, stealing or getting into scrapes by the 'blanket' application of punishment.

This is not to say that these children were not reproved for their pilfering, or that simple explanation about the unacceptable nature of this behaviour was not made; they were, and it was. It has to be remembered, however, that children of this age do not deal in abstractions, and make little sense of verbal explanations. Long talks about morality, honesty or the kind that start 'how would you feel if' are pointless. Short and firm verbal sanctions are not only kinder and less waste of educational time, but are likely to be (if any verbal treatment is) more effective. Questions about why the child pilfers are equally meaningless – for he does not know; if he did, he would not pilfer. Exacting promises that he will not do it again only serve to give the child a lesson in the meaningless nature of words; and one has only to compare the frighteningly solemn promises of the marriage ceremony with divorce figures to see how many adults find the keeping of promises an impossible ideal. A child of five to seven, before ability to deal in abstractions has even begun to be possible for him, is not likely to do any better than tens of thousands of adults. At best, he will just not understand what is asked of him; at worst, he will be left with a feeling of guilt at having 'let down' the adult in some further and inexplicable manner.

The minor pilfering of small children who have just entered school, and who are very vague about what is their own in the classroom – often, indeed, they are given tins of crayons, books etc. with their names on and are told 'these are yours' – has not been dealt with. It is assumed that this will be understandable to the teacher, and that she will deal with it unemotionally as part of the social education she gives to every child. Mothers are sometimes upset by this (to them) naughty behaviour of their five-year-olds, and need the teacher's reassurance that it is very common and very normal. The device of emptying her own pockets at the end of the day, and returning the odd crayons, pieces of equipment and pencils to their rightful places as part of the tidying-up process in which all the children help, is usually enough to give the practical guidance that children need. Allowing them to take home work that they have done, and letting mothers come into the classroom after afternoon school to see equipment, specimens and work that cannot, legitimately, be removed from the classroom, demonstrates to the child where things belong, to whom, and why. Even a child who pockets some attractive small article will usually yield to the well-known device of the teacher asking who has sharp eyes and can find the missing object. (Such a child will often find things before they are lost, so to speak, in order to gain the praise of his teacher; and from this she knows that he has a special need, which she must try to analyse and meet.)

In a very poor area almost every child will be a pilferer at first. Not only will many be without material goods, but some will be without affection, also, and will want 'bits of the adult' to keep and take home. In such a place a teacher needs a greater stock of those oddments described in discussion of Tessie than she might normally use. Only by convincing the children of her stability in affection and her generosity in provision can she hope to get them to the stage when they do not need to pilfer – because there is enough to go round, and it is always there. But the social problems of such an area are complex and frightening, and must be studied as a whole; pilfering is only one of the problems with which the teacher in such an area has to contend. It is not confined to 'poor' areas, however, nor to 'bad' families, and its roots are more often emotional than they are financial – even in poor areas and bad families. Whether he comes from a privileged home in a good area, or a bad one in a slum, the first social agency likely to have to deal with the pilferer is the Infants' school. It is possible that something may be done at that stage which may prevent his appearance in court five years later; at least many teachers will feel that the effort is worthwhile, whether there is actual evidence of their actions being successful or not. Such approaches as have been suggested in the cases quoted above may be all the more effective if made in the humane, sometimes unorthodox and empirical manner in which most teaching and learning is conducted in the Infants' school.

Suggestions for Further Reading
Aichorn, A. *Wayward Youth* Hogarth (1957)
  Delinquency and Child Guidance Hogarth (1964)
Glueck, S. (Ed.) *The Problem of Delinquency* Houghton Mifflin (1959)
Glueck, S. and E. T. *Family Environment and Delinquency* Routledge (1962)
McNally, J. *Delinquency and the Schools* Educational Research Vol. VII, No. 3 (1965)

Stott, D. H. *Delinquency and Human Nature* Carnegie U. K. Trust (1950)

Wills, W. D. *Throw Away Thy Rod* Gollancz (1960)
Common Sense about Young Offenders Gollancz (1962)

Wilson, H. *Delinquency and Child Neglect* Geo. Allen and Unwin (1962)

Chapter 8

Children with Sex Worries

There is perhaps no more suitable manner in which to introduce this chapter than by the words in which Dr. Winnicott introduces his chapter on 'The Child and Sex' in ('The Child, the Family and the Outside World' – 1964). He writes:

'Only a little while ago it was thought bad to link sex with childhood "innocence". At the present time the need is for accurate description. As so much is as yet unknown the student is recommended to carry out research in his own way, and if he must read instead of making observations let him read descriptions by many different writers, not looking to one or another as the purveyor of truth. If special difficulty is found in allowing even for the possibility of childhood sexuality, it is better to turn one's attention to another subject.'

Infants' teachers who are themselves normally stable and loving will not need the psychoanalyst to tell them of the intensity of feeling experienced by small children in regard to those they love, nor of the dreadful damage done by withdrawal of love. If Freud had not delineated that set of relationships he named the Oedipus complex, observant and permissive teachers of Nursery and Infants' school children would have delineated it for themselves. And beyond the bounds of the Western family-pattern, in places where it takes a form not 'Oedipal', Margaret Mead and Bronislaw Malinowski (among others) found that young children have attachments, fears, habits and inclinations that it would be mealy-mouthed to call other than sexual in origin.

Yet this word 'sexual' is narrowed, in many Western adult minds, to cover only the act of coitus in adults, as though the whole sexual relationship were confined to that act alone, and successful marriage sprang ready-made out of no previous experience of loving. This, as Erich Fromm points out, is as foolish as for a person to say that although he has never looked at a subject, handled a paintbrush or mixed paint he knows that he will be able to execute a masterpiece in paint as soon as he feels like it Full adult sexuality has a long history, (as has full adult knowledge of language, craftsmanship or anything else), of growth through play, experiment, enquiry, instruction and application. The child producing a dazzling 'live' painting is not called either a mature painter or precocious or abnormal. His effort is seen as a step, valuable however in its own right, towards an adult appreciation (or perhaps execution) of very different, because mature, work. In the same way, the sexual interests, experiments and expressions of young children have only distant connections with adult sexuality. Yet, as with all other knowledge and skill, the future use and expression of sexuality is dependent on satisfying experience at their own level of childhood sexuality. To call his experiments and relationships nonsexual because of a narrowed use of a word is as silly as to say that his work with brush and paper is not painting.

In the normal family infantile sexuality passes almost unnoticed. The child has deep attachment to his mother, expressed quite naturally in physical ways; he includes the other parent in his affections early in life; he goes through a phase of trying to shut one parent out and being possessive about the other; he asks about his own sex, comparing his body with that of brothers or sisters; he tries to sort out partnerships and generational relationships in the manner already discussed in connection with Gareth (p. 101). If puzzled he sometimes asks a child of the opposite sex to show him her body, and sometimes displays his own. Girls and boys have different lessons to learn, and each has complex adjustments to make in regard to parents; but both boys and girls must make them if they are not to be gravely disturbed later. In all their play they practise what they see as male and female rôles, according to how these are expressed in the culture – boys go out to work while the girls do the housework in the Wendy House, each sex tries on the clothes and the trappings of the other at some time, and plays at being an adult of the opposite sex, and so on. If all this cannot be fairly described as 'sexual behaviour' it is certainly difficult to know what to call it.

By the time they arrive in the Infants' school most children from ordinary families have sorted out the preliminaries, as it were. Their own emotional upheavals in relation to identity and their standing with each parent are largely resolved for the time being; they know to which sex they belong, and some of the implications of this fact. They look interestedly at adults outside their homes, and want to know if they have children, too. They go on playing-out male and female rôles in increasing complexity for a year or more after they start school – but the games gradually become vehicles for other kinds of skills. By the age of six, in many cases, children are beginning to form like-sexed groups, and to continue their learning of 'how to be a boy' (or a girl) by playing with other boys (or girls).

It is with the child whose growth in sexuality has been impaired or distorted that the teacher will have to be concerned, although her friendly explanation to mothers of quite normal children who indulge in some forms of sexual play (perhaps because they have no siblings of the same sex) may be a valuable part of her job.

27. Roderick

A tall, well-built boy, admitted to the school at the age of five-and-a-half after having moved from a neighbouring town. Of average intelligence, as found on later tests by the Educational Psychologist, but thought to be deeply disturbed. Performance in most skills below average, but spoken language very well developed. Believed to have had little opportunity to practise such skills as drawing, painting, cutting etc. and experimented avidly with them when given the chance.

Roderick had been in trouble at his first Infants' school for what was described as 'gross indecency' during his second term there. He had, it appeared, persuaded both boys and girls to drop their pants and let him look carefully at their genitals; and for this he had been caned. He had repeated the offence a few days later, and his mother was asked to remove him from the school. She was an intelligent, determined woman, very aware of her rights and insistent upon them. Roderick was entitled to education, since he was not defective, and education he was going to receive, angry as she was with him. She was later thought by a psychiatrist to be paranoid; but she was nevertheless an amusing and lively woman, and certainly justified in thinking that it was 'a bit much' to ex-

133

clude a five-year-old from school on such grounds. She insisted that he remained there until the family moved – and this he did.

Roderick's behaviour was bizarre in the extreme, and his speech – despite an extraordinarily mature vocabulary and great facility with words – very odd, being high-pitched and forced, as though he were pressing every word through the top of his head. He flitted round the head's room touching everything lightly and saying such things as,

'Oh! What a beautiful ship! I shall take it, shall I? No, I won't. Oh! You can see clouds out of your window! Shall I look?' He tiptoed and pirouetted, seeming anxious despite his attempts at ease, until his mother gave him a sharp tap on the leg, when he subsided into a chair and stared at the head teacher.

He was put into the small class while his readjustment to school was made, but found it impossible to stay in the room for more than a few minutes at first. So erratic and demanding was he, that it was arranged that he should come into the head's room to play whenever he liked in order to relieve the class teacher who had several other difficult boys at the time. This he liked to do, and over a period of several weeks was able to persist for longer at such activities as building with blocks, cutting paper or threading beads. His play was like that of a younger child, and he had an avid, feverish attitude to it. He scattered wooden beads across the floor on one occasion, and said that they were millions of stars, and then that they were not stars at all, but children. On another occasion, he built a tower and said it was to catch the thunder-bolts. He was obsessed with weather, sang strangely tuneful songs that he made up about rain and clouds, and would look at a weather-book for many minutes together. He also pulled plastic dolls to pieces, naming the parts as he did so. One day as he was doing this he said suddenly,

'This doll doesn't have one. It doesn't have a little thing. It didn't like it. Perhaps it didn't like it?' To the question,

'What doesn't it have?' he made no answer, but hurled the pieces at the door. A little later he burst out with,

'Am I a funny kind of woman?'

One of his problems was on the surface at last. His mother had divorced his father, and his grandmother had long been separated from her husband. An unmarried aunt lived with

134

the family, which thus consisted, apart from Roderick, entirely of women – grandmother, mother and aunt. His mother's determination that he should not play with what she called 'the riff-raff', and the lack of uncles or close men friends of the family, meant that Roderick had hardly seen a man at close quarters since babyhood. It was little wonder that he felt it necessary to find out about other children, for his physical difference from everyone else in his household must have worried him for years. In addition, the contempt his mother expressed for men, echoed by his grandmother and aunt, must have meant that even if he had vague notions that his 'difference' only meant that he was male this was not a very satisfactory thing to be.

A well-illustrated and simple book about sex, designed for young children, was found for him, and sitting on the head teacher's knee he had the basic facts explained to him. He was also encouraged to talk to the schoolkeeper, who was told a little about the boy's situation and was sorry to think, as he said, of a 'boy with no dad around the place'. Roderick simply did not know how to treat this ordinary, friendly man, and was at first shy and then rude; but after a few weeks he behaved quite normally with him. A friendly relationship was set up by the headmistress with the mother, and visits made to the home, for it was felt important that she should, if possible, be helped not to despise or reject her son, as she had her husband and father.

There were many other disturbing features about this boy, however, and he was eventually referred for psychiatric examination and sent to a school for maladjusted children. This step was taken in friendly and complete co-operation with his mother, who, it was hoped, would also receive some guidance and advice about herself. There was no doubt that Roderick's early experience had been very different from that sketched above as being the normal. Far more, and deeper, damage had been done than was expressed in the sexual confusion of this boy, bad enough as that was. The whole emotional climate of the family, through two generations at least, seemed deviant; and there was little doubt in looking at Roderick that the pattern bade fair to be repeated in a third unless it could be broken by therapy. It is rarely that a child in such a state will be found, but when he is it is surely the function of the Infants' school to take such steps as it can to deflect what looks like 'fate'. Far less disturbed children than Roderick, however, have the same kind of sexual problem. If a child comes from a home where opportunity is lacking to find out about the opposite sex, not only physiologically but socially and emotionally as well, he or she is likely to be in a state of some confusion. Extreme parental modesty, of a kind fairly rare in these days, or a punitive attitude towards questioning, allied with absence of like-sexed siblings, can give rise to the same kind of problem as that faced by Roderick. If the child is not so otherwise disturbed it may be that the straightforwardly educative approach described above may be of great help. But this must not be forced; the child must be allowed to ask the questions, and he is likely to do this if the atmosphere is friendly and all knowledge is regarded as worthwhile.

28. Ingrid

A tiny, anxious-looking, but aggressive child, who appeared in the playground from the age of three and would not go home until her older sister came out to take her. Of average intelligence, but very retarded in reading and writing and not very much better at number skills. A very good painter, however, producing colourful and mature-looking work from the age of five. Otherwise interested only in active, outdoor games, at which she was better than average.

Ingrid was a problem during her first year in school on account of her interfering with other children, and her apparent inability to sit at the simplest task for more than a minute or two. In a classroom she was very disruptive, but longed to stay there, and did not like having to work even a yard or two away from other children. She did not object to working in the head's room, however, since she seemed to enjoy the attention of one adult. It was thought that she might be in more than usual need of affection, and this was discussed with her mother. There seemed no reason for Ingrid to feel rejected, but rather the reverse. She was the youngest child of four, having a sister four years older than herself and two brothers already in their teens who made a great fuss of her. Her father and mother seemed to get on well together, and her mother said that Ingrid had always a special time with her parents when she went to bed, and they took turns to read a story and play with her. The mother admitted that Ingrid had never been a very 'cuddly' child, but said that she did not seem to like being touched at all of late years and had been spiteful and generally naughty at home over the same period – since she was about four.

There seemed no explanation for the child's increasing aggression towards other children, nor for her occasional fits of weeping. She had never been a popular child, because of her constant interference with the activities of others, and she was now positively disliked by some girls in her class. This was hardly surprising, for she pinched and punched them without mercy on occasions, while all the time begging them to let her play with them. She was obviously in a very disturbed state, and her work, as she neared her seventh birthday, was very retarded indeed. Talks with her mother, remedial reading sessions with the head, encouragement to her to play sensibly with others, had all failed to improve her, and the parents agreed to referral to the Child Guidance clinic. It was felt that they had been a little guarded about Ingrid from the beginning, despite the co-operation they had shown, and it was wondered if, perhaps, she were an adopted child, which they did not wish to admit, or if there were some family circumstance which had not been revealed.

No such 'mystery' was uncovered at the clinic, however, and it was felt there that the mother had been helpful and open – as she had been at school – but a little strained. This was hardly surprising, for Ingrid was being very tiresome at home, and for long periods would not talk to her mother. At her second session with the therapist the truth emerged. Her older brother had been interfering with her sexually for two or three years. This was not as physically serious as might have been thought, for the boy was young enough to be un- certain of his own powers; but emotionally much damage had been done because he had sworn her to secrecy, and threatened her with punishment if she told her mother. The parents were naturally shocked by this finding, and relied on the psychiatrist to talk to them about the best course to take with the boy. Ingrid was encouraged to tell her mother all about the matter, and her mother helped to accept the con- fession with calm. She was also advised on means by which she might indicate to the child that the parents were now in control, and that the brother was not 'wicked' so much as unkind, wrong-headed and himself in a muddle.

137

So far, it looked as though Ingrid's problem would be solved after a few more sessions with the therapist, and a few more weeks of support and advice for the parents. But this was not the case. As the psychiatric sessions continued it became apparent that Ingrid, not the adolescent brother, had made the first overtures – and this at the age of four. It looked as though a fairly normal attempt to sort out sex-differences had gone badly wrong in a manner it would not, perhaps, have done if a much younger brother had shared her bath-time and so on with her. Moreover, by this time (and she was now seven) Ingrid was very sexually precocious. In the words of the psychiatrist,

'Her head is as full of sex as an egg is of meat.'

This psychiatrist said that in thirty years of practice she had never met a young child so sex-conscious, and was thankful that the therapy was not being conducted by one of the young male doctors. It was thought that long-term therapy was needed for this very disturbed little girl, and it was still in progress when she left the Infants' school. It was hardly surprising that her work remained poor, for most of her mental energy must have been expended on her problem.

Some teachers may find such a case almost unbelievable, and it is true that they are mercifully rare. It must be faced, however, that adolescent boys have sexual experiments with young sisters (and brothers) far more often than is commonly accepted, and that many of these are not as harmful in their effects as adults might suppose. It is guilt rather than physical experiment that does the harm, unless, of course, there is gross sexual assault. (This appears to be rare; something very much more like sexual play is the usual behaviour.) Nevertheless, the emotional needs of adolescents are very different from those of small children, and their experiments quite different in quality and nature from those described as normal for four-year-olds. This means that even if little harm is done some inevitably must be; and the adolescent who cannot, or dare not, make his experiments with his own age-group is badly in need of adult guidance. The young child needs protection against not only the physical experience but the 'alien' needs of a disturbed adolescent. Even in a good home, (and Ingrid's was this, by any of the criteria usually applied), such a confrontation may occur.

There was nothing specifically sexual in Ingrid's behaviour

in school, but her case is an example of the wisdom of referring for psychiatric assessment a child who is unable to relate with fellows, very retarded, and has inexplicable fits of weeping. That a sexual problem lay at the heart of this disturbance no one in school could have guessed, but it was a function of the school to refer the child and to receive the explanation of the therapist without censure or blame for parents or child.

29. Walter

A most odd-looking child, thought to be suffering from some glandular misfunction, since he was as nearly square as a child could be, and had shorter limbs, fingers and toes than the body-length would suggest as normal. Speech hasty, slurred and babyish; movements clumsy; approaches to other children enthusiastic, but violent. No apparent training in ordinary social skills such as using cutlery or taking himself to the lavatory. No persistence and no apparent appreciation of the uses of tools, toys or materials. Much more like a two-year-old, in fact, than a five-year-old in almost every aspect of development. Masturbated continuously unless given something in his hands or distracted to look at something interesting. An only child of young parents.

It was difficult at first to get any information about this boy. His mother appeared only to enter him at school when he was already five years old. This meant that he had not visited the school before his entry, and there had been no opportunity to talk to his mother about him. After he had started school he was brought by a succession of *au pair* girls, and left at the gate. It was difficult to contact his mother, for she and her husband ran a successful business together, leaving home before Walter came to school in the morning, and coming back only when he was ready for bed. They also led a busy social life, and it seemed that Walter had been left to the care of *au pair* girls ever since he was a few months old. Only the attendance of his mother at the medical examination made the gathering of this information possible.

The doctor was concerned about the boy's backwardness in speech and social skills, as well as about his odd physique and poor muscle tone. The mother's answers to the doctor made it apparent that she had not thought the child in any way backward for his age; but she was defensive about his having been left so much to the care of inexperienced and often reluctant

139

girls, and blamed them for what she called Walter's 'nasty habits'. That she should have made herself responsible for him she did not admit, saying that she was a very busy woman and that the business would suffer if she abandoned it.

Much discussion with Walter's mother had to take place over a period of months before she was able to accept some responsibility for him, and to co-operate with doctor and school in discovering his needs with a view to meeting them. The loneliness and boredom he must have experienced as a baby and toddler were admitted finally, however; and it also emerged that more than one of the foreign girls who had had charge of him had tied his hands together, slapped him, and taken other punitive action when he played with his genitals. The mother seemed not to have realized either the disturbed and bored state which had led him to excessive play of this nature – he had been given nothing else to play with, and had been strapped in pram, chair or bed for long periods throughout his life – or the danger in making him feel dirty, naughty or unloved on account of it. Whether she ever fully appreciated the situation was doubtful, but she was shocked to realize how much Walter differed from other children, and how much his future as schoolboy and even adult might be jeopardized by such an early experience.

Walter's problem was not, as Roderick's and Ingrid's, a specifically sexual one, but since it involved masturbation is included here rather than under another category. He could be justly described as having some of the features of an anxious child; his behaviour about the classroom was certainly bizarre, and he could be categorized thus; and he was undoubtedly immature to a pronounced degree. Nevertheless, he represents, in an extreme form, many of the features of children who resort to the infantile comfort of genital stimulation, and is thus included here. His unfamiliarity with other forms of physical pleasure (such as running freely in a large space, riding a tricycle, kicking a ball and climbing) was pathetic, and his response to such opportunities understandably excited and vigorous. His apparent feelings of rejection also typify the feelings of many, if not all, children who masturbate, and his teacher made special efforts to relate to him at a level which is more usual with two-year-olds. She sat him on her knee, played finger-games with him, gave him little things from her bag, and held him by the hand while taking him about the school. He was encouraged at the same time to develop those skills normal to a five-year-old, such as using a knife and fork, dealing with his own clothes and washing himself, for he had to accept the requirements of the Infants' school however emotionally immature he might be.

Such training, although intensive in Walter's case, is not so alien to that given in the Reception class as to make it impossible for an interested teacher with not too large a group. It was fortunate that a small class (of, at the time, twenty children) was available for him. His masturbation decreased as he found more activities to engage his attention and a stable, consistent adult to relate with him. He was still prone to rub his genitals and rock backwards and forwards during story-time, and it was not until he had adopted a soft toy to nurse that the habit disappeared. (Thereafter, he clutched at his trousers if worried or thwarted, but no more. This is one of the commonest gestures of anxiety, fear or uncertainty among small boys, and cannot properly be classed as masturbation in the manner of Walter's earlier manipulation.) In connection with the nursing of a toy it has to be appreciated that this is *learned* behaviour, as is most other, and that Walter, as far as could be ascertained, had never learned it. In cuddling and nursing a toy a child can externalize, symbolize and deflect much of his own need to love and be loved. It can never be a substitute for being loved and giving love, and this may be why it was not part of Walter's play until several months of relationship with his teacher, and (during those months) a more constructive approach by his mother had given him the idea, so to speak.

The problem presented to teachers by children whose parents have taken so little practical part in their upbringing is immense. Obviously, neither the attitudes nor knowledge of the parents, nor the five previous years of damage to the child can be rectified in school. The co-operation of parents already feeling guilty has to be gently sought; the school doctor can play a most important advisory rôle to both parents and teachers; and the ordinary opportunities of the classroom can be made available to the child in ways in which he can use them. His damaged relationship with the parents, reflected in the self-comforting and infantile habit of masturbation, is better dealt with if possible by the Child Guidance team than by the teacher. It is unlikely that teachers

141

will have the knowledge, resources or time to 'take on' so major a family problem as that instanced by Walter. Yet masturbation is a distress-signal to the teacher, (at least, if it is pronounced and persistent as in Walter's case), and like persistent nail-biting, enuresis and aggressive outburst, should be seen as such, and not as a predominantly 'nasty' habit requiring stricture or suppression.

30. Arthur

A thin, tense, bespectacled boy, of average intelligence according to tests taken in school, but retarded in reading at the age of nearly seven when he entered the school. An only child, of parents older than the generality, well-loved and eager to please his parents. Said by his mother to have nightmares and to be prone to bed-wetting. Solitary in school until after start of treatment at the Child Guidance clinic, but friendly with his teacher from the start.

Arthur represents a problem fairly commonly found among children of Infants' school age, and in some ways resembling that of Roderick. His poor school performance and his apparent inability to make friends were the first causes of anxiety to his teachers, and were mentioned at his medical examination. His mother's account of his nightmares and enuresis, and her own anxiety in regard to the boy's health were further cause of concern to the doctor. It appeared that Arthur had always been a rather anxious boy, but that his tension had increased after he started school at five. His mother had had a miscarriage at about this time, and since she had been very ill Arthur had gone to stay with relatives for several weeks. It was his first separation from his mother, and he had been very upset at first, relapsing into withdrawal from his aunt and uncle thereafter, and being inept and tearful when his lively young cousins had wanted him to play with them. He had started having nightmares at this time, and screaming that 'he couldn't get out'. It appeared, from the mother's later telling of the story, that Arthur's cousin had told him that his mother had been going to have a baby, and that it would not now be born. There was no evidence that this had been done maliciously or with any intention other than to impart information; for these children were between nine and twelve years of age, fond of their little cousin, (whom they saw rarely), and themselves quite open in discussion of where babies come from and so on. Nevertheless, to Arthur, who had no brothers and sisters, and whose rather shy, middle-aged parents had not told him anything of such matters, the knowledge was a great shock. The separation-anxiety no doubt heightened the impact of quite matter-of-fact information, and his own uncertainties about sex-differences seemed to have been the final destructive factor in the situation.

Even in telling the story to the doctor, and later in enlarging on it to the head teacher, Arthur's mother was slightly embarrassed at first. She was not a prudish woman, in fact, but Arthur had seemed to her such a baby, and her own upbringing so unhelpful in giving her words in which to talk of sexual matters, even at four-year-old level, that she had obviously not tried to explain her pregnancy, much less her absence in hospital, to the boy. It is almost certain that Arthur knew that his mother was 'different' before the miscarriage, and probably associated her condition with some abdominal condition. He had been a rather costive child and his mother had worried about this, giving him old-fashioned laxatives such as senna tea, and telling him that he would be ill if he did not 'go' every day. The confusion in this boy's mind between the dangers of constipation and childbirth, between the rôles of the sexes, and his own place in the scheme of things was tremendous. Fortunately, his essentially loving and intelligent mother was very willing to accept expert psychiatric advice for him, and he was referred to the Child Guidance clinic immediately after the doctor's visit.

At the clinic he expressed, clearly and soon, all the fears sketched above. He had indeed confused his own constipated state with his mother's 'baby', and believed that he, too, would be taken to hospital to have something taken away. He had seen his youngest girl cousin in the bath, also, and told his therapist that Sandra had had her penis taken away, which added another confusion to his already muddled mind. He had phantasies that *he* was the baby who could not get out of his mother, and it was this that was the main content of his nightmare. In fact, in his play at the clinic, and in his ready verbalization of his fears once he knew there was someone to whom he could express them, he effected most of his own cure within a few weeks, complex and phantastic though his troubles had been.

143

His school work improved slowly, but his tension, night-mares, enuresis and even constipation cleared-up within a matter of months. (Straightforward advice to the mother from the school doctor in regard to the latter included a recommendation to 'stop worrying about it' – admittedly difficult for such a parent – and to increase Arthur's intake of fruit and liquid. The mother's anxiety about the state of the boy's bowels was typical of that of many parents, and often led to tension and other complications in the children.) It was possible, since Arthur would have been as young as possible on leaving the Infants' school, to retain him for a further year, and in that year he put on weight, became friendly with several other boys, and learned to read. He left the Infants' school eventually as an unnoticeably ordinary boy, of average performance, and confident in his own powers.

It is not often that such a combination of common misunderstandings and fears will be found in one child, but many children will have one or the other of them. In the case of the child where this becomes known, for any reason, there is an educative task for the teacher, (as in Roderick's case), and usually a place for advice and help to the mother from the school doctor. In some other cases resembling Arthur's but not involving such disturbance, it was found that the mother's relief at talking-over the problem with the head or class-teacher, and finding that problems about the origin of babies are common between the ages of three and five, seemed helpful in itself. That one's child is not abnormal or a sexually precocious monster of some kind, that one is not alone in being a little worried about how to explain, without giving too much information too soon, are in themselves comforting findings to many mothers. The teacher is in a peculiarly strong position to give such comfort, for she knows many children – and a mother usually knows only her own.

Considerations

There can be few reasonably well-educated parents in these days who find themselves unable to deal with the sexual questions of young children. The finding of one's own rôle of the three-year-old, the questions about physiological differences common to four-year-olds, and the enquiring about babies from the age of three upwards, present little difficulty to the modern parent. The teacher of Nursery and Infants' school children has no problem of formal 'sex instruction', and it would surely indicate that something was wrong with parents, schools or children if she had. In most cases, there is nothing wrong, and interest in sexual matters will be only one of the myriad interests that young children have in the normally interesting classroom and environs of an Infants' school. Attitudes of tenderness to baby creatures, human and otherwise, can be set-up by the example of the teacher and the opportunity to see animals, (preferably not closely caged), birds and human families at close quarters. This is as an important a facet of 'sex education' as factual instruction, and will enlarge for children that already wide view of sexuality which in most cases they have brought into school from good, loving homes.

There are, however, the homes where perhaps due to punitive attitudes of parents, absence of one parent, (as in Roderick's case), unfortunate encounters between siblings, (as in Ingrid's), deprivation of some fortuitous happenings in regard to marital relations or birth of a baby, children are confused and miserable. There are also distinct differences of attitude to genital play according to class,[1] and teachers in some areas will have to be aware that their own enlightened view of infantile sexual behaviour, including masturbation, is not shared by the majority of the parents in the neighbourhood. There are almost certainly similar class differences in attitudes to children's questioning, and the degree to which they are allowed to share bath-time and bedrooms with siblings of the opposite sex. Some parents may be so 'frank' as to give their children far too much information, and allow far too much sharing of bathrooms with adults, confusing the younger child by giving him explanations for which he did not ask, and denying to older ones (from about the age of seven) the development of that natural modesty which is so different from prudery or prurience. On the other hand, and predominantly among working-class parents, there will be a great reluctance to discuss anything remotely 'sexual' with the child, and a shocked reaction to the suggestion that parents are ever seen undressed. That this set of attitudes may, by reason of housing conditions, be accompanied by far

[1] See 'Patterns of Infant Care in an Urban Community' J. & E. Newson (Penguin) 1965.

more opportunities for children to see and to know more about adult sexual behaviour than is possible to the middle-class child, is yet one more consideration for the teacher if problems arise in the Infants' school.

It would be foolish to look for a sexual basis to every learning difficulty and every piece of deviant behaviour – a tendency arising from a misapplication of Freudian theory to the behaviour of 'problem' children, and perhaps a misunderstanding of much of what Freud himself said. It would be equally foolish, however, to ignore the fact that children with problems of the kind discussed above do enter our Infants' schools every year, and that in many cases they, and their parents, need skilled help. It is important that the teacher of young children be aware of the possible difficulties of a sexual nature that children meet, and of the ways in which they may be helped to overcome them. She is not likely, if she is of ordinary sense and sensitivity, to see sex in every problem; but she must not hesitate to mention the difficulties of a particular child because she is afraid of the accusation of doing just that.

Suggestions for Further Reading
Very few texts, beyond clinical and medical, deal specifically with children's sexual development, questions and difficulties. Relevant passages, comments and implications are, however, to be found in the following:

Bowley, A. *The Natural Development of the Child* E. and S. Livingstone (4th Ed. 1963)

Carmichael, L. (Ed.) *Manual of Child Psychology* John Wiley (2nd Ed. 1954)

Gabriel, J. *Children Growing Up* U.L.P. (1964)

Gesell, A. *The First Five Years of Life* Methuen (Reprint 1954)

Lowenfeld, M. *Play in Childhood* Gollancz (1938)

Isaacs, S. *Social Development in Young Children* (1933) Routledge & Kegan Paul (7th Impress. 1952)

Stone, L. J. and Church, J. C. *Childhood and Adolescence* Random House (1957)

Chapter 9

Immature Children

The title of this chapter may well appear to be tautologous, for all children are immature organisms, by definition. Yet there is a sense in which the biologically immature human being, the child, can be more or less mature than others of his chronological age. It is a common-sense proposition, which every wise teacher will endorse, that no two children of the same chronological age are at exactly the same stage of development in *every* aspect. Some five-year-olds will appear physically older than others, and their motor skills will seem advanced; there will be speech immaturities in one, allied with quite normal development and skills in other directions; another may be unusually socially poised, but slower than the generality in learning to read. Between child and child, and within an individual, there will be anomalies of development which are natural and normal – which give, in fact, that 'pied beauty' to life of which Manley Hopkins writes, the '. . . things counter, original, spare, strange;
Whatever is fickle, freckled (who knows how?)
With swift, slow; sweet, sour; adazzle, dim . . .'

In a quest for uniformity, conformity, measurement and norms of development it might be possible to lose sight of other, more subtle values; to view the slow as inferior to the swift, dimness as a nuisance rather than a gentler version of light, the original as an affront and those outside our arbitrary limits for growth and learning an irritation.

This is not to say that wisely applied measurement, wisely interpreted is not of use, nor that the establishment of some 'norms' is a waste of time. It is possible to discern ways in which the *majority* of five-year-olds or seven-year-olds are more like each other than they are like members of another age-group – their general size, body-head proportions and muscular development, for example, are characteristic of an age and stage. (Even so, this most basic resemblance of members of an age-group to each other may need a different set of age-norms for children of a different culture or stock.) We base much of our work with children in school on the justifiable assumption that at certain ages *most* children will be ready for certain interests and skills, and our standardized tests may be useful in determining which children are 'exceptional' and need special attention. But variations and anomalies *within the individual* are not so easily measured by single tests nor possible of expression in direct scores, and Ruth Griffiths' concept of developmental profile is a useful one in considering these.[1] It is thus possible to conceive of maturity in terms of the physical growth attained, the kind and range of motor skills developed, the command of language and thought-processes that are apparent or measurable, and the social-emotional stability achieved; a conception which depends upon observation, standardized tests and scales, and the generalized concept of 'like-characteristics' for particular age-groups.

There is, however, a sense in which maturity is not measurable, since it is a unique achievement and a subjective experience for each individual. In this sense, a five-year-old may be 'mature' in not only his achievement of the characteristic skills of his age-group, but in that inner harmony with himself-as-he-is of which Anthony Storr writes.[2] Allport, as Storr, thinks of the achievement of maturity as more than the growth of muscle and bone or the achievement of skills, and also speaks of it as a subjective experience, with a personal version for each individual. He suggests however, that there are common features of 'maturity' no matter how individually these may be arrived-at or expressed: comfortable relations with the self and with reality, acceptance of self and others, spontaneity and creativity are some of them.[3] These could be as applicable to a three-, four- or seven-year-old as to an adult – if one appreciates that the 'reality' of a young child's world is necessarily different from that of an adult's, and that his relations with 'others' are appropriately less sophisticated and reciprocal. Most writers dealing with the concept of maturity lay stress upon the need to be comfortable with and accepting of the self while having awareness of goals (or ideals) which impel constructive striving. The mature adult individual is

[1] See 'The Abilities of Babies' (1954).
[2] 'The Integrity of the Personality' pp. 170-171.
[3] 'Pattern and Growth in Personality' ch. 12.

not a smug and static creature who has 'arrived', but a dynamic being in a state of sound equilibrium between himself-as-he-is and himself-as-he-would-be, able to create and to command, to lead and to follow, to wait and to initiate – and always aware of himself as part of a dynamic human whole, with a responsibility for it which he must express in his own personal, cultural and vocational manner. In this sense, as Erikson points out, '. . . a wise Indian, a true gentleman, and a mature peasant share and recognize in one another the final stage of integrity.'[4]

Erikson's listing of eight stages from birth to old age reminds us that childhood is, in its own right, important to the achievement of a well-spent and gay youth, a creative middle-age, and an old age of strength and wisdom. His stages in childhood are those of:

basic trust v. basic mistrust.
autonomy v. shame and doubt
initiative v. guilt
industry v. inferiority

These are envisaged *not* as representing appropriate 'achievements' at various ages, but as part of the life-work which is continuous. Trust may be learned in babyhood, as the child learns to rely not only on the sameness of the providers but on his own capacity to cope with his urges. The quality of these experiences will affect his response to all situations involving trust, enabling him to incorporate more sophisticated kinds of confidence into his relationships, intellectual activities and whole life-style as he matures. According to Erikson, the individual does not learn to trust (and, when appropriate, to mistrust) once and for all at the first stage, but rather lays a basis, in the experience of satisfactory mothering, for a sense of identity and of being able to meet the demands of others in regard to himself. The experience of being able to trust oneself and able to rise to the expectations of others in the society is thus constantly being renewed.

In the same way Erikson's other stages are seen as basic experiences, occurring in the first instance at certain ages, (as

4 'Childhood and Society' (Pelican Edition) p. 260. The succeeding paragraphs are based on chapter 7 of this book.

ability to be aware of and to control the body's parts, powers and limits develop), but continuously experienced with ever more sophisticated meaning and intensity. To the teacher this concept of development to full psychic maturity is a valuable one, for it highlights her responsibility for providing situations, encouraging relationships and making materials available which will help children to build on the past, make full use of the present, and not jeopardize their future. It reminds her, also, that the eventual achievement of maturity in adulthood is best served by allowing full exploration and expression in childhood. The child who is helped to be mature *for his age* is more likely to reach eventual full maturity and integrity than the one who is denied the needs of a particular stage. This denial may take many forms: doing too much for a child, doing too little, putting a high premium on self-control too early, or not helping him to control himself at all – as well as that insistence on sterile academic standards, meaningless to the child, of which Jersild writes so bitterly. (See p. 96 above).

The work of Piaget may give all those concerned in the education of children another concept of maturity, for he sees it as the development, in an orderly sequence, of *ways* of thinking – ways which cannot be taught 'ahead' of physical maturing, but which are dependent also on experience of a first-hand, sensory nature. For example, by the processes Piaget calls assimilation and accommodation the child's experiences of size, space, weight, time, quality, quantity, and so on, are internalized, extended to incorporate new phenomena, and give rise to concepts of conservation, serialization, categorization and causality. From the sensorimotor stage when the sensory experiences are the most vital, to the 'mature' stage of being able to deal in formal logic and think in abstractions, judge, reason and classify is a continuous development. Each stage of thinking is dependent on a satisfactory achievement in the previous stage; and the first steps to full intellectual maturity are practical experience and personal discovery of the world. The work of Piaget is obviously too vast to be dealt with in a few brief comments, and is familiar already to teachers. Like the work of Erikson in another field, it represents deep insights into the growth and development of human beings, and into the needs of children for full development. It is mentioned here as an indication that there is now another major criterion for the use of teachers when the difficult assessment of a child's 'maturity' is to be made. Piaget's findings neither supersede nor contradict the developmental norms of Gesell and similar scales, or the psychoanalytical interpretation of Erikson, but rather add another dimension to our thinking of what constitutes maturity.

The children already discussed in this book all showed signs of being immature in one or more particular. Indeed, their inability to 'act their age' in some way was what brought most of them to the notice of their teachers. The children who are the subject of this chapter, however, were immature in a 'total' way that the others were not. They may have been aggressive, anxious, prone to pilfer or to have sexual worries, but they were predominantly noticeable because they looked, moved and behaved over a very wide area like much younger children. In an Infants' school, where eagerness to grow up, to become more adequate, and to be given more and more responsibility is characteristic, these 'Peter Pan' children present the teacher with something of a problem. They are apparently denying the fundamental purpose of childhood – which is to grow out of it – and this being so they obviously are in special need of adult help.

31. Alan

A small, fair, chubby boy, looking at the age of seven very like a five-year-old, and having similar movement. Tests applied by the educational psychologist showed him to be of average intelligence (I.Q. 104), but he was totally unable to read, despite extra, individual help during his last six months at school. Not reliably dry at night by the age of seven, given to solitary play, day-dreaming and flitting from one activity to another in and out of school. The youngest child of five, the other four being from twelve to fifteen years older than he at his birth and including twin sisters who adored their baby brother and 'mothered' him from babyhood.

Alan's mother was a warm and intelligent woman, who had been delighted to find herself pregnant again in her forties, and enjoyed Alan's birth and babyhood. He had been a good baby, receiving the affection of two big brothers as well as of adoring sisters and parents. He said himself that he had three 'mummies' and 'two men brothers and my dad'. He had, moreover, slept in the parental bedroom until the age of six

when the family moved to a larger house, and still had bedtime rituals of a kind more appropriate to a baby than a boy of
school age. He was not, apparently, ritualistic in the usual
way but obviously liked the attention to his wants which was
represented by the babyhood comforts. In school he played
alongside other children rather than with them, and this was
not particularly noticeable in his first year, when so many
other children were also just beginning to move from
parallel to co-operative play. By his second year, however,
his markedly babyish appearance and his inability to share
tools or equipment without outbursts of rage was a matter
of some concern. Since he had shown no signs of being interested in reading, in writing or in any of the many experimental activities of his classmates his mother was consulted.

She was worried about him also, and said that he took
money from her purse or from his father's pocket in an
almost 'open' manner, and spent it on sweets, seeming quite
unable to appreciate that it was not his to take. His bed-
wetting was a matter of concern to his mother, too, and was
becoming a source of friction between him and one of his
brothers who teased him about it. He bit his nails, which
earned him some disapproval from his sisters, and was generally not as permissively treated by the four elder siblings as
he had been as a baby – although there was no doubt that
they were still very fond of their young brother. His failure
to learn to read was not regarded by his mother or his
teacher as too grave at this point, but was beginning to worry
his father who remembered the older children being able to
read early, and who was himself a particularly literate person.
No pressure had been put upon Alan, and he had not been
questioned about his performance in school, but the mother
felt that it would not be long before her husband began to be
seriously concerned about Alan's lack of progress in formal
skills. No other clues to the boy's patent disturbance were
forthcoming, however, and it was agreed that he should have
extra help with his reading in school, that his brother should
be restrained from teasing him, and that he should be read-to
at bedtime. An appointment to see the school doctor about
Alan's enuresis was made at this time.

During the next few months Alan became the inciter of
aggression in several groups of boys, always running away
when threatened himself or when an adult intervened. It was

now apparent that this quiet, chubby little boy was a serious disturber of the peace, inciting other boys to all sorts of mischief in which he would not join. It was difficult to see why bigger, more vigorous boys took notice of Alan's suggestions; perhaps his greater intelligence, and his undoubted imaginative powers, impressed them. His reading was non-existent as he neared his seventh birthday, and his bed-wetting had stopped only temporarily after the doctor had arranged for the provision of a patent apparatus to help him to wake himself up. It was decided to refer him to the Child Guidance clinic, and he was seen there just after he was seven.

Alan's mother was as co-operative with the clinic as she had been with the school, and impressed the psychiatrist and the P.S.W. with her warmth and good sense. She agreed to various suggestions made about Alan's routine at home, including introducing a slightly later bedtime, and refusal to yield to his 'blackmail' despite the temporary antagonism this might arouse in him. She was not thought to need more than occasional visits from the P.S.W. To his therapist Alan revealed much of his trouble immediately. He started by using his normal piping voice and the wheedling (but engaging) manner of a five-year-old, but soon changed voice and manner in vigorous play with small dolls. He enacted scenes of family life in which a little boy escaped from his parents and had gay adventures on his own; he allowed the boy to be caught by both parents and taken home, to be put to bed in the largest bed in the house; he then played at 'witches', using the mother doll as the witch, but soon switched to his former themes again.

The psychiatrist felt that Alan was not too deeply disturbed, but was at the emotional level of a three-year-old, and needed a great deal of play in order to come to terms with his rôle as a growing boy and his relationship with his large grown-up family. He had always made bold, colourful pictures at school, and continued to do this at the clinic, using the themes of his doll-play: boys running over hills, witches leaping over rainbows, ships full of boys being pirates, and so on. The psychiatrist was impressed by the quality of his imagination, and believed his intelligence to be rather higher than the tests had suggested. There was no doubt, however, that he had many problems to work out, and was not willing to face growing up. His babyhood, after all, had been a particularly favoured one and it was hardly surprising that he was something of a Peter Pan. Yet there was a real desire in him to be adventurous, in charge and 'big', and this was considered a healthy sign. His view of his mother as over-protective, which seemed indicated by his 'witch' play as well as by his conversations with the psychiatrist, was also felt to be a favourable sign, and was discussed as such with her. It was obvious that Alan had little mental energy to give to the work of formal learning while he was still struggling to achieve a measure of initiative and independence, and this was explained to his father, who accepted the suggestion with understanding and interest. Much provision for imaginative play was available in school, and Alan was encouraged to make full use of it; he was also encouraged by his mother to ask home friends of his own age – which he did with reluctance at first, but with growing enthusiasm.

Transfer to the Junior school posed a problem. Alan still looked, spoke and moved like a much younger child; but he was beginning to grow up, and to keep him with children chronologically younger than himself for another year seemed inadvisable. On the other hand, the pressures of a large, Junior school upon a child so ill-adjusted as yet to his rôle, and a complete non-reader in addition, were thought to be too much for him to cope with. It was arranged that he go to a much smaller school very little farther from his home than the one to which most of his classmates were going. As several other children went there each year this did not strike Alan as 'special' treatment. He was to continue attendance at the clinic, and to receive remedial teaching within the new school if his lack of progress in the following term seemed to warrant it.

32. Bobby

Brought to school before the age of five by a very worried young mother who said she could do nothing with him at home. Admitted a few months earlier than he would otherwise have been as there was room in the small class and the mother did seem to be in special need. A tiny, dark boy appearing very much younger than his actual age, with a light, piping voice and many speech immaturities. Later tests by the educational psychologist showed him to be of average intelligence, but there were indications that he was a some-

154

what disturbed child. In school seemed like a three-year-old – solitary in play, but interested in other children, chatty, affectionate, not able to concentrate for more than a minute or two, and predominantly concerned with large motor skills. An occasional tantrum, and stubborn refusal to do anything he did not wish to do also more typical of a three-year-old than a child nearing five.

Bobby's mother had been only nineteen when he was born, and his father barely twenty-one; they lived for the first three years of their marriage with Bobby's maternal grandmother. For the first eighteen months of his life his young parents had not had to come to terms with their son, for the grandmother had helped with him from the start, and had encouraged the couple to go out and enjoy themselves while she sat in with Bobby. When the parents had a house of their own, and the grandmother was too far away to visit more than once a week or in an emergency, they had found adjustment to full responsibility difficult. Both parents were very fond and proud of their son, but indulged him to the point at which he was the real power in the house; and as he grew older their efforts to undo the damage seemed to make matters worse. He defied his mother, kicked his father, and ran away laughing after causing his mother to lose her temper. He was a vigorous and healthy little boy, but so 'naughty' that his mother felt that she dared not let him out of the house to play – and confinement made him naughtier still. Both parents ended by bribing him to be 'good', smacking him or taking him with them for long drives to tire him out, apparently without any consistency between themselves or with regard to a particular piece of behaviour. By the time he was five, and had been at school for nearly a term, he was still a wilful and difficult child, and it was thought that psychiatric advice should be sought.

The psychiatrist found him willing to co-operate with her, very affectionate, and quite remarkably like a three-year-old in his responses and in his phantasies. He did not want to play with small toys, however, and most of his treatment was carried out while he cruised round the playroom on a tricycle, pushed a truck or sat on her knee. 'He revealed very plainly a longing to be controlled,' wrote the therapist, inviting her to push the truck or to tell him where to ride on the tricycle; he frequently resisted attempts to be pushed, however, and

155

drove the tricycle in the opposite direction, laughing and looking slyly over his shoulder to see what she would do. He was able to interpret his own meaning, and became proud of performing feats of skill and control. It was thought that only long-term help for the parents would ensure Bobby's progress, and this was started. The P.S.W. visited the home frequently, and said that the parents were such 'babies' themselves that it was hardly surprising that Bobby did not show the poise and work-attitude of most five-year-olds. There was, moreover, some indication that Bobby had felt deprived when the family had left the maternal grandmother's house, and that the young mother had herself felt lonely and abandoned for a period. Support and advice from the P.S.W. for this couple in regard to their own relationship seemed as important as advice about Bobby's upbringing.

In school he continued to be a problem, since he would not come in when wanted, even if it was raining, would not leave a room if he were engaged in something that interested him (and this was often something destructive), and would not get off tricycle, truck, swing or seesaw until he was tired of it – which made him unpopular with other children. If called, he ran away; if picked up, he kicked; if lifted from a tricycle he wound his legs round it so that it came up with him. In fact, he transferred to the school the tactics that had driven his mother to bring him there before he was due for entry. It looked as though the habit of doing the opposite to that which he was told needed to be broken; that it was probably habit was shown by his non-malicious, affectionate behaviour to the person he had just defied and his stopping in mid-step when he realized that it was to his advantage to do so, (as when a teacher called his name and held out a sweet – he was half-way across a long hall before he checked his habitual response).

It was decided that every time he was called he should be rewarded, even if this meant catching him to do it. The psychiatrist agreed that this would be a reasonable course to take in school. Accordingly, his class-teacher and the headmistress took to having sweets in their pockets, and when it was necessary to call Bobby indoors for a meal, or out of the classroom to wash, or into the cloakroom to change his shoes he was captured and rewarded. The technique was that used to train a puppy to come to the call, in fact, and it worked

156

very well and surprisingly quickly. He liked to be picked up and swung round, and after a few trials with the sweets he was running towards whoever called him with his arms out ready to be swung off his feet, this apparently being of more value to him than the material reward. He would clasp his arms round the back of the adult's neck and hug hard before being put down to trot off, seemingly happily, to do whatever it was that was required of him.

One of his most negative and tiresome responses appeared, after only a week or so to have been 'extinguished,' and it was possible to start to educate him in other behaviour fitting for a five-year-old. With the co-operation of the psychiatric social worker his mother was advised to take the same sort of course as the school was taking, and in the same areas of learning, and although there was no doubt that she found this difficult she attempted to do so. If he went into a tantrum he was firmly held with his back to the adult, and his shoes off, while ʌg gently and insistently talked-to until calm. When he ran away from the meal-table he was asked if he wanted to eat any more, and if he said 'no' (as he usually did, at first) his unfinished meal was removed without comment. As his mother had begged him to eat, or had become very angry with him for leaving the table, mealtimes had provided him with plentiful opportunities to test his own and his parents' limits. In school limits were clearly set: children may leave the table, but they do not eat until they sit down again; and they do not cause disruption of other people's mealtimes since no one minds whether they have finished the meal or not. The active outdoor life possible to children in the Reception class gave Bobby an appetite, however, and it took only a few trials at mealtime to demonstrate to him that his teacher meant exactly what she said. He appeared to feel that it was not only better to eat one's meal sensibly than to go hungry, but it was also a pleasure.

Bobby improved considerably in the next half-year, becoming more persistent in his activities, able to co-operate with other children for short periods, and skilful in many more directions. He remained a most lovable and warm-hearted little boy, and this positive side of his nature was encouraged to the full. He was to be seen helping the schoolkeeper, chatting to the cook, and carrying books for the secretary, as well as climbing on the fence to talk to the men in an adjacent garden. Perhaps because he was treated like a five-year-old by more adults he began to act like one, and to lose some of the markedly immature characteristics that had previously set him apart from other children. He was still 'young' for his age, however, and learned to read late. It seemed as though he needed to work through the social as well as motor skills he had failed to achieve earlier before he could take an interest in the more sophisticated skill of reading. His birthdate made it possible to retain him in the Infants' school for an extra year and still be only a few months older than his classmates when he arrived in the Junior school. He was, by this time, only a little retarded in reading, and in other respects not markedly different from any other seven-year-old.

33. Jeff.

An only child of parents very much older than is usual, being in their early fifties when Jeff entered school at five. A delicate-looking child, of a little below average intelligence according to group non-verbal and verbal tests performed when he was nearly seven, but with performance in all skills considerably below what would have been expected. Reluctant to do anything with other children, and alternately sulky and defiant with all adults.

Jeff was noticeable in school, at least during his first year, for his unsuitable and old-fashioned clothes. At the age of five (in the "fifties") he was wearing velvet bib-and-brace trousers and satin or lawn shirts with wide collars, white socks and black, strap shoes. In cold weather he would be so wrapped in cardigans, scarves and woollen hood that undressing was all but impossible for him to achieve alone. He was escorted to school from a very short distance, either on his tricycle which his mother controlled from behind with a walking-stick, or in a 'pusher' on wet or snowy days. He had been at school for over a term before he was allowed to walk the short distance by himself, and probably owed his emancipation to the fact that his mother developed very painful varicose veins at about this time.

He was said to have frequent bouts of bronchitis, but the school doctor found him to be a very fit child, despite his delicate appearance, and suggested to his mother that she wrapped him up a little less and let him run about a lot more.

158

His attendance was, in fact, good, and he had only the usual childhood illnesses while he was in the Infants' school – none of them in a serious form. Nevertheless, his mother continued to worry about him, and to dose him regularly with laxatives, cough mixture and cod-liver oil. She was prevailed-upon to leave him at school for his midday meal, and it was found that he had a hearty appetite and appalling table-manners. In the classroom Jeff was so immature as to be a nuisance to other children, since he could not share, would not wait, cried if requested to do either, and hit or pushed others without the least provocation. His motor skills were poor, especially those concerned with holding pencils, brushes or any form of tool, and he rarely tried in consequence, to produce any of the pictures, patterns, writing or models so popular with other children.

During his first year matters improved a little when he came to school alone, possibly because he then had opportunity to play with other boys before school. He also struck up a friendship with two very 'tough' little boys in his street and played with them on the common after school – and before going home. This caused his mother considerable concern, and Jeff had to be told to go home first and tell his mother where he was going to be. It was thought necessary to point out to his mother that if he presented himself at home only to be kept there and forbidden the safe and suitable play he craved it was unlikely that he would ever go straight home from school. She was not an unreasonable woman in many ways, and admitted that she wanted to 'keep him a baby' while knowing that she couldn't. But his freedom was still very limited and his response to his teachers unsatisfactory, since he seemed to transfer to them the resentment (and probably guilt on account of it) that he felt for his mother.

Such a situation presents considerable difficulty to teachers. Older parents, with little or no appreciation of the educational changes since their own childhood, any more than they have of the mode of dress, manners and interests of contemporary childhood, are difficult to help without teachers appearing dictatorial or censorious. Jeff's mother was fortunately able to come to school for all open days and other 'occasions', however, and a long, gentle process of introducing her to new ideas was begun. She greeted casually-introduced information about the value of outdoor games, painting, modern ways of teaching number, and the importance of attractive books with 'Fancy!' and 'Well, I never!' but so long as Jeff approved of such activities she was not herself antagonistic to them. As she became more used to the relaxed and child-centred attitudes of an Infants' school she became more confiding about her own feelings. It appeared that she had had several miscarriages early in her marriage, and had not expected to have a child. Jeff had been a great joy to her, therefore. Her husband had not viewed the baby's arrival with quite such enthusiasm, however, and she described him as 'set in his ways' and 'like a baby himself' if his routine were upset. He was proud of his son, but probably felt that he had been ousted from the central place in a childless home – an understandable and probably quite common feeling in such a father. His resentment had expressed itself in his making quite unreasonable demands on a small child, and the mother had counteracted her husband's sternness by protective and over-indulgent behaviour.

Over a period of a year, and in scraps of conversation, Jeff's mother interpreted the whole situation to herself, and even began to laugh sheepishly about still wanting a baby and not a boy. She admitted that she had kept his baby-things (cot, pram, rattles and bath) in the 'front room' but thought she might as well sell them now. Perhaps she had hoped for another child. Or perhaps in keeping them she had had a 'magical' idea that she was keeping the baby, too. Whatever the reason, she acknowledged its unreality and disposed of the objects in Jeff's last year in the Infants' school. In this year, too, she made the symbolic gesture of clothing him in more suitable shirts and trousers – although she still wrapped him like a cocoon on cold mornings, pinning a large woollen scarf at the back after crossing it over his chest. Only steady, regular insistence on completion of small tasks, and realization of his need to 'play through' all the experiences of most normal three and four-year-olds (as, for example, giving him opportunity for block-play, riding tricycles and splashing water even when he was past the age at which most children were employing these materials in such a 'young' manner), seemed to help the boy himself. His apparent resentment at being over-protected, and his exploitation of it, diminished as his mother became more permissive; and there was some evidence that his father was more interested in and less jealous of him by the time he was seven.

Despite his difficulty in establishing himself with other children, his poor attitudes to adults, his wheedling and whining, sulks and tantrums, and his extraordinarily 'young' appearance, Jeff did not give the impression of being as deeply disturbed as Bobby or Alan, and the school doctor did not feel that psychiatric help was necessary. There was also the difficulty, had such a course been taken, of dealing with the entrenched attitudes and fears of these parents; it was left to the school staff to 're-educate' a pleasant, limited woman – and in this case the effort seemed fairly successful. With the father success was more dubious, but may have been achieved ultimately by the mother herself. Jeff was a poor reader on leaving the Infants' school, having a 'reading age' of 6:1 on a Schonell R.1 test, and failing to register at all with a Neale Analysis. Nevertheless, the progress from a 'reading age' of 5:2 to 6:1 which was reflected, too, by ability to read most simple primers and 'first' readers in the class library, had been made in the six months of the mother's growing insight into the family situation, and the increased freedom the boy enjoyed. He was well over seven before he left, and there was no question of his being retained in the Infants' school – although this might have been beneficial, particularly as two of his friends were not old enough to leave until the next year. The lack of literacy (beyond the most elementary level) in his home might have made the achievement of reading difficult in any case for Jeff. That he was kept as a baby, in addition, must have accentuated the difficulty, and meant that he faced demands of the Junior school less adequately prepared than his teachers in the Infants' school would have wished.

Considerations

In the cases described above it is possible to discern resemblances. Each of these boys was well-loved and had had, in babyhood, what a baby needs – close, warm mothering. Each of them was 'salvageable' probably because each had reserves of affection and trust on which to draw. The growth from babyhood to a stage of autonomy had in each case, however, been in some way distorted or denied, and initiative had not developed in any real sense by the age of five. Nevertheless, support and varying degrees of interpretation for the parents seemed in each case successful in helping them to accept the child's needs for growth; and the acceptance by teachers of these needs where growth had been distorted or denied meant that a programme was devised which would enable Alan, Bobby and Jeff to 'work through' the stages and phases previously inadequately catered-for. No child chooses his immaturity, says Janice Dohm[5] – and it ill befits teachers to blame children because of it. To tell a child he is 'too old' to play with this or that, or that his preferences are 'babyish' is never helpful. With children such as those described above it may be positively dangerous. Alan was probably, in a sense, afraid to grow up, and to leave behind a peculiarly 'safe' babyhood. Bobby seemed not to know *how* to grow up, perhaps because his loving, young parents were themselves so naïve and immature. For Jeff to grow up may well have meant 'losing' his mother, and (perhaps as frightening) challenging a severe father by being another 'man about the house'. The stages to maturity for such children must be taken gently, and in such a way as to demonstrate that the fears are groundless, and that the paramount ambition of all children – to be grown-up – is not taboo. The parents need to be helped, too, and the children not hurried through the experiences they need, and that other children probably assimilated a year or two before them.

It is possible in the ordinarily permissive Infants' school to allow for such growth and to give such support, directly or by referral to the Child Guidance service, to the parents. As each child is at a slightly different stage of growth, in any case, and as opportunities for free experiment are always available, it is possible to 'carry' a child like Alan or Jeff in the normal class of thirty or forty. A child similar to Bobby presents more of a problem, since he is inevitably more disruptive and noticeable. But co-operation between members of staff, and the help of the head teacher, can provide an 'answer' even in such an unusually difficult case. Admission a little earlier than usual, as in Bobby's case; retention for an extra year; the placing of a child in an appropriate Junior school, as in Alan's case – these are some of the purely administrative ways in which schools can help to solve

[5] In 'Young Writers: Young Readers' ed. Boris Ford (1958) p. 106.

what is always a complex socio-personal-psychic problem. It is essential to try to solve it, for as has been argued by many investigators in many aspects of human development, maturity in adulthood cannot 'just happen'. It is rooted and grounded in appropriate childhood experience – and in some cases, at least, the teacher of young children has a part to play in offering that experience.

Suggestions for Further Reading
In addition to those works cited in the text and at the end of chapter 1 (p. 30):

Buhler, C. *From Birth to Maturity* Routledge (1935)

Gesell, A. *The First Five Years of Life* Methuen (Reprint 1954)

Gesell, A. *The Child from Five to Ten* Hamish Hamilton (1946)

Gabriel, J. *Children Growing Up* U.L.P. (1964)

Griffiths, R. *The Abilities of Babies* U.L.P. (1954)

Tanner, J. *Education and Physical Growth* U.L.P. (1961)

Stone, L. J. & Church, J. C. *Childhood and Adolescence* Random House (1957)

Most standard textbooks in psychology also contain relevant material: e.g:

Hilgard, E. *Introduction to Psychology* Methuen (1957)

Munn, N. *Psychology: the Fundamentals of Human Adjustment* Harrap & Co. Ltd. (1961)

Chapter 10

Bizarre Behaviour

For present purposes bizarre behaviour is taken to mean any markedly odd phenomenon such as weird gesture, gait or other movement, garbled speech or strange language-use, and failure to interpret reality in a normal manner. Children displaying some or all of these characteristics are easier to recognize than define, and are not easily, or soon, diagnosed as being brain-damaged, epileptic, psychotic or mentally defective. They can baffle pediatricians, neurologists, psychiatrists and psychologists – much less ordinary General Practitioners or teachers. If given the benefit of the doubt about their educability, as they should be, they appear in the normal Infants' school and are in special need of the teacher's help.

Although some of the children already discussed had some bizarre characteristics, they differ (except perhaps for Roderick) from the children of this chapter in that they had an apparently normal comprehension of reality – even withdrawn children have an only too tragic realization of some real problem, as a rule. Bizarre children, while coping fairly normally over a wide area of their lives, often fail to make sense of some skills, have major irrational fears, yet do not apprehend some real dangers, and although often capable of making warm relationships are apt to express these in odd ways. They often have a 'fey' appearance and strangely disconnected thoughts.

Since bizarre behaviour arises from so many causes it is not feasible to outline a theory, or discuss the literature as is possible, for example, in cases of aggression. Faced with a child whose gesture, speech, gross movement or view of reality is so odd as to deserve the description of bizarre, a teacher may find herself involved in considerations of brain-damage, epilepsy, mental subnormality or autism; and only familiarity with the child and knowledge gained from parents, doctor and, perhaps, Child Guidance clinic would indicate areas in which she might read with advantage. What is becoming increasingly recognized is that bizarre children can often respond to help in school. Of brain-damaged children, whose behaviour is almost always odd in the extreme, an American doctor says:

'Even the interested and able teacher is handicapped because there is so little systematic research into the special problems and methods of remedial education for this group of children.'

After stressing the importance of pre-natal care, adequate welfare after birth and cultural opportunity, he adds:

'. . . enriched preschool and school programs, and the like can be expected to lessen the burden of neuropsychiatric complications that assails these children.'[1]

Certainly, they can be 'held' in the normal Infants' school, and given a chance to enjoy the company of other children and the sensory experiences that a modern school offers. That their 'oddness' often gives rise to a sense of inadequacy is another point made by Birch, and one which teachers will appreciate.

34. Branwell
A tall, thin, loose-jointed boy, retained at a Nursery school until the age of five and six months, as he seemed so odd in his ways and slow to adapt himself to the ordinary routine of the Nursery school. An only child of cultured parents, said to have been an affectionate baby but very slow in learning to talk.

When Branwell entered the Infants' school he was breathless with excitement, and approached adults and other children with a wide, engaging smile and shout of,

'I'm at school! I've come to school!'

He coped fairly normally with school routine, but was slow in doing up buttons and putting on shoes, even by five-year-old standards, and had jerky, clumsy movements in performing such operations. He was deeply anxious to please, and frequently asked whether he had done something 'right' or was 'being a good boy'. At the same time, he was obviously unaware of his deviance from normal behaviour, as when he took himself off for a walk outside the school without telling his teacher, or sat on top of the lavatory block eating an ice-

[1] H. G. Birch 'Brain Damage in Children: the biological and social aspects' (1964) p. 71.

cream which he had left school to buy. This sort of behaviour was taken, during his first term, as indication only of the independence he had learned at the Nursery School, and was not viewed too seriously. It was only after two terms, and many explanations, that his teacher came to the conclusion that Branwell was not really registering the existence of rules, much less their meaning. He was patently puzzled by her reproofs, and repeatedly told her that he was really a good boy. A few minutes later he would be standing in the rain, sitting on the coke dump, or good-naturedly dismantling the work of another child.

In a curiously disjointed manner, he would skip everywhere, singing to himself, joining a group playing with balls for a few moments, before moving off to join another group somewhere else. His powers of concentration were minimal, and yet he obviously enjoyed most of his fleeting activities. There was no suggestion in his behaviour of wilful inattention or destructiveness; he was in some ways more like a two-year-old than a boy of six, in fact. His conversation, however, was in a bizarre way quite mature. He would talk, in a breathless, slightly garbled manner, about aeroplanes, cars, the games he played at home with his toys and the doings of other children in school much as most of his age-mates were able to do; but interspersed with his factual accounts and descriptions were non-typical remarks such as,

'And, you see, that witch – she really said it. She did, John gave me his tractor and we had a smashing game. But she didn't like it. Witches aren't true, are they?' For a period he was obsessed with witches, and played at being one as well as talking of them. It was as though half of him realized the unreality of what he was saying and believing, but that at another level he was convinced of the reality of witches, bogeymen and giants. His phantasies were probably those of most children at a younger age, expressed overtly and with the vocabulary of an average six-year-old, but with more realization that any younger child could have that they *were* phantasies. Moreover, on some days he seemed markedly more 'fey' than on others, his movement more prancing and darting, his voice higher and his conversation less rational than on the preceding or the following day. No pattern of disturbance at home or in school could be discerned in these incidents;

their occurrence seemed quite erratic, and suggested some innate 'trigger'.

He was obviously something of a problem in school, since his teacher could never be sure where he was or what he was doing, but it was possible to keep him for two years in a small class with the same teacher – to whom he was very warmly attached – and to let him have a considerable degree of freedom allied with the gradual learning of essential rules. As he moved towards his seventh birthday the tenor of his play changed. He had been very friendly with a rather disturbed but intelligent boy since Nursery school days, and the two of them now played wild games of cowboys and soldiers in the playground, and co-operated to build large structures with bricks and waste materials in school. From largely parallel play, lasting a few minutes at a time and with materials such as sand, water and small toys, Branwell progressed to essentially co-operative play with his friend John, and even imitated him in trying to read. Branwell's teacher noticed, however, that he had no real idea of what John was doing, and would sit with a book upside-down, peeping at his friend and turning pages as the other did so. The teacher's attempts to get Branwell to match pictures, pick out words or join in the reading of a wall-story had been abortive from the beginning, and despite the boy's apparent longing to be as other children he could not even begin to see the point of print at nearly seven.

A programme of active play with all sorts of sensory materials had been possible for him from the beginning; and as much unobtrusive stress as possible was laid on activities involving matching, sorting and contrasting different shapes, colours and weights. Every teacher of Infants will appreciate that most of this experience can be provided easily in the normal classroom. There is some evidence that children of bizarre response sometimes have *perceptual* difficulties and can be helped by just this kind of experience to distinguish relationships in a world of real colour, shape and size.[2] Certainly, eighteen months at the Nursery school, followed by two years of continuing experience with such materials in the

[2] '*Special Education*' Vol. 48 No. 4 (Sept. 1959) p. 34. Article by G. D. Clark.

Infants' school ended by Branwell's being able to play normal games, make reasonably accurate pictures and models, and talk interestedly of his doings. It is possible that a progressive sense-based training in perceiving relationships between shapes, and continuing encouragement of rational conversation, would in the end make it possible for a child like Branwell to make sense of print. The ability to read involves a symbolic process, however, as well as appreciation of fine differences in shape, and for this such a child is unlikely to be ready before the age at which he normally leaves the Infants' school.

Branwell was retained in the school until nearing his eighth birthday, and was then transferred to a remedial class in a Junior school. His parents were not happy about this, since the boy seemed increasingly tense and liable to outbursts of tears or temper after transfer. He was seen by a specialist who confirmed an earlier tentative diagnosis of minor brain-damage, and recommended that Branwell go to a school specializing in the education of children with very unusual difficulties.

35. Billy

Admitted to the Infants' school a term later than usual because of difficulty with speech, clumsy movement and poor sphincter control. The fourth child of interested and intelligent parents, and an affectionate and confiding child. Apt to sit very still as if thinking hard and not notice when spoken-to, but not withdrawn.

Billy was a plump, jolly child, with the straddle gait and puppy-like tendency to roll about on the floor of a two-year-old. He was a child who really could laugh until he cried, almost always at some 'physical' joke (such as a funny hat, or somebody pulling a face) -- again, very like a two-year-old. His speech had the rather charming immaturity of a three-year-old's, but was improving fast, and there seemed no doubt that contact with other children of his age was a great stimulus to his conversation. He often had wet pants during his first two terms, but responded well to encouragement to take himself off to the lavatory at rather frequent intervals, and he was reliably dry by the end of his first year. His teacher, accompanying him on one occasion, discovered that he could not stand to urinate in the usual male fashion, and showed him how, as she had done with her own sons.

His parents were rather startled to hear of this, but thought that as his three older siblings were girls and his father was away from home a great deal he may simply have not realized what to do.

'You know, it just didn't occur to me,' said his mother, 'I suppose having the girls first . . . I thought he'd *know*!' Billy certainly improved greatly in the matter of wet pants from this time, although obviously there were other factors than 'knowing how' involved in his incontinence.

This cheerful, affectionate boy flung himself into the vigorous physical activities offered by the school with great zest. He climbed and chased, kicked balls, rode on trucks and followed other active boys about in an interested manner. Indoors he sat on the floor, (rarely on a chair), building towers or sandcastles, or pushing small cars along with appropriate noises. He loved playing with water, but had to be thoroughly overalled when he did so, for his large, clumsy gestures resulted in a lot of spilling. Unlike Branwell, he could concentrate for ten minutes at a time, and was very proud of his achievements. He listened to stories with eyes like saucers, and burst out with comments and questions in a manner most flattering to the story-teller. Every activity, in fact, would have been fairly normal for a child two years his junior; but his clumsiness was abnormal, and his whole 'style' worrying if one thought of him as nearing the age of six.

His occasional trance-like stillness in the most unlikely situations – on top of the climbing-frame or when watching the drain-cleaner at work outside the school, which was a very popular event with small children – gave the first clue to an 'oddness' that had worried his parents for several years. His mother agreed to mention it to the school doctor, who referred him to a specialist. It was then discovered that Billy was a minor epileptic, and also had a slight glandular disturbance; the specialist attributed the late talking, clumsiness and poor sphincter control to minor, but very frequent, attacks of an epileptic type. Billy was treated with drugs and some of his symptoms cleared up – he was less clumsy, and the trance-like states were not seen again. (It must be remembered that these had been fleeting, and did not involve the rigidity or foaming at the mouth which would have suggested even to a layman that he was epileptic.) He did not make much progress in acquiring normal skills, however, and it was con-

169

sidered wise to send him to a special school. The educational psychologist found his I.Q. to be 80, but was cautious about placing much credence on tests applied to such a child as Billy. He suggested that an E.S.N. school might be a good place for the boy to make up the lost years rather than strictly necessary on doctrinaire grounds of his having a certain I.Q.

Billy's parents were at first unhappy about this recommendation but talks with the psychologist, the head teacher, and the head of the E.S.N. school were helpful in enabling them to see that Billy needed time, a gentle pace, and the opportunities similar to those he had so enjoyed in the Infants' school if he were to 'catch up' with other children. Everyone concerned with this cheerful and willing child felt that the ordinary pace and pressures of a normal Junior school might be too much for him at seven, and might well give rise to anxiety and feelings of inadequacy of a sort he had previously been spared. It is a possibility, too, that a programme of this kind – late entry into the Infants' school and transfer to an E.S.N. school – might result in such a child's being able to join the 'normal stream' well before school-leaving age. An over-early insistence on 'normal' behaviour and learning, and a rigid adherence to transfer age, as well as refusal to allow the benefit of special schooling, can do a child like Billy no good. It may, in fact, do a very great deal of harm, and make return to the mainstream of education an impossibility.

36. Gavin
A very tiny, thin child, with exceptionally high colour and feverishly bright eyes. A slight tremor of head and hands was noticeable, and seemed almost continuous. Speech fairly normal, but very hurried and sometimes incoherent in consequence. Language markedly poor for a child of six, the vocabulary being limited and sentences ungrammatical – usually on account of their brevity, since words were missed out, and a sort of verbal 'shorthand' used. Admitted to Infants' school at the age of six, having previously attended the kindergarten department within a large Children's Home. Aggressive and withdrawn by turns, prone to fits of anguished weeping for no discernible cause, but noisy and active in outdoor play with other boys. Movements all somewhat jerky, and ability to concentrate negligible.

Gavin was brought to school by a couple who were prospective
170

adoptive parents. They had a daughter many years older than Gavin, but could have no more children of their own, and the father in particular dearly wanted a son. They were a well-intentioned but anxious couple, who set high standards for themselves and their daughter, and were already setting them for Gavin. (He was told to take off his cap, say 'good morning', stand up nicely, and be very quiet in the first minute of entering the room, for example.) It appeared that they had had the boy with them for several weeks, but had been on holiday, and had therefore not entered him at school earlier. He had also seemed what the mother described as 'a bit nervous' and the father as 'just a bit new to us, like' so the holiday had been taken to give the boy a chance to settle down with them before facing the further strangeness of school. These parents gave the impression of being a little guarded about the boy, but this was attributed to their sensitivity about being adoptive parents, and therefore knowing relatively little as yet about Gavin.

When, after several weeks in school, he was still alternating between withdrawal of a marked kind and wild, noisy outbursts, in which phases he was vicious with other children, the mother was informally consulted. She maintained that he was 'a very good boy, quite a model' at home, and was slightly resentful at the suggestion that he was in any way deviant in school. When his tremor, and his jerky movement were mentioned she denied having noticed these symptoms, and suggested that the school was producing nervousness in the boy. It was decided to leave him to settle down further, and to raise the matter with the school doctor at the medical examination. The doctor was concerned about the tremulous condition, and asked if anything was known of the boy's previous history. With Gavin out of the room the adoptive mother said that the Children's Officer (of an adjacent authority) had told her that Gavin's mother had had a schizophrenic breakdown after his birth, that the boy had been in residential nurseries and Homes all his life, except for three short and abortive fosterings. This child had, in fact, had six changes of mother-substitute before he was six and offered for adoption to this couple. The possible significance of this had apparently not struck the mother, although the doctor asked, cautiously, about the boy's emotional responses. Neither had she any idea what the illness of schizophrenia involved, and asked the doctor if it were serious or could be inherited. Only guarded answers can be given to such questions, especially when the well-being of a child is at stake, and in this case the doctor was most cautious, confining himself to giving general advice about warm mothering and patience being necessary in such a case.

Gavin did not improve, as did Branwell and Billy, but continued to appear bizarre in movement, and limited in language. His attacks on other children were sporadic and apparently 'cold-blooded', since they seemed motiveless. He failed to make the kind of warm relationships with other children and with adults that were possible to Branwell and Billy, and flitted from activity to activity without seeming to develop any interests or skills. At intervals he withdrew completely, sitting in a corner with his head hanging down, and making no response to invitations to come out and do something else. Only if reproved for hurting another child did he show positive realization of another person, and that by trembling all over, and waiting with a quivering lip for (as it appeared) a physical blow. As he had not been smacked in school, and it was thought unlikely that his adoptive parents would have so punished him, it could only be thought that he had, at some time, been severely punished in this way, and was still frightened.

By the age of six and nine months he had made no progress with reading or any other 'formal' skill, which was perhaps not surprising in view of his past history and his poor command of language, and so his adoptive parents were again consulted. They were, in fact, still waiting for the adoption process to be completed, and were rather 'edgy' about the whole, slow procedure, which may have accounted for their unhelpful attitude. They maintained that Gavin was a perfectly normal boy, 'brighter than most', and that he was 'incited' to hurt other children. They had not noticed any tendency to withdraw at home, and still denied the tremor and jerky movement. Of his backwardness in formal skills and inability to concentrate, the father said that the school was entirely to blame, and that if more work and less play were the order of the day the boy would learn. When it was gently pointed out to him that under this 'free' programme other children learned to read, the father made the extraordinary accusation that Gavin was being 'picked on' by his teachers

172

for being adopted. He maintained that he would undertake to teach the boy to read in a week. Throughout the interview it was difficult to be patient with a man who, however well-intentioned, was so determined to form the boy in the image he had of 'my son'. That a man should determine to make an adopted son truly his own is obviously praiseworthy; the utter denial of almost frightening reality is surely unintelligent. A school doctor, two experienced teachers and the Health Visitor, (who met Gavin during a routine weighing and inspection session), were perturbed by the increasing oddness of the child; the prospective adoptive parents would see no flaw in the boy, and refused all suggestions of medical, psychiatric or educational examination aimed at helping him.

The Children's Officer of the authority from which Gavin had come was accordingly contacted. She was evasive about the history of the child, but eventually acknowledged that he had been 'something of a problem' to place, and that it had been suggested that he was either unstable or affectionless, or both, by a psychiatrist visiting the Children's Home. When asked about the tremor, jerky movement, alternating aggression and withdrawal and the fear of reproof, she was vague, saying only that Gavin had had several 'little difficulties' and that she could not say whether these had been among them – probably they had been. She seemed quite satisfied with the proposed adoption, saying that the parents were the sort to do their best for a child (which was undoubtedly true), and, in any case, had taken to Gavin strongly on sight and insisted that he was the son for whom they had been looking. It is understandable that a hard-pressed Children's Officer with a difficult child on her hands should be grateful for the appearance of sound, comfortably-placed adoptive parents with a special feeling for the child. Yet, one is left feeling a little uneasy by such a case. Perhaps, to quote Bettelheim, 'love is not enough' when dealing with so strange (and probably disturbed) a child. Another Children's Officer might have acted differently – leaving the boy in a small residential school or unit to make some 'roots', at least, while perhaps having psychiatric treatment; or fostering him on people who *understood* the implications of a mentally unstable mother and several changes of mother-substitute, and were prepared to co-operate in treatment of some kind to make good some of the possible harm; or offering him for adoption only on those same conditions. Be that as it may, Gavin presented his teachers with a problem in terms of both behaviour and learning that they had to carry alone, since no outside help was obtainable, and no past history of any use was available to them.

He was accordingly allowed a great deal of freedom to play in ways already described as helpful to other children, and although not making any noticeable progress did not, at least, get worse. He was given help with his reading by the head-mistress – but he trembled violently all the time he was looking at pictures and words, and seemed not to understand what was being said or expected of him. It emerged that his father was indeed teaching him to read – although he had not succeeded in the week he had set himself, nor, in fact in several months – and that every evening the boy had to 'do six pages'. There seemed little point in taking the matter up with the adoptive parents, for Gavin was in his last term in the Infants' school, (suggestions that he might benefit from an extra year there, since he would be barely seven on transfer to the Junior school had met with unqualified refusal on the part of his determined adoptive father), and there were conflicts enough in this child's life already. He was handled very gently in his extra reading sessions, – indeed, they became more like 'Listen with Mother' sessions than anything else – but made no noticeable relationship with either teacher or head in the rest of his time in the school.

For a child like Gavin there is probably little a school can do. Certainly, his is not a success story from the point of view of his Infants' school, despite sincere efforts with both the boy and his adoptive parents for nearly a year. The adoptive parents could hardly be blamed for refusing to see any ab-normality in the boy. There may even be advantages in main-taining that a child is 'normal' and setting normally high standards for him, for it is not unknown for a child to become what he is expected to be – although in Gavin's case one could not be sure if the adoptive parents were being defensive and therefore wilfully 'blind' or genuinely seeing him as the little boy they had always wanted. The school does no service to a child in such a case by pushing the parents to the point of open antagonism and contradiction – and perhaps this point was reached, or nearly so, in Gavin's case. The mess of his earlier life is possibly also not a matter for blame. Without a full history it is impossible to know whether his unstable mother refused to let him be fostered or adopted, and thus made satisfactory arrangements for him impossible to the Children's Officer. Whether so badly damaged a child should ever be offered for adoption is a question that has already been posed; but those concerned with the placement of children like Gavin are all too aware of this problem, and teachers can only be sympathetic when they consider the involved legal and personal problems with which Children's Officers are faced every day. It might be helpful to the schools to know something of past histories of such children, however, (under seal of professional secrecy goes without saying), so that they are not working completely in the dark. It might also be possible to ensure, before adoptive or foster-parents take charge of the child, that they fully understand any deviance from the normal, and in some cases undertake to have the child treated by specialists. Gavin's adoptive parents were obviously not in possession of all the facts, and of those they had been given they understood little. One cannot escape the fear that such parents may be exposed to great anxiety, even grief, as the child grows up. Again, this is not directly the concern of teachers; yet, as the child goes to school, and worried adoptive or foster-parents approach his teachers, it is a problem of which they should at least, be aware.

37. Amanda

A tall, well-grown girl, with a very small head, but attractive features. Ungainly in movement, having the unco-ordinated, stiff gait and counterbalancing arm-swing of some spastics. Speech 'scrambled' and difficult to follow, but impossible to define as of any particular order of defect. Prone to sudden high squeals and throaty mutterings on occasion – rather alarming to other children. The second child of a well-to-do professional family, having an older sister said to be unusually gifted. Some suspicion of brain-damage from soon after birth when she was seen at a famous children's hospital. All development had been slow, but by the age of five Amanda was a reasonably capable child – reliably dry and clean, able to handle cutlery, deal with simple fastenings, play with most toys, and make herself understood. Not sent to school until

*the age of six, and then initially for half-days, on account of
both the speech and movement abnormality.*

By her second term in the Infants' school Amanda was making some progress. Her speech was not good, but her vocabulary was increasing rapidly, and she had something approaching an obsession with new words. She would say, 'What's 'at? Say it! Say it! Panderlomum! Panderlomum! Mi' Tanner say panderlomum!' or some such on hearing a new word that caught her fancy. She was a great worry in a classroom, for she flitted from child to child, touching their work, babbling, and occasionally giving a child a poke or thump for no reason that could be discovered. On such occasions, she would set her mouth, frown and glare in what can only be described as a baleful manner while she was reproved, sometimes looking at the victim as if he or she were a particularly dangerous or frightening animal. One sometimes had the impression that Amanda was truly hallucinated, for some of her hurried 'explanations' of such attacks seemed concerned with dogs or witches, or other creatures which were certainly not there but which she pointed at and attempted to describe. In this sort of irrational fear she somewhat resembled Branwell, but had not his sunny temperament and ability to make friends. After hurting a child she would sometimes chant the child's name over and over, and hug him or her very hard saying she was sorry – but her peacemaking was almost as savage as her attacks, and she was not a popular child.

She developed skills very slowly, as was to be expected, and such tasks as washing brushes, or dressing a doll, or putting out milk-bottles took her a very long time and many dashes away to do something else. A patient teacher protected the other children as much as possible but gave Amanda many little jobs to do, and talked to her a great deal. This teacher developed a technique of occupying the child while she told stories to the rest of the class, in order that quiet times would not be too disrupted. There was usually something new that Amanda longed to look at, pull apart or otherwise play with, and a succession of simple materials and occupations were introduced at carefully-timed intervals to keep Amanda out of mischief at least for short periods. She was also very fond of playing with water, splashing and crooning to herself while she did so; and this occupation usually ensured up to five minutes' constructive play at a time. The large dolls' pram was another attractive plaything for this odd little girl, and she was allowed to push it up and down the hall, and out in the playground as she would. Anything, in fact, which served to give her practice in persistence and to divert her attention from children engaged in quiet activities was welcome.

Not only irrational fears of (apparently visible) creatures, but also of quite ordinary and seemingly harmless things were evidenced in Amanda's case. She screamed at the sight of a black doll brought to school by another child, and could not, on another occasion, be got to touch a blue Teddy-bear. When the children in her class were making paper animal-faces to wear while they sang the Rocking Carol Amanda wished to make one, too, and seemed delighted as her teacher helped her to paint, cut and then fix tape on a pale grey 'donkey' face. As soon as this was put over her face, however, she screamed, and continued to scream even when it was immediately taken off. She shouted that she hated to be a donkey, and tore off the masks, (quite naïve and unterrifying in themselves), from other children, shouting that they weren't to be cows and sheep and donkeys. Such a scene had to be terminated as quickly as possible, and the other children calmed, so Amanda was removed to sit quietly and talk to the headmistress. On the head's knee she made ugly faces and talked in a random sort of way about the coming Christmas party – until she seemed to remember the paper masks when she screamed, but half-laughing, that she wasn't going to wear a paper hat.

It was fairly apparent from early in her schooldays that Amanda was going to need special schooling, and this was arranged when she was seven, with the co-operation and understanding of her parents. There is no doubt that these pleasant and intelligent people were sad and worried about Amanda, but they accepted the help and opportunities offered both by the Infants' school and the E.S.N. school to which Amanda was transferred, reinforcing at home the training (perhaps one could hardly say 'education' in its usual sense) of school. Amanda was later said to be not only brain-damaged but possibly microcephalic, and to have some emotional disturbance in addition. But this is largely irrelevant to the Infants' teacher faced with any child so abnormal as

Amanda. Such a teacher's task is to occupy the child fruitfully, and with such materials as will promote some learning, however little and however simple; to help in whatever ways she can to get the child to relate with others (in Amanda's case no mean feat) and with adults; and not to add to the strange conflicts and feelings of inadequacy that almost always accompany such abnormality.

Children do not normally enter special schools of the type to which Amanda went before the age of seven – it is a wise and humane provision that such a child is not to be labelled as ineducable without the benefit of many expert opinions, nor ascertained as educationally subnormal before having the chance to benefit from the stimuli offered by an Infants' school. In consequence of such caution most Infants' teachers will have, occasionally, to do their best for a child who will need special education later. This must surely be seen as one of the functions of an Infants' school, and accepted as such – unless such children as Amanda are to be relegated to 'solitary confinement' away from children of their own age, until they are seven. This is as unthinkable as it is illegal, and much may be done in the Infants' school to help even so damaged a child as Amanda.

Considerations

There is no real pattern of either cause or effect to be seen in the four cases discussed above, as might be expected when one uses the term 'bizarre behaviour'. It is true that in the cases of Branwell and Amanda there was a definite diagnosis of brain damage; but this could mean in any of several brain areas, of more or less severity, caused by pre-natal or post-natal disease, injury or inexplicable failure to develop, and thus affecting the afflicted child in a multitude of ways from severe impairment of movement or of speech to subtle personality disturbance – or all three. With causes the teacher cannot be concerned, although she will often be interested, and must deal with brain-damaged children while they are in the Infants' school in ways indicated above, or any others that seem to offer fruitful effort to the child. In Billy's case the minor epileptic condition could also be called a sort of brain-damage, in the sense that the rhythm of the brain is abnormal in such cases, although this is a term not used for the fairly easily diagnosed epileptic condition as a rule. It was suspected by at least one doctor that Gavin might be pre-psychotic, but this was a tentative and unverifiable opinion, of academic interest only to the teacher who had to cope with him. Referral to the Child Guidance clinic, and skilled treatment, or even a period of education in a psychiatric unit, might be the most satisfactory course to take with a child in respect of whom a diagnosis of pre-psychosis has been made.

What concerns the teacher when dealing with so bizarre a child as any of those described is that he *may* be suffering from such a serious condition as brain-lesion, epilepsy or incipient chizophrenia, and not 'merely' be wilful, naughty or mentally subnormal in the manner of a true mental defective. It is interesting that for none of the children discussed above was there a reliable I.Q. at Infants' school age, since their responses were so erratic, and their general behaviour so odd, that educational psychologists put little credence on the test-results at this stage. Amanda's estimated I.Q. on transfer to the E.S.N. school was 65 – but this figure was hedged with reservations and furnished only as an administrative necessity. Patently, she was educationally subnormal – but in many ways she did not resemble a dull child. For Branwell no test result was ever given to the school, his 'scatter' on tests being such as to make scoring very chancy. Billy, with an I.Q. of 80, quoted with reservation, was admitted to a special school largely on the grounds that he was an epileptic who learned slowly rather than on grounds of dullness. This is to underline the extreme difficulty presented to expert testers and to doctors by such children; and also, perhaps, to make a plea for humane and not too doctrinaire use of both measuring instruments and special school provision in such cases.

For the teacher the task has already been indicated. At least she can do something towards giving such odd children a sense of adequacy and the experience of success; as Birch says:

'Many of these youngsters come to think of themselves as bad, stupid and doomed to lifelong failure. With such a self-concept they may simply abandon any effort to restrain the behaviour that gets them into difficulty. Viewing themselves as incompetent, they behave as incompetents, even in circumstances within their coping capacity.'[s]

s *'Brain Damage in Children'* p. 70.

This, at least, the teacher can do something to prevent, and by use of no more than her own specialist skills and intelligent appreciation of the difficulties such children face.

Suggestions for Further Reading

Birch, H. G. *Brain Damage in Children: the biological and social aspects* Williams and Wilkins (1964)

Cleugh, M. F. *The Slow Learner* Methuen (1957)
Teaching the Slow Learner Methuen (1964)

Rimland, B. *Infantile Autism* Methuen (1965)

Walter, Grey *The Living Brain* (1953) Penguin Books (1961)

The journals:
Maternal and Child Care
Special Education

often contain articles useful for the teacher of children similar to those discussed in this chapter.

Chapter 11

Children with Physical Limitations

Physical handicap is well covered by literature in almost all categories.[1] For many years specialist education has been available for the deaf and partially-hearing, the blind, delicate and crippled child; finer discrimination between types of affliction in all these categories, and greater medical skill have made possible the establishment of units catering for particular types of difficulty that at one time would have been found in one large institution. The work of voluntary societies, such as the National Spastics Society, has brought the needs of handicapped children to the attention of the public, and of education authorities, and it is unlikely that any handicapped child in this country goes without specialist treatment and education for long. Nevertheless, there is a growing realization that not every child needing to wear a hearing-aid or a leg-iron, or even an artificial limb, is so handicapped as to require a place in an institution or even education in a special school. Many children with physical limitations now come into the Infants' schools. Their handicaps may not be very severe, but they do present teachers with certain difficulties in the normal classroom situation.

The teacher who is drawn to work with more severely limited children will hardly need the suggestions of this chapter; but for the teacher of normal children, who has a handicapped child in her class, some discussion of the difficulties and needs may be of use, and the list of works at the end of this chapter may enable her to follow-up the particular type of handicap with which she is faced. Some general considerations may also be useful in helping her to induct the handicapped child successfully into the life of normal children in a normal school. Although some of the children who had physical limitations were categorized (p. 31) as 'unclassified' they are discussed here for purposes of indicating the sort of minor problem they may present to a teacher.

[1] It is also discussed in relation to children in normal schools in 'Children and their Primary Schools' ch. 21.

It must be firmly stressed that *all possible information from parents and doctors should be available to teachers who have the daily responsibility of educating a handicapped child.* Only if such information is available can a teacher be expected to give the right kind of help – to know how much to leave a child to help himself, whether to use gesture to help a partially-hearing child, when to challenge and when to allow the child to rest, for example. Much harm can be done, inadvertently, by expecting too much and by expecting too little. The variable pace and the possibility of individual or small group work in the normal Infants' school make such consideration of special needs less difficult than it might be in a more rigid situation, and the physically handicapped child who is able to attend normal school will not usually find the years in the Nursery and Infants' school much of a strain. Given adequate information and an informal routine, teachers usually find that such children are much less of a 'problem' than emotionally disturbed children.

Young children do not have criteria of 'oddness' unless adults cause them to acquire such criteria. They accept without judgement a vast range of difference in colouring, size, level of attainment and play-preferences. It is true that they sort themselves out into groups having common interests and approximately the same intellectual ability by the end of their Infants' school years; but unless these spontaneous groupings are given special significance by rigid streaming, separate treatment in regard to the borrowing of library books (for example), or adverse comment on the performance of one group compared with another, they co-exist harmoniously and even co-operate in many projects, absorbing into this group or that the emotionally disturbed, the dull and the handicapped child. The 'tone' that the teacher engenders in her class is thus important if a handicapped child is to be happily 'unnoticeable'.

Children are curious, of course, about such apparatus as a hearing-aid or a leg-iron, and perhaps the best way to satisfy this inevitable curiousity is to let them ask (polite) questions about it and understand its use. If they know what it is for and how it works they are likely to lose interest in it, and thereafter make unselfconscious allowances for the limitations it sets on the wearer in some situations. As far as helpfulness is concerned, young children are likely to be *too* helpful to the handicapped child rather than not helpful enough – at least initially – and may need to be tactfully restrained from doing too much for an afflicted classmate. This is certainly a fault on the right side; but teachers need to be aware that it is a fault that could do the handicapped child no good if carried to extremes.

Compassion and tenderness are learned, not innate qualities, and are only in their earliest and most crude forms in the Infants' school. Since compassion involves the ability to put oneself in the position of the other – in which it might be said to differ from pity – and since young children are naturally in an egocentric stage of development when this is a literal impossibility to them, it is unrealistic to expect them to rise to the adult ideal of empathy. Only the most mature adult can be expected to have such quality, and to demand it of children can have unpleasant consequences: there is a certain parrot-like repeating of rather pious platitudes about 'poor little children' and 'cripples' and 'children not as lucky as us' which grates on the ear because of its patent lack of roots in real understanding. This is not to say that young children have no feeling for others. They have – but at their own level, just as they have the ability to reason at a 'concrete' level which is different from that of adults. The achievement of compassion in adulthood is more likely to come if appropriate expectations are presented in childhood than if the purely verbal 'propaganda' is all that is given. Courtesy to each other, ordinary kindness in everyday dealings, and tolerance in mundane matters (as discussed on p. 182) are appropriate expectations in respect of children in the Infants' school. Long talks about handicapped children or exhortations of the kind that depend on the 'how would you feel if' gambit are likely to give rise to two undesirable consequences; the repeating of the 'patter' without understanding, already mentioned, and a positive dislike of the children whose handicaps are thus receiving so much of the adults' attention. It is possible that in a few cases there may be a third danger in appeals to children's 'sympathy' – the guilt that may be felt by a young child when he vaguely apprehends that something is expected of him in terms of feeling but has no real understanding of what it is. That he cannot 'oblige' the admired and loved adult constitutes a burden for the child, and one which wise teachers will not add to those he already has to carry as a growing and learning human being. In helping her class to accept a handicapped child as one of themselves a teacher will find that honesty is certainly the best policy – straightforward explanation, ordinary appeals for consideration if some circumstances seem to warrant it, and thereafter no comment unless the children ask for further information or explanation.[2]

There may be some forms of handicap, rarely met in the normal school, it is true, for which a teacher feels some aversion. This is best acknowledged and dealt with than denied. The more mature a person is, the less likely is she to flinch from some handicaps; but it is a doctrine of perfection to expect every teacher to face with equanimity every affliction. Some may be irritated by the deaf child; others may wince at the gait of a child with a dislocated hip; a few may find asthma frightening – and so on. No blame attaches here. Few teachers could face the work of a nurse in a defective colony; few nurses could stand the cheerful racket of a normal Infants' classroom; and many thoroughly good teachers of normal children could not cope for long in a unit for autistic children or even in an orthopaedic hospital school. It is the responsibility of the teacher to acknowledge her feeling, and of the head to take such feelings into account when placing a handicapped child in the school. Most Infants' teachers take the few cases of physical handicap they meet in their stride, however, and personal problems of the kind mentioned above probably affect only a few.

38. Sheila

A lively, quick-thinking child, small for her age, but healthy and active despite having had congenital dislocation of both hips. Still wearing a support on one leg, but requiring only one more operation to complete treatment. Intelligence rated as above average by the psychologist at the orthopaedic hospital where she received her first schooling, but no figures supplied. Admitted to normal Infants' school at the age of six. The older child of two on school entry, and of three by the age of

[2] See 'The Emotional and Social Adjustment of Physically Handicapped Children' by M. L. Kellmer Pringle in 'Educational Research'. Vol. VI, No. 3 (1964).

seven, with well-educated parents who took great interest in her progress.

Sheila was delighted to come to school. She wanted to look at everything, do everything, and know everybody, giving an impression of social poise beyond that normally expected at six. She was popular with her classmates at first, and they were interested in her leg-iron for only a few days. Thereafter, they would rush to help her if she had any difficulty in getting up or down a step, but otherwise seemed to forget her disability. Sheila made a particular friend of a girl of her own age and of similar family background, and it was with this friend that the first difficulties arose. The two girls were playing what was at the time a very popular game of comparing and 'swapping' what they called 'jewels' – bright beads, buttons, pieces of sea-washed glass etc. stored in small tins – when Sheila was overheard to say, 'You've got to give me your diamond or my leg will hurt.' Her friend Sally, not being of an age to foresee results of actions, or to yield to such patent blackmail, shut her tin and got up to leave Sheila – whereat the latter pinched her friend very hard, and made her cry. The incident lasted only a few seconds, and the teacher immediately went across to intervene, reproving Sheila and comforting Sally. Sheila sulked, accused Sally of stealing her beads, and was generally very tiresome. Within a few minutes, however, the two girls were playing together again, in the manner of six-year-olds (who seem to be able to maintain this sort of 'friendship' over long periods), and nothing more was said about this ugly little incident.

It was the forerunner, unfortunately, of similar incidents, and of a difficult period for Sheila. She used the weapon of her incapacity in a much more sophisticated manner than might be expected of a young child, and was able to run rings round' other children. She went so far, on one occasion, as to tell a boy who had accidentally bumped into her that her leg would fall off if he did that again! Despite this naughty behaviour, she did not give the impression of being deeply worried about her handicap, and indeed did almost everything other children could do, including climbing on the high frame and riding a tricycle. She was expecting a bicycle for her birthday, and seemed limited only in respect of fast running and skipping with a rope. She was not thought to be over-tired, nor to be having any pain, and her specialist was pleased with her continuing improvement. It seemed unlikely that her exploitation of other children with due directly to jealousy of the skills of others, for she was brighter than average in formal skills and received due praise for her efforts, as well as taking part in physical activities.

Her parents were consulted about her behaviour, and said that she had been more 'difficult' at this homecoming from hospital than on previous occasions. She had shown more open jealousy of her young brother, and was resentful of her mother's pregnancy. She had openly said that she didn't want 'an old baby' in the house, and it was difficult to escape the conclusion that this was because she was the one who wanted the 'babying'. Despite her social poise in some respects she had probably suffered earlier from feelings of rejection when left in hospital, and the conscientious visiting and loving assurances of her parents could hardly be expected to mitigate such feelings altogether. Later periods in hospital had meant a great deal of close contact with her parents, as though she were an only child; and it was thought likely that she found the ordinary sharing and hurly-burly of normal family life less satisfying than the 'intense' relationship inevitable while she was in hospital.

It was agreed that the parents should tell Sheila exactly what the specialist had said about the scope and probable date of the next operation, in order that she should have a realistic idea of the situation, and probably less anxiety. The parents asked that the teacher should 'have no nonsense' with Sheila about her leg, and should reprove her firmly if she exploited her handicap to the distress of other children. Further, they undertook to explain the whole situation to the parents of Sally, who had been a little worried about Sheila's treatment of their daughter. Their ready understanding of Sheila's difficulties did much to comfort her parents, also, for the parents of a handicapped child often feel guilty (on quite irrational grounds as a rule) and find outside disapproval hard to bear. The application of consistent treatment and honesty about her handicap from all those with whom she came in contact certainly seemed to help.

She accepted the new baby with more grace than might have been expected, attached herself with particular warmth to her father – a normal attachment for girls of this age, and a very helpful one when the mother is coping with a new

186

baby – and continued to do very good work in school. She ceased to exploit her handicap, and became very popular with the girls in her class on account of her liveliness in play and a growing ability to devise dramatic versions of popular games. It was not anticipated that she would need special consideration in regard to transfer to the Junior school, but it was suggested that as she would need to be in hospital again during the early years there the parents discuss her case fully with the head on transfer.

39. Marlene

A tiny child of very active nature, who had been partially-hearing since birth. The only child of affectionate parents, who were of slightly limited understanding but very co-operative with specialists and teachers. Retained at Nursery school until nearly six years of age in order to give her practice in using her hearing-aid under the rather difficult conditions of the classroom. Taught by the peripatetic teacher of the deaf while at Nursery school, and continuing under weekly supervision by the same teacher in the Infants' school. Considered by this teacher to be slightly below average in intellectual ability, but by no means really dull.

Marlene was well-used to school by the time she entered the Infants' school, and found the atmosphere and opportunities of the small class she entered not very different from those of the Nursery school. In her ordinary dealings with other children she was friendly, rather excitable, and always busy in some physically active game. She had a harsh, rather unpleasing quality of voice, due to her hearing impairment, and her excited shouting and 'bossing' of other children was thus something of a trial when she first came to school. However, as she became more used to the new situation her excitement diminished, and her voice consequently was less loud. One effect of her voice was to cause other children to raise their voices, and if asked not to shout they would say that Marlene could not hear unless they did, or that they were talking 'to Marlene's hearing-aid', or that she had shouted at them. Help in understanding the use of the hearing-aid was given by the peripatetic teacher, who let children listen through the earphones of the audiometric apparatus, and talk softly into the aid. He explained the nature of Marlene's defect to

187

the teachers, and indicated the limitations of the aid. Careful forming of sounds, and the practice of speaking directly to the child, were also helpful, and even other children gradually learned to put this advice into effect. In Marlene's case her handicap was lessened if staff and children remembered and made full use of her aid; whereas the opposite policy was pursued in respect of Sheila's leg-iron, which was better forgotten except under special circumstances.

Marlene herself was apt to switch-off the aid rather than persevere in some difficult situations, and it was not always easy to know when she had done this. Only experience with the child was of use here. A high, old-fashioned classroom, with brick walls and high windows is not a good place in which to teach a partially-hearing child. Sound ricochets and shatters against such surfaces, making voices difficult to hear even for the fully-hearing child, and magnifying the ordinary chatter of an Infants' class to sometimes unbearable proportions for the partially-hearing child. The parents said that she seemed to hear everything at home, and this was probably true. Some sympathy and understanding of the difficulties under classroom conditions must be extended to a child such as Marlene, and steps taken to reduce echo, distortion and volume of sound if possible. Even mounting of friezes and paintings etc. high on brick walls can result in quite astonishing improvement of the acoustic properties of a classroom of the type described.

Although Marlene could not be described as intellectually gifted, and there is evidence to suggest that such impairment of hearing does result in intellectual retardation,[3] she learned to read by the age of six-and-a-half, and by phonic methods. It was necessary for her to have regular and systematic training in making sounds, and in recognizing and naming objects in bright and interesting pictures. She was also given pictures accompanied by words that could be analysed phonically, and thus given a training that would in most schools come after initial reading by 'look-and-say' method. The primer series most commonly used in the school also lent itself to use of phonic approach,[4] although not usually used in this way initially, and Marlene would take her primer to the specialist

[3] M. M. Lewis 'Language, Thought and Personality' (1963) p. 75.
[4] The 'Gay Way' Series – E. R. Boyce (pub. Macmillan).

teacher and read it with great pride. Perhaps there is an ironic lesson here for hard-pressed Infants' teachers: an absolutely *systematic* approach to the teaching of reading and the early use of phonics under individual guidance, even though this may take place only once a week for a short period, can result in even a not-very-bright child with a hearing impairment learning to read effectively before many 'normal' children. The class teacher found it necessary only to reinforce the work of the specialist teacher, and learned something of value for all children from the experience.

Full co-operation with the parents, the doctor and the specialist teacher ensured for Marlene a very happy, normal life with classmates in the Infants' school. This probably enabled her, in turn, to be transferred successfully to the Junior school at the normal time, and to take her place in it as easily as other children. It is commonly found that partially-hearing adults are socially inept, being shy or awkward or even 'difficult' in relationship. The work of the Nursery and Infants' school may well be a factor in preventing such social disability, as Marlene's case suggests.

40. Bertie

A child of such multiple handicap, physical, mental and cultural as to be entered as 'unclassified' in the table on p. 31 and of a kind very rarely met in the Infants' school. Only the migrant nature of the family made it possible for Bertie to 'slip through the net' of medical and social services until the age of five and some months. Included for discussion because of the particular steps that need to be taken in the school if such a child is entered.

Bertie was brought to school by a dull-seeming mother on the arrival of the family from the north of England. It appeared that his father moved about the country taking jobs such as potato-picking or road-work and accompanied by his family as often as he could find accommodation for them. At the time of Bertie's entry to school the family of two adults and three children were living in a caravan rented from the road contractors. The mother was pregnant with her fourth child, and was in a poor state of health. Although both mother and child were reasonably well-dressed and clean in appearance they presented a disquieting picture of poor physique and ill-health. Bertie was wizened and very small for his age; his speech was indistinct and very limited; his jaw was underslung and tremulous; and his feet were so appallingly turned inwards that he literally fell over them if he attempted to run.

These were no reasons for refusing him entry, however, and he was accepted in the usual way, and seen almost immediately by the school doctor – who conducted a medical examination in the next month. The requirement of medical examination was explained to the mother, who seemed to have little idea of what was involved in a child's starting school and did not seem very familiar with medical services, either. Before the day of the examination, however, Bertie proved to be an even more difficult 'case' than even his poor appearance would have suggested. He was incontinent in regard to both bladder and bowels, and appeared to have had no training at all. After the third 'accident' in school the mother was sent-for. She at first maintained that school was making Bertie nervous; next that his teacher would not 'let him go'; then that he was 'a dirty little devil' and did it on purpose; and finally, after some firm talking-to, said that she had not bothered much with his training, and often let him wear nappies at home. The rare and extreme step of excluding him from school until he was clean was taken – but with the co-operation of the Health Visitor the exclusion did not last long. Under the firm guidance of the nurse, and with as much encouragement as is possible to get such a mother to give to such a child, Bertie was 'clean' in two weeks. He was then re-admitted to school, and his other behaviour noted.

This was gravely abnormal. Obviously, he could not walk or run easily, but he seemed never to have played with outdoor toys and hardly knew what to do with a truck or tricycle until shown. Thereafter, he seemed to enjoy trundling wheeled toys about, and was allowed to do so. He seemed not to register other children, even when they pushed his truck or, as on one occasion, put him in the middle of a pile of tyres and invited him to jump out and chase them. He would say, 'la-la-la' to himself for long periods, flapping his hands in a weak gesture to accompany his murmurings, and rarely answered when spoken-to. His answers were monosyllabic when made at all, and it seemed doubtful whether he understood what was said unless it was also monosyllabic – such as 'Sit in the truck' or 'Take the ball' in a very firm voice.

The medical examination revealed many defects. He was underweight, had an ear infection, had slight malformation of the jaw and roof of the mouth, and needed immediate orthopaedic treatment for his feet. The mother seemed dully surprised at this catalogue of defects but agreed to take him as requested to the local hospital. The school doctor thought that the boy was mentally defective, having regard to his low level of response, and asked for special examination on these grounds also. Poor Bertie was indeed a 'mess', and it seemed pointless to keep him in the normal Infants' school. Yet until ascertained ineducable he had to stay somewhere, and at least he probably received a little stimulation from the toys and contact with teachers that a school offered. Other children either ignored him, or said he was 'daft' – and this despite the teacher's efforts to maintain that good 'tone' already mentioned. With a child like Bertie it is almost impossible to communicate under normal school conditions, and no efforts are likely to be fruitful if contact and response are completely lacking. It was hoped that his ascertainment would be not long delayed, and that he could receive the specialist help of an occupation centre as soon as possible.

Before this was obtained, however, the family moved to the midlands, and all trace of them was lost for several weeks. Then came a request for information on Bertie from another head teacher. Bertie's mother had taken him to another Infants' school, and yet another school doctor had asked for specialist opinion on him. His educational and medical records were immediately forwarded – and presumably the machinery of ascertainment and for treatment of his feet was set in motion in the next area into which the family had moved. This is surely a justification for the keeping of full records, for a child of such a migrant family may well 'start at square one' each time the family moves, unless teachers and doctors make immediate demand of the mother as to the previous place of residence and send for records.

41. Edward

An undersized but active child, the oldest of three, and of indulgent working-class parents. He had been found to have an operable heart-abnormality at the age of two, and was expected to undergo the operation some time in his seventh year. Meanwhile, authorized by his doctor to attend normal school, and to be watched only for overtiredness during vigorous physical exercise. Found to be of somewhat below average intelligence on a group-test, (I.Q. 85), but verbally fluent and with quite average ability in most skills except reading. A slow starter in this respect, but only slightly retarded by the end of his Infants' school years.

Of Edward there is little to say that could not be said of most lively boys of his age. He was used to playing with other children, and enjoyed being one of a group in school. He was noisy and grubby, fully involved in all normal classroom and playground activities, with a particular skill and delight in football – a taste he shared with many other boys who, like himself, had been allowed the freedom of the quiet backstreets and the common. Such an active child was obviously something of a problem when his physical condition was remembered, and his mother had not succeeded in planned limitation of his vigorous play before he came to school. He had, however, in his pre-school years complete freedom to come indoors and rest when he felt like it, and this he had apparently done quite often. Faced with the extra company and stimulus of school it was feared that he might overtire himself; he certainly took as little notice of a teacher's suggestions that he should 'slow down' or change his activity as he had taken of his mother's. The only sensible courses were letting him stop when he felt inclined, with a firm sanction on further activity if he seemed to be getting overtired. For so previously indulged a child the second course was at first irksome; but he needed, in any case, to become used to the ordinary discipline of school and to learn that his teacher meant exactly what she said and was prepared to enforce her sanctions if necessary – as his mother was not. Even had Edward been an entirely fit child he would probably have been somewhat wilful during his first term.

With the support of the school doctor Edward's mother became firmer with him in general, and this made her insistence on his resting occasionally more effective. She had, not unnaturally, been inclined to indulge him from the time his heart condition was diagnosed, and to withhold from him the odd slaps with which she (on her own admission) enforced her somewhat casual discipline of the other children. When she realized how her very indulgence had made it difficult to limit Edward's activities she was prepared to take a

192

18

more consistent and firm line with him – a policy which was helpful with her other children also, as it turned out. In school the boy continued to be interested and active, but much less wilful, and increasingly sensible about his own condition. In Edward's case there seemed little danger of his becoming over-sensitive about his limitations, for he cared too much for vigorous physical activity to retreat into 'invalidism'. The early freedom may well have stood him in good stead in this connection; a child who had never discovered the pleasure of playing with balls and trucks may have the more easily 'given up' when required to think of his physical limitations.

The operation to restore his heart to normal functioning was carried out before Edward was seven, and after nearly a term's absence from school he returned to resume his lively play and his good relationships with other children. The period in hopsital seemed to have had no adverse emotional effects on this boy, probably because he was secure in the affection of his parents and of an age to accept temporary parting from them with good sense. Like many children of his age and essential stability, he enjoyed the 'fuss' made of him in hospital, and the new toys, endless supplies of sweets and so on which being there brought him. Only for a very short period after his return home did he 'play up', and this seemed, in a similar manner to Sheila, to be because he had less attention there than he had had in hospital. Certainly, on his return to school he showed no tendency to misbehave or to exploit his experience.

Considerations

There were other children very similar to Edward in the degree of limitation imposed on them, asthmatics being among them. These presented little problem in school, and if they did so are numbered among the 'unclassified' in the table of special needs since their difficulties were usually of short duration, as often mildly emotional as physical, and sometimes involved problems of parental attitude in addition. It is, of course, necessary to exercise a little reasonable care in dealing with an asthmatic; it is not wise, for example, to let him sort out the feathers for head-dresses, or arrange the fluffy seed-heads on the nature table. But parents of such children are surprisingly often of the very intelligent kind who are informative and helpful about their child's condition, and indicate the kind of situations in which attacks might take place. It is only the 'mild' asthmatic, in any case, who is likely to be in school; very severe cases may need special schooling from the start, although modern treatments tend to control the condition well. As with the cases of heart abnormality, overactivity is inadvisable, and the teacher needs to be aware of when the child is 'overdoing things' or getting excited. Asthmatics do tend to be anxious by temperament, and particularly anxious about their own condition which is, after all, a terrifying one even for adults. It is now generally recognized that asthma (as eczema, which also imposes physical limitations on the child in school) is a psychosomatic condition. This certainly does not mean, however, that the asthmatic child can 'pull himself together' or that he 'does it on purpose'. Barton Hall quotes Bray (1937) as saying that the psychic trauma is 'the trigger that fires the already loaded allergic gun'.[5] Only full discussion with parents and doctor can help avoidance of some risks, allergic or emotional, in school.

Other physical handicaps may include diabetes, mild epilepsy, (of a kind, however, more noticeable than in Billy's case), and the handicap associated with thalidomide. All the above-made considerations apply to these as to all handicaps: the necessity for full information; the recognition of and, if possible, allowance for some less helpful parental attitudes; maximum use of the child's real capacities in order that he may be constantly aware of what he *can* do rather than what he cannot; and the maintenance within the class and the school of desirable attitudes on the part of other children. As far as curriculum and timetable, organization and provision are concerned there is unlikely to be much difficulty in making the necessary allowances for handicapped children – so long as the proportion of these to the normal in any one class is low.

This raises another consideration: how many handicapped children to accept in the normal school. Fortunately, this is not a common problem, but it may arise, as it does in the Nursery school, if a particular Infants' school becomes known as a place that has a small class (or extra room, or particularly suitable staff) that makes acceptance of handicapped children

5 'Psychiatric Examination of the School Child' p. 130.

more feasible than it might be in other schools. Many Nursery heads are under unfair, if understandable, pressure to accept handicapped children in perhaps larger numbers than they feel their schools can carry. It is an unfortunate misunderstanding, even in quarters where the purpose of the Nursery school might be thought to be understood, that such schools exist largely to cater for the underprivileged of every kind. Difficult as it is for a head to turn away a handicapped child, many take a courageous stand, against even implications of lack of sympathy, in order to maintain their schools as places of appropriate education for normal children, accepting only that proportion of children with very special needs that might be expected not to 'unbalance' the rest. Only the provision of Nursery education on a much vaster scale will remove from the head teachers the burden of difficult decisions about handicapped children. Under some circumstances the heads of Infants' schools may find they have a similar responsibility to decide how many handicapped children a school can 'carry'.

The provision of units for partially-hearing children within the normal Infants' school is one of the means by which the difficulty of providing normal social experience for handicapped children can be overcome. In such units the children share mealtimes, much free-play experience and all entertainments, open days etc. with the rest of their age-mates, having in addition specialist teaching in properly fitted rooms and with a trained specialist teacher. In the same way, the benefits of a normal Infants' school might be shared with children who are mildly spastic, diabetic or even non-communicating. Obviously, such provision depends on there being a school with an unused classroom, an authority willing to equip it with (often) expensive apparatus, and a teacher trained to deal with specific handicap. Yet none of this is impossible, and the reward in human efficiency, happiness and general improvement in learning would seem to outweigh the mere cost. In any case, a child needing to be kept in a residential school costs an authority much more than he does if attending a day-school; and the risk of abnormal emotional and social development is enormously reduced if a child lives with his family and goes to school every day as others do. Many a head teacher of a normal Infants' school who has a particular interest in one or another type of handicap would undoubtedly welcome the opportunity of pioneering a 'small class' or a unit for such handicap within her own school. Perhaps provision for such fairly mild handicap as has been described in this chapter will, in the future, increasingly take this form. In the meantime, the teacher in the normal school must cope as well as she can with children who have physical limitations – and she usually finds she can cope very well indeed given information, a flexible organization and normal Infants' school provision.

Suggestions for Further Reading

Ayrault, E. W. *Take One Step* Methuen (1965)

Central Advisory Council for Education (Plowden Report) *Children and Their Primary Schools* (Chapter 21) H.M.S.O. (1967)

Lewis, M. M. *Language, Thought and Personality* Harrap (1963)

Robertson, J. *Young Children in Hospital* Tavistock (1956)

Schonell, F. E. *Educating Spastic Children* Oliver and Boyd (1956)

Watson, T. J. *The Education of Hearing-Handicapped Children* U.L.P. (1967)

Chapter 12

Children with Cultural Handicap

It is difficult to choose a term which will at once cover the handicap of the child from the feckless, inadequate and poverty-stricken home and the child from an essentially middle-class background who, for example, having one foreign parent finds it difficult to come to terms with the outside world where not only customs and usage but even language may be different from those within his home. Children can be handicapped on school entry by each of these situations, different though they are – and perhaps the most reasonable description of this handicap is 'cultural'. Immigrant children, whether from the Caribbean, India, Pakistan or Cyprus, must obviously find themselves handicapped in similar fashion[1] – but there were no immigrant children in the five hundred who are the basis of this work, and the particular problems connected with their induction into English society cannot, therefore, be discussed here. It is possible that much that is applicable to children from other backgrounds having elements of cultural deprivation is also applicable to immigrant children, but the reader is referred to specialist literature on immigration problems, some of which is listed at the end of this chapter.

Not every child from a working-class home is deprived of linguistic and social experience of the kind that makes school entry so much easier for the middle-class child – but some undoubtedly are, as the following brief survey of some recent findings suggests. Neither are poverty or fecklessness necessarily accompanied by lack of affection and reasonable discipline – although, again, the sheer difficulties of life may result in both. Despite the many exceptions, however, there is little reasonable doubt that social class in this country can be a handicap to many children, at least as far as their schooling is concerned. If poverty is added to the class factor the teacher is faced with considerable difficulty, since she has to

[1] See 'Children and their Primary Schools' Ch. 6.

deal with children whose needs are for acquisition of those elementary skills of communication, those habits (such as use of cutlery, hand-washing etc.) expectations and attitudes most children have already acquired by the age of five.

It might be thought unnecessary to include a chapter on such handicap, since many children discussed in connection with other difficulties and needs (Duncan, Brian, Tessie and Mary are examples) were also handicapped by limitations of one kind and another arising from cultural factors. The children who are the subject of this chapter, however, were primarily noticeable in school for their lack of those 'normal' language skills, habits and attitudes already referred-to above. They were not aggressive, withdrawn or prone to pilfer; they showed no excessive anxiety, and were markedly free of the kind of worries or bizarre behaviour which drew the attention of teachers to the needs of some other children. That they had special needs, however, was undeniable; and it is the purpose of this chapter to discuss these in isolation from other factors – an arbitrary device which, in the classroom, does not preclude consideration of any other special difficulties they may have. There does seem to be a 'cultural syndrome' – poor speech, limited vocabulary, uncouth manners, non-involvement in the interests of school and deviant appearance, as well as poor health – which might be considered, justifiably, apart from other difficulties. It is probably not amenable to remedy by education alone; but teachers have an obvious contribution to make to the improvement of the children who are characterized by these 'symptoms' as this discussion attempts to show.

At the end of his survey of the primary school careers of 3,809 children from all social classes, and all born during one week in March, 1946, J. W. B. Douglas makes the following comment:

'Over a period of three years in the primary schools, there is a substantial loss of ability in the manual working-class children which could be prevented, it seems, by teaching, even if the attitude of working-class parents towards education does not change'[2] Douglas speculates on the greater gains to be derived from improvement of education at the primary stage, rather than at the secondary, perhaps, and then writes:

[2] *'The Home and the Scchol'* (1964) p. 128.

'Perhaps we should think in terms of nursery schools which aim to give small children the stimulus that is so often lacking in their homes.' He concludes this factual and thorough account by adding that there is need 'to measure more fully the impact of the family on the early processes of learning and on the acquisition of incentives before children reach school.'

It is true that the three years in which this loss of ability referred-to by Douglas takes place are those between eight and eleven, and might be thought by some to be the responsibility of the Junior schools. But children take into the second stage of their primary education what they learned of school in their first, and it is the responsibility of Infants' teachers to ensure that this view is an interested and hopeful one. There is then at least less chance of a child becoming relatively less and less efficient as he moves through the Junior school.

Douglas is by no means alone in finding that what is for the purposes of this chapter called 'cultural handicap' is probably the greatest waster of ability ever found in an educational system. Children whose *test-scores are identical or very similar* at the age of eight pull steadily and (it seems) irrevocably away from each other in the next stage of their education – those from homes generally described as middle-class finally gaining a disproportionate number of grammar school places compared with their age-mates from the manual working-class.

The practice of streaming by ability seems to aggravate this tendency, and is discussed by Daniels, Jackson and, more recently, the Plowden committee in ways which are beginning to influence many head teachers towards 'unstreaming' their schools.[3] It looks sadly, also, as though a predominantly middle-class teaching profession tends to judge – perhaps unconsciously – the strengths and potential of children as much by social class as by actual performance in school or by test-scores. Floud and Halsey found that when objective tests of ability were abandoned in one division of a local authority,

[3] Daniels, 'Effects of Streaming in the Primary School' B. J. Ed. Psych. Vol. XXXI, No. 69 (1961) Jackson, B. 'Streaming: an Education System in Miniature' (1965); 'Children and their Primary Schools' ch. 20, paras. 806-824.

in favour of teachers' assessments and interview, the proportion of working-class boys going to grammer school fell and that of middle-class boys rose.[4] It is difficult to escape the suspicions that social bias was a factor here; and that some 'wastage' might be avoided if some preconceptions about intelligence and social class were abandoned.

In addition to this rather worrying evidence of 'built-in bias' for or against some children in our schools, according to the social class from which they come, there is the contribution of Bernstein to the relationship between social class and linguistic development, which is of major importance to teachers of young children. That poor speech and limited language-facility, in terms of vocabulary and fluency, are characteristics of many children from what may be called underprivileged homes has been well-known to teachers since such children were admitted to schools at all. What may once have been attributed to poor heredity, however, or accepted as a 'natural' limitation of the 'lower orders' is now seen as being, in part at least, amenable to good teaching in the very early years. This is not to deny that there may be a hereditary factor, but recent research has not been concerned with the older argument of what proportion of a child's intellectual ability might be due to his inheritance and what due to environmental factors. This has been seen as a fruitless and largely academic question, and many investigators of human learning have abandoned it in favour of the more promising researches into *how* children learn. In discussing the 'proportion' findings Hunt writes:

'The fact is that between-family and within-family variations in environment within the full range of the social classes in the culture of America constitute but a small part of the variation that has existed historically on the face of this earth. Moreover, if the assumptions that intelligence is largely fixed and that development is largely predetermined are discarded . . . who knows what the limits are? It is inconceivable that they are to be fixed by any given set of existing conditions.'[5]

Bernstein's theme is that opportunities to develop certain

---

[4] Floud, J. E. and Halsey, A. H. '*Intelligence Tests, Social Class and Selection for Secondary School*'. B. J. Sociology VIII, p. 33 (1957).
[5] R. McV. Hunt '*Intelligence and Experience*' p. 327.

language facilities early (i.e. in the pre-school years) is vital not only to the child's ability to communicate, but, and even more importantly, to his ability to *think*. Between what Bernstein[6] calls a 'public code' and a 'formal (or elaborated) code' of language lies all the difference between an order to a child to 'Shut up!' and a request framed as, 'I wish you would make less noise with that hammer, darling!' The former leaves the child no room for what one might call manoeuvre in his responses, holds no suggestion of proposition, invites no come-back in the form of question or explanation. The latter tends to invite various responses, and moreover, is couched in such terms as to imply some courtesy on the part of adult toward child. In a similar manner, a child's question of 'What's that?' (identified by Piaget[7] as demonstrating a transitional phase between verbalizations accompanying actions, and descriptions of action) may be answered in such a way as to leave no further experiment with words possible – or in such a way as to help the child to develop not only vocabulary but the ultimate human skill of classifying, categorizing and identifying 'things' by 'names'. Communication as well as abstract thinking has its roots in this stage, and according to recent work by Bernstein the Nursery school has an essential function to perform[8] for children deprived of the linguistic, exploratory and social advantages of the middle-class home.

In an article in *'New Society'*[9] the writer describes the very different views of mothers of different social classes on the function of toys in the pre-school years:

'Here, 68 per cent of the middle-class gave top ranking to the statement that toys help the child 'to find out about things'. Only 29 per cent of the working-class gave this statement top ranking.' There is obviously something of great significance here for the teacher of young children, for, as the writer of the article points out, middle-class mothers 'have a concept of toys and play which harmonizes well with that of

6 Bernstein, B. *'Social Class & Linguistic Development'* in *'Education, Economy and Society'* by Halsey, Floud and Anderson.

7 *'Play, Dreams and Imagination in Childhood'* (1945) p. 223.

8 See also *'Children and their Primary Schools'* ch. 5 para. 165 and ch. 9.

9 Vol. 8 No. 221, December 22, 1966 *'Social Class and the Under-Fives'* by Jean Jones p. 935.

the infant school'. Between the language and attitudes of home and school there is little difference, and hence minimum upheaval at school entry for the children from homes where play has been seen as a means of furthering learning, language facility encouraged, and the very toys chosen with regard to the child's age and sex as well as to their intrinsic quality as articles.

The child from the underprivileged home, whether this is technically working-class or not, is not only hampered by his language and conceptual limitations and by his unfamiliarity with the possibilities of many kinds of play and play-materials, but also in very many cases by the inadequacy of his parents when dealing with the school. As the writer of the above-quoted article points out:

'They are hampered by not knowing school requirements, and they do not know what to do about it. Their well-meaning enquiries may even be construed by the school as interference, and politely discouraged. The result is that they see the school as an institution that is hardly worth tangling with.' The same point was made by Marsden and Jackson in *Education and the Working Class*. The helplessness of some parents when faced by the comparatively simple requirements and aims of the Infants' school is even more apparent if their children are among the relatively few who enter grammar schools – and the wastage in the Primary schools of which Douglas speaks is once more evident in the secondary stage. Not only greater opportunities to develop language and conceptual skills, to play with interest and curiosity with a variety of materials, and to make the sort of social relations with their age-peers which are acceptable at every level of society, but good relations between their school and their parents from first stage are among the most urgent needs of children such as those to be discussed in this chapter. That they have other, practical, needs is undeniable; and that the school can go some way towards meeting them by the provision of meals, milk and even clothing hardly requires stressing. It is in the saving of human intellectual potential, however, that we now need to be concerned as well. No society in a technological age can afford the 'drain' once considered normal; it is, perhaps, in the Nursery and Infants' schools that the first steps can be taken, with both children and parents, to ensure that we lose no more.

The children whose 'cases' are in the category of cultural handicap were not in every instance underprivileged in the sense that is implied in the foregoing paragraphs. There are other hampering circumstances of a cultural nature, as has already been mentioned, and one such case is cited here.

42. Roy

A small, pale, anxious-looking child, found to be underweight at his first medical examination in school, and also suffering from bronchitis. The second child of four on school entry, and of five before the age of seven, the oldest child having been transferred to a special school just before Roy's entry. Parents appeared limited in understanding, and father said to be violent with both his wife and children at fairly frequent intervals. No intelligence score available for Roy, but he showed signs of being rather below average after a few months in school.

When Roy was first brought to school by his mother he was already five and three months, his mother having forgotten, or perhaps simply not bothered, to bring him previously. She was a large, untidy, but not unaffectionate woman, who dragged him in to the head teacher's room with a threat of, 'Teacher'll 'it yer if yer don't stop snivelling,' which did not make rapport with Roy easy for some time. She was obviously rather ill-at-ease in school, and sat on the edge of a chair as though ready for flight while she gave particulars of Roy. The boy himself squeezed against his mother, who absent-mindedly, as it seemed, held his hand and gave him several little pats on the thigh. As he had not been to the school before, and was apparently very frightened, it was suggested that he and his mother come and have a look round, and that he be brought back to start full-time school on the next day. This proposition took several repetitions before his mother appeared to understand. When she did, she shook her head, saying that she had had the 'other two' outside in the pram, and that she was on her way to 'the welfare', after which she was going shopping. It was as much as anyone could do to persuade her that Roy needed his mother to accompany him to the classroom, and that this was a quite normal practice. Still tearful, and clinging to his mother, the boy was taken to the Reception class, where the children were playing with the usual materials and equipment. He looked without interest at the room, ignored the teacher who came across to welcome him, and clung tighter to his mother. She pulled away from him, gave him a push towards the teacher, and told him to be a good boy before hastily ducking her head at the head teacher and hurrying out of the door. Since Roy was so upset, and had begun to scream, he was taken back to the head's room, and sat on her knee until he calmed down. Such a beginning to his school career was not promising, and he took several weeks to settle to school, being tearful every morning after his mother had pushed him through the gate. Several suggestions that she should come in with him were ignored; she seemed afraid and resentful by turns, and treated head and staff as though they were inimical strangers.

Nothing had been said at his entry about his clothes and footwear, for it was felt that his mother's confidence must be won before attempts were made to improve these. He wore a ragged, sleeveless pullover, many sizes too big, a torn and filthy shirt, a pair of trousers so small and tight that he must have been in constant discomfort, and a pair of boots with literally no soles in them. When he put his foot up to have the knotted, dirty laces tied his teacher realized that his bare feet were showing through the bottom of his boots, and she took him at once to the head mistress. He had by this time been in school for nearly two weeks, and apart from wearing a long-sleeved pullover on several occasions was wearing the clothes he had originally worn on entry. Of underwear he had none, and only occasionally wore socks. It was not possible to allow him to walk virtually barefoot, and some shoes and socks left by a parent for just such an emergency were found to fit him. The problem of how to get his mother to accept such clothes without either developing resentment against the school, or coming to rely entirely upon such 'charity' in the feeble manner of so many women of her kind, or even of selling the nearly new shoes and socks for a few coppers to a neighbour was, as always, a difficult one to solve. In the end, it was decided that the head teacher should take Roy home that evening – his mother left him to come alone, as only a short distance was involved – and explain the situation.

The home was very much what one would expect, being shabby on the outside, with rubbish in the garden, a broken latch on the door, broken panes in two windows, and a general

204

air of dilapidation although a council house. Several heavy knocks were necessary to bring Roy's mother to the front door; the boy himself had wanted to go round the back, but it was felt that it would be an impertinence if the headmistress did likewise, and both waited on the front step. Inside, the house was grubby, untidy and almost without furniture. The two toddlers were naked from the waist down, and both sucking dummies; they looked as though they had not been bathed for days. On the table were empty and half-empty milk-bottles, a few cracked cups, bread in its wrapper, knives, pieces of food, and a baby's bottle. The rest of the room was in a similar mess, and there were no toys or other signs of normal allowance for children.

Yet Roy's mother, after initial embarrassment, offered her visitor a cup of tea, and was friendly, if a little ingratiating. Much could be learned directly, and much inferred, from what she had to say, and from the appearance and behaviour of the children. Roy said nothing at all throughout the short visit, but gave an uncertain smile when the visitor included him in the conversation; the toddlers clung to each other, staring at the visitor with wide eyes, and not once uttering a sound. Their mother glanced at them occasionally, as she made reference to the way in which they 'broke up everything', but did not speak directly to them at all. Neither, however, was she cold or harsh with them, and it looked as though they might have occasional rough attention when she was alone with them. The linguistic poverty, and the lack of opportunities for children to learn in such a situation hardly need stressing. Roy was monosyllabic in school for a year after entry, and his response to playthings was one of mixed surprise and apparently unintentional destructiveness for over a term. When it is remembered how *few* were the everyday articles in use – cups, cutlery, chairs, even kitchen utensils – it was not surprising that he was slow and uncertain about simple counting, and the difference between three articles and four or five.

After the initial contact, relations with Roy's mother were moderately friendly, and there was no evidence that she sold or otherwise disposed of the clothes that were regularly sent home for both him, his older sister and the two younger children. The Health Visitor kept an eye on the clothing of the smaller children, and said that they were usually properly clad after the school started to supply clothing regularly. The Children's Officer, approached in the matter of shoes, (since it was felt unacceptable to continue to give Roy used footwear), provided these at regular intervals, and also saw to the provision of winter coats for all the children. It might be thought by some that this amount of help is both uncalled-for and dangerous, in that it encourages a feckless attitude. Yet, it must be remembered that such a woman as Roy's mother is feckless to start with, and will hardly improve if left to find the children's clothing for herself. Where, in fact, will she find it? A man who works as an unskilled labourer in a small factory earns rather less, in some instances, than he would draw from National Assistance, and this was true of Roy's father. Such a man is rarely one who 'manages' his money well – indeed it would tax the wit of an intelligent man to make so small a wage feed, clothe and house a family of seven adequately. To take a punitive view of such families, to suggest penalties, limitations, even sterilization, is of no help to the children. No matter what strictures are made, a child like Roy will come to school in rags, and with his feet bare to the pavement unless some straightforward help is given. It is surely the task of the teacher to make it possible for a child to benefit from his education, if she possibly can. This a child cannot do if he is cold, hungry, isolated from his fellows by a dirty and unprepossessing appearance, or just very uncomfortable in ill-fitting clothes. Nothing could be done for Roy until he was adequately shod and clothed, and his mother was 'on the side' of school.

The school doctor, concerned at the boy's frailty, made an order for free halibut-liver oil capsules to be taken every day, including during the holidays: and, although his father was employed, free meals at school were also granted on medical grounds. Extra milk, and biscuits, were given to him daily before he left school in the afternoon, which went some way towards ensuring that he had more than his one meal a day. It was found that this improved diet could be provided with a minimum of publicity, and thus no embarrassment to Roy as he grew older and more aware of other children. As with the question of clothing, the provision of free meals and such other dietary additions as the doctor thought suitable in Roy's case, are sometimes thought to encourage laziness in parents. But it is a singularly unfeeling policy to try to bring feckless parents to a sense of their duty by letting their children go hungry, underweight and prone to infection, (which, incidentally, they pass on to their more fortunate class-mates), and it was not felt in this school to be a fruitful or even allowable policy. Only contact with the parents, in the form of constant help and advice of Health Visitor, head teacher, class-teachers, school doctor and Children's Officer, is *likely* to 'reform' such inadequate people as Roy's parents – and, even then, only over a very long period, if at all.

A year of play in the Reception class, a great deal of attention to his speech and to the extension of his extremely limited vocabulary, and the beginning of social behaviour of a kind expected in a rather younger child, made it possible for Roy to enter his second year in the Infants' school appearing much less deviant than when he had arrived. He had put on weight, and developed a pleasant manner, which, together with his 'normal' clothes and willing disposition, made him a popular playmate with one or two rather slow-learning boys from his street. It would have been helpful to this boy, perhaps, had he had the stimulus of play with 'brighter' children – but this is hardly possible of manipulation in the ordinary free situation of the Infants' school, even if it were ethically allowable to dictate to a child with whom he should play. His teacher made a special effort to engage this little group of boys in stimulating activities and conversations, which were necessarily at a 'younger' level than many in the class. Puppets, and the making of a shop, a model railway after a visit to the station, and such joint ventures, were not very different from the pursuits of the rest of the class, and gave the sort of opportunities for speech and exploration that Roy so sorely needed.

In social skills he was markedly proficient in his second year, his teacher taking particular pains with what she called his 'manners' – in the same way as she had with Brian, and with equal success. But from the point of view of learning formal skills Roy's Infants' school career was not a success. He left a term before he would normally have done so, as the family moved and all contact was lost, and at that stage was quite unable to read. It is unlikely that he would have learned in his last term even with the help of a teacher who took a particular interest in him, and with whom he had a good relationship. As far as his linguistic skills were concerned he had progressed to moderately clear speech, had extended his vocabulary, (although it was still limited for a child of nearly seven), could sustain attention through a simple story, and could write and recognize his name and one or two words. He had probably progressed faster in two years than he had done in the previous five – at least as far as language skills were concerned – but the handicap of such early deprivation of linguistic experience may be too much for the ordinary school to overcome. Special facilities and programmes, either before or during an extended Infants' school stage, may be the only solution to the problem posed to teachers by children like Roy. In number skills he was slightly less retarded than in language, but by no means anywhere near the level of understanding of most seven-year-olds when he left the school. Nearly two years of opportunity to handle objects in abundance, to sort, sift, weigh, measure, compare and count – an opportunity his home had not been able to offer at all – seemed to result in his having reached the understanding-level of most five-year-olds. But he lacked their curiosity and 'drive' in the face of numerical and mathematical phenomena, and again it is possible that the ordinary school cannot 'make up' the lost years for such a child.

43. Robert

A plump, rosy child, of apparently average intelligence. The fourth child of seven on school entry and of eight by the age of seven. Parents very cheerful, apparently affectionate with each other and with the children. Previous members of the family who had attended the school – an older brother was barely seven, and still there on Robert's arrival – had been popular with other children and with their teachers on account of their cheerfulness and good nature, but had been slow learners. Robert seemed as even-tempered and obliging as the rest of his family, and rather more able; but, perhaps because more children had been born, the standard of clothing and general care had fallen, and Robert was ragged and poorly shod when he arrived.

Because the family was well-known to the head teacher and staff of the school, and relations with the parents had always been friendly, the matter of Robert's appearance was dealt with at once, and before comment could arise from other children. His mother was visited in her home, (a chaotic, grubby place, very similar to Roy's but with perhaps a few more possessions, including toys for the children), and presented with enough pullovers, shirts, trousers and socks to see Robert through the winter. She was cheerfully grateful without being either ingratiating or embarrassed by this provision, and declared that Robert should be 'kept nice', as the older children had been. The next day, however, the boy appeared in the most ragged, shrunken clothes, with broken boots and no socks – and his older brother was wearing some of the clothes that had been left for Robert. These were much too small for him, and both brothers looked dreadful. Asked where his own clothes were, (they had been shabby but warm and moderately clean); the older boy said he did not know. There seemed only one thing to do, and that to pay another visit to his mother.

This good-natured, inconsequential and feckless woman at first said she did not know what had happened to any of the clothes, and looked vaguely round the room as though they might suddenly appear; but she subsequently admitted, after some very plain talking about the discomfort she was causing her two young sons, that she had let a neighbour have the 'spare' trousers and shirts for half-a-crown, and that Robert's older brother had insisted on wearing what was left. It appeared that the family was in danger of eviction for non-payment of rent, that small sums of money were owed to every tradesman foolish enough to let either parent have credit, and that there was no food in the house for that evening's meal. Fortunately, the family allowances had not all been drawn for that week – a surprising omission on the part of this mother – and the situation was saved for the immediate future. The problem was, as is so often the case, a multiple one, and involved (eventually) the housing committee of the local council, the National Assistance Board, the husband's employer, the Children's Officer, the school doctor, the Health Visitor and the local vicar to whose Sunday school all the children above the age of three went regularly. The initiating agency in this case was the headmistress of the Infants' school, who had most direct contact with the family and was not, as some other agencies were, either the dispenser of money or the demander of it. It is with someone in this 'neutral' position that such parents can sometimes discuss problems that they cannot, or dare not, discuss with anyone else. The Health Visitor had not been aware of the extent of the family's financial troubles, but having been informed by the school was able to offer help with the under-fives, and put in a plea to the housing authority. The threatened eviction did not, then, take place, Robert's father undertaking to pay off the arrears of rent by instalments. In order to do this he took an extra, evening, job – mainly obtained through the good offices of the Children's Officer – and the family was once more fairly solvent.

Clothes, free meals, extra milk and a supportive attitude to the parents gave Robert a chance to lead a normal life in the Infants' school, and to be relieved of the threat, (of which he and his older siblings had been quite aware), of being taken into a Children's Home if the family had been evicted. He blossomed into a most able and popular child in his first year, learning to read much sooner than had his older brother and sisters, and having a particular flair for number and mathematical work of all kinds. His father visited the school on several occasions, usually with offers to help in some way, (not very realistic offers, but very kindly meant), and was told of his son's good progress. As the older brother had progressed much faster since Robert's arrival at school, and was near-average in performance by the time he left, the parents were increasingly well-disposed towards the school, and even gaining, it was thought, a little understanding of what education could mean to the children.

Robert showed great interest in almost everything, and was a joy to take to local museums, the zoo, an old church or some famous ruins. He asked questions, wrote long accounts of his visits, and illustrated them in a lively manner. It was arranged for him to accompany the young family of one of the staff on an outing to London during a holiday, and to be taken by another family with children in the school for a day at the seaside. Together with other children, Robert was taken to places of interest by the vicar, and responded in a lively fashion to every opportunity. His linguistic experience had not been so limited as Roy's, perhaps because his parents were more talkative, if not very 'bright', and his older sisters had talked to him. Nevertheless, he had been markedly less able to communicate and to conceptualize than most of his age-mates on school entry, and his need for extra stimulation was nearly as great as Roy's. As has already been suggested, it is a fruitless exercise to try to assess the relative contributions of heredity and early environmental factors to a child's intellectual ability. Perhaps Robert had started with some favourable genetic endowment lacking in Roy; or perhaps the happier 'temper' of this whole family had made possible the extraction of maximum benefit from even limited opportunity. Whatever the reason might be, the extra opportunities offered to this boy seemed to accelerate his progress beyond what had been expected. (It is not possible to say what would have happened if the opportunities of school, and outings, had been less – perhaps he would still have done better than previous knowledge of the family suggested.)

When Robert was just over seven, and nearing the end of his Infants' school years, the family once more ran into financial muddles. Robert's mother was pregnant, and his father lost his evening job after a silly quarrel with a foreman. The rent was weeks in arrears, and once more Robert, (and the younger sister now in school), began to look ragged and dirty. As before, the family was supported by several agencies, including the school. Visiting the mother, the head teacher found the usual muddle and vagueness about what was owing, and to whom, and tried to help a now very distressed and tearful woman to sort things out. The Health Visitor assured her of a supply of essentials for the new baby, and reminded her that there would be a maternity grant to pay for more. The father was encouraged to seek another evening job, and reminded how well his children had done, and how generally successful his own previous efforts had been to keep his family 'on even keel'. It looked as though a sceptical housing committee might once more accept payment of arrears by instalments, and this cheerful, if not very adequate, family be put into a position where the children would at least have a chance to grow up less feckless than their parents.

During the summer holidays, however, the mother entered hospital to have her baby, some complications having developed, and the children were sent away by the Children's Officer for a seaside holiday. What happened to precipitate it remained obscure, but it was an undeniable fact that an eviction order was served on the father, and that his wife and new baby did not come home from the hospital but went straight into Part III accommodation, together with the two toddlers on the completion of their holiday. The five older children were taken into care, put into three separate homes,

211

and presumably attended different schools. No request for records was received from anyone by Robert's first school, and enquiries of the Children's Department elicited little information about the children's whereabouts, and none about the possible duration of the separation of the family. The staff of Robert's school were concerned and somewhat angered by the affair, for the family had been known to them for many years and its ups-and-downs followed with friendly, if sometimes exasperated, interest. In such a case, however, it is not possible for teachers to do more than re-establish contact with the family if it returns, and to give the children, under such circumstances, a sense of being welcome in their original school. Records, if asked-for by schools elsewhere, would obviously be of some help to teachers not knowing the family, and might make induction into 'new' schools easier than if nothing were known at all about the children's levels of performance and the family's characteristics.

The two children discussed above represent that surprisingly large proportion (for a prosperous and generally 'middle-class' neighbourhood) of children culturally deprived. Others, living under similar circumstances, also had few toys, poor linguistic experience, and the constant hand-to-mouth existence sketched in connection with Roy and Robert. Threats of eviction, or its actual happening, debt to tradesmen, desertion of the home by men simply unable to shoulder the responsibility of their families, and in one case desertion by the mother, occasional fights with the neighbours, and a total inability to manage (admittedly) meagre incomes and ordinary household tasks were the commonplaces of these parents' and children's lives. Yet, as the modest progress of Roy, and the more rapid and promising progress of Robert suggests, the Infants' school may have an important part to play in bringing the children of such families closer to the 'norms' of the majority. Whether the key factor is the practical help given with meals, health and clothing; or the imposition on previously undisciplined children of routine, and consistent rewards and sanctions; or attention to language; or the stimulus of materials; or the acceptance of the parents, 'with all faults', by the adults of another social class, is immaterial. It is highly probable, though incapable of proof, that the application, simultaneously, of all the above remedies would result in improvement

212

in school performance at the first stage – and increase the chances of success in the second, when children enter the Junior school or department. Such an 'attack on a wide front' might be particularly effective with younger members of the family, for the possibility of 'feed-back' into the family of attitudes, habits and skills learned by the first members of it to attend school should not be overlooked.

44. Kurt

A very fair, well-built, pleasant-looking boy, apparently of good intelligence, but speaking only German on school entry of the age of five. Father an Englishman, mother German, and the German grandmother also living with the family. Mother, a well-educated woman, spoke English moderately well when giving particulars of Kurt, but only German spoken at home, including by the boy's English father.

Kurt was a friendly child, and during his first few weeks in school seemed unworried by the language barrier between him and other children. He chatted away about what he was doing, and addressed his remarks to his teacher in German, apparently without noticing that she either misunderstood him, asked him to repeat himself, or (when she did understand), answered in English. He must have heard English spoken often enough in shops and by callers at the house, and the resemblance of some common words in the two languages was apparently of help to him. Yet he continued to use German almost exclusively, and became, after a few weeks, resentful of attempts to get him to make simple requests in English. On one occasion he threw a new and attractive book on the floor, apparently because it was not written in the language of his books at home – the first intimation his teacher had that Kurt, at barely five and a half, could read at least well enough to recognize the difference between some words in German and English.

Other differences between Kurt and his class-mates became noticeable as the first year in school passed. He was dressed very well, but in leather breeches and jackets, with shirts of an attractive but unusual kind in this country; and his winter outer clothes were of the kind worn by skiers, (much more commonly seen on small children in England now than they were at the time Kurt was in the Infants' school), which attracted the interest of other children. This attention was by no means unkind, but Kurt resented children examining his padded jacket, long trousers and 'tough' coloured-leather boots, and on one occasion 'swapped' his gaily-coloured woollen hat for a dull green school cap. In the spring, his class-mates being more observant than they had been six months previously, they commented on his new leather trousers, and caused him to shout rudely at them. Except for an occasional request in English, or a comment when listening to a story, (he seemed quite able to follow a simple narrative), he persisted in speaking German and refusing to try to read English words. He was inevitably becoming isolated from his class-mates, although he joined in games that involved a minimum of talking, such as chasing round the playground or climbing on the frame, and it was felt that the matter of his language difficulties should be discussed with his parents.

This was not a difficult matter, for both were interested in Kurt's education, although they came to school rarely. When the question of his continued use of German in school was raised the mother was somewhat defensive. She explained that she wanted him to retain the language and ways of her own family, and that his grandmother, who was very fond of him, treated him always as though he were German. It appeared that this elderly woman had not taken kindly to her daughter's marrying an Englishman, and was exerting a powerful influence over her to bring the grandson up in a positively non-English manner. Kurt's father was a little puzzled by the boy's resentment in school, and said that he had talked to him in English during the last few months – at least on occasions when doing so would not precipitate adverse comment from the grandmother. He was sure, as were the teachers, that Kurt understood almost everything said in English, and, like his wife, wanted the boy to be bi-lingual. They agreed to talk seriously to Kurt about accepting the necessity to speak English in school and German to his grandmother; and it was suggested that this be put to him as a matter of 'being kind' to people both in and out of his home.

The conflict this child faced between home and school was undeniable. It was slightly aggravated by such simple differences between his mother's way of doing housework and that of her English neighbours as her practice of throwing open the bedroom windows and hanging the bright red, down-filled quilts over the sills every morning. ('Kurt's mummy

214

hangs the beds out of the window!' said one child to the teacher, having observed them from the bus-stop.) She kept her house phenomenally clean, even by the exacting standards of a 'good' neighbourhood, and insisted that Kurt wear a smock if he did any painting or other 'dirty' work in the house or in school. Her cooking was well-known for its continental excellence and the unusual nature of the cakes and bread she baked – but, again, Kurt was slightly resentful of other children's comments when his mother brought some of her delightful cakes to school for a party or a sale-of-work. It seemed that the conflict would be long in resolving itself, and that this potentially very able little boy might not be able to take advantage of his own ability. The parents were probably aware of his difficulties, but somewhat hampered by their understandable reluctance to hurt the grandmother, who had no friends outside her family.

By the beginning of his second year in school, however, Kurt resolved some of the difficulties himself. He demanded, and was given, a school cap and blazer, of a kind worn by many children, although a uniform as such was not obligatory, and was very pleased with them. He announced, in English, that he had a new winter coat, also, adding, 'Like Gregory's. It's a duffle coat!' Shiny black wellington boots, although probably much less comfortable and attractive than his 'ski' boots of the previous winter, also seemed to give him great pleasure – and it is likely that the 'conforming' characteristic of five- to six-year-olds was of some significance in his exercise of choice now that he was older and more aware of standards outside the home. Following the request of his parents that he learn to read and write in English while at school – and a reminder that 'Daddy learned like that' – he began to co-operate with his teacher in reading simple primers, demonstrating, (as she had suspected), that he already recognized a great many words. Perhaps a tendency to identify with his father rather than with his mother and grandmother was reinforced simply by his being with other boys, and not so much at home. Or perhaps he would have made this 'transfer' regardless of school or outside experience. For whatever reason, he talked much more of his father than hitherto, and even joked kindly sometimes about his grandmother. By the time he was half-way through his second year in the Infants' school he was, as he had been on entry, a friendly and popular child. His parents visited the school more often in order to help the mother to understand its aims and scope. She had, of course, found English schools baffling, and it is very possible that some at least of Kurt's earlier refusal to have anything to do with 'English learning' stemmed from his mother's inevitable lack of knowledge of what was expected in school.

By a combination of friendly relations with the parents, some extra attention to Kurt's formal language skills, the child's own independence of mind in regard to what he wanted to wear, and unobtrusive restraint on other children's remarks about him in the early stages, it is likely that a fairly painless resolution of conflict was engendered. Had the parents been less willing to discuss his schooling, (or less intelligent), had his mother been as insistent as the grandmother on the boy's appearing very 'foreign', or had Kurt himself been less able, especially linguistically, there might have been a less successful outcome of his difficulties. There is some evidence that conflict between the language, manners, dress and domestic usage of home and the wider society can result in grave neurotic disturbance. This conflict sometimes arises from severe religious sanctions (see, for example, the case of James, p. 79), sometimes with mental illness of one or both parents, (as in Adrian's and Dennis's cases, pp. 86 and 81), and even more often with the deprivation of early experiences described in the cases of Roy and Robert.

The circumstances of Kurt's life were very far removed from any of these 'extreme' cases of conflicting mores, expectations and language – but there are elements of the same kind of difficulty when a child has to reconcile the behaviour however intrinsically sensible and sound, of his mother, with the rather different, and probably just as sensible and sound, behaviour of his teachers. It is not surprising that a young child, even of Kurt's stability and intelligence, sometimes casts in his lot with his mother (or father, as the case may be), and seems to reject the most reasonable demands of school. Fortunately, it is well within the professional skill of teachers to start on the task of building a bridge between the child's 'two worlds' before he is too bewildered, isolated or retarded for the task to have much hope of success. It is possible that had no one taken any interest in Kurt's difficulties, he might have resolved them spontaneously, since he was apparently a gifted child. But it would seem heartless, and a failure of ordinary teaching skills, to expect spontaneous resolution of such a problem; and there is always the possibility that a child who had become unpopular with classmates, and failed to learn to read, at the Infants' stage may have lost too much ground to make up in the Junior school.

Considerations

Some considerations of the plight of children from underprivileged homes of the poverty-stricken and/or feckless kind have already been made.[10] The school would seem to have a large responsibility for providing maximum opportunities, of all kinds, for such children, some such opportunities, perhaps, of an unorthodox kind. It is usually possible to 'bombard' children with language, even by getting the schoolkeeper, the cook, the welfare helper and the secretary to chat to a child like Roy on every possible occasion. It is not beyond the ingenuity of most head teachers to arrange for more secure children such as Robert to go on outings, perhaps with a Sunday school, or with other families, and thus extend the range of their experience. It is surely reasonable to expect a longer period of exploration and free play in school than is usually needed by more fortunate children, in order that some of the 'lost years', at least, may be compensated for; and the insistence on ordinary good manners, so effective in turning uncouth little boys like Brian and Roy into acceptable members of the group is not as superficial as it sounds. It is important for children from grossly underprivileged homes not to feel rejected as they move to other schools, and in groups outside the school – and the ability to handle cutlery properly, to eat quietly, to use grace-words, and to greet others with courtesy are among the most important of all the means of making a favourable first impression. No amount of complaint or reproof or chastisement is likely to turn a child like Roy into a pleasant, sensible and attractive person with whom to share a desk or a meal. Patient insistence on ordinary good manners, encouragement to 'look nice' and have clean hands and tidy hair, and praise for achievement of these modest skills, however, might conceivably start that upward spiral of improvement so noticeable in both Brian and Roy.

10 See 'Children and their Primary Schools', ch. 5.

It is not rational to expect a child from a very poor background to 'pick up' the manners and standards of others. A lot of previous learning is required before a child is even aware that there are standards other than his own; he has to be 'set' to pick up clues; to *own* a comb, soap and shoe-brush before he can be expected to use them – and so on. It might be argued that the Infants' school, hard-pressed for staff, often inadequately supplied with washing facilities, and given no allowance for toilet articles is not the place to do this most elementary training. Yet where else is there while parsimony in the provision of Nursery schools remains the policy of government after government? The alternative to some training of this kind is for teachers to put up with unprepossessing, often dirty, children, who are shunned by their fellows and no pleasure to anyone – least of all to themselves. It should not be overlooked, moreover, that using grace-words, feeling clean, smelling of soap, experiencing the comfort of smooth hair, and viewing the self dressed in 'new' clothes are among the sharpest stimuli to a sense of adequacy and heightened awareness of the senses. Many children left dirty, uncomfortable, chilly and unattractive to look at must have markedly blunted sensibilities by the time they reach school. It is surely among the legitimate aims of education to re-awaken awareness at all levels – and if the starting-point is at the child's body-awareness the teacher gains nothing by ignoring this need. Clothes and lightweight foot-wear, (heavier cast-off shoes were not thought to be suitable for transfer to another child), were collected in the school on which this study is based from parents who were willing to help less privileged children than their own. Many of them noticed a poorly-clad child as they brought their own child to school, and in many cases went immediately to their homes to fetch sound but outgrown clothes for such a child. The cupboard was never empty; and some of the proceeds of sales of work was spent on articles such as combs and brushes which were not supplied by willing and generous parents.

The ethical question of how far such provision encourages fecklessness has already been discussed; the only criterion that can be applied, in the writer's view, is the well-being of the children who are in such need. Some means of dealing with feckless parents, in a non-punitive and totally unpatronizing way, can usually be devised. But the ragged, dirty, cold or hungry child is not a weapon one can legitimately use against even the most inadequate and stupid mother; she has allowed him to be in this state, and is hardly likely to be able to change her ways after harsh verbal stricture. Were this true, such children as Roy and Robert would no longer exist as a problem in our schools.

It is, at the moment, an academic question, but it is possible that a special 'enrichment programme' in Nursery school from the age of (say) three would render unnecessary many of the courses that have been suggested as necessary in the Infants' school. Hunt surveys the most modern findings in regard to the development of intelligence, including the enormous contribution of Piaget. He reviews also the major contribution of Hebb to our understanding of intelligence as being associated in some way with variegation and mobility of cell assemblies in parts of the brain not concerned with 'reception' of information from eyes, ears, skin, etc. or with motor responses. Hebb's work led to demonstrations that intelligence is closely associated with *experience*, and that adult intelligence appears to be partly, at least, a function of 'strategies' (similar to computer programmes) which are, as it were, available in the brain for the 'processing' of new experience and the solution of new problems. It begins to look as if these 'stored strategies' arise in the first instance from a rich perceptual experience in early childhood – although proof of this hypothesis is not likely to be forthcoming without a wide application of 'rich' environments for many thousands of children.[11]

'The discovery of ways to govern the encounters children have with their environments for this purpose (i.e. to maximise each child's potential for intellectual development) would require a great deal of expensive and difficult investigation of the effect of various kinds of early experience on later intellectual capacity at the higher levels.'[12]

There is, however, suggestive evidence already from the studies made of children relatively unstimulated in impersonal institutions for the first months or years of their lives;[13] and more from studies of very retarded children 'exposed' to

[11] R. McV. Hunt 'Intelligence and Experience' pp. 352-359.
[12] Ibid. p. 363.
[13] Dennis, W. quoted by Hunt; also Ainsworth, Bowlby, Lewis and Wilkins – refs. at end of chapter.

Nursery school experience, and showing marked acceleration of intellectual development in 70 per cent of cases, when compared with similar groups not so 'exposed'[14], to encourage teachers to give culturally deprived children more, not fewer, opportunities than their more fortunate age-mates. Even if scientific proof of the value of 'enrichment programmes' is not forthcoming, commonsense and ordinary humanity suggest that increasing a child's ability by giving him intensive sensory, linguistic and social experiences is at least a possibility that must not be ignored.

Suggestions for Further Reading
I. *Social Class and some of its implications for the teacher:*
C.A.C.E. *Children and their Primary Schools* (ch. 5) H.M.S.O.
Douglas. J. W. B. *The Home and the School* Macgibbon & Kee (1964)
Floud, J. E. Halsey, A. H. & Martin, F. M. *Social Class and Educational Opportunity* Heinemann (1957)
Jackson, B. and Marsden, D. *Education and the Working Class* Routledge & Kegan Paul (1962)
Lovell, K. and Woolsey, M. E. *Reading Disability, Non-Verbal Reasoning and Social Class* Educational Research Vol. VI, No. 3 (1964)
Newson, J. & E. *Patterns of Infant Care in an Urban Community* Penguin Books (1965)
Willmot, P. and Young, M. *Family and Kinship in East London* (1957) Penguin Books (1962)
Willmot, P. and Young, M. *Family and Class in a London Suburb* Routledge & Kegan Paul (1960)
Women's Group on Public Welfare *The Neglected Child and His Family* Oxford U.P. (1948)

2. *Parental Deprivation:*
Ainsworth, M. *Deprivation of Maternal Care* W.H.O. Public Health Papers No. 14 (1962)
Bowlby, J. *Maternal Care and Mental Health* W.H.O. Monograph 2nd Ed. (1952)
Lewis, H. *Deprived Children* Oxford U.P. (1954)

[14] S. A. Kirk (1958) quoted by Hunt, *'Intelligence and Experience'*, pp. 333-335.

Wilkins, L. T. *Delinquent Generations* H.M.S.O. (1961)
Wynn, W. *Fatherless Families* Michael Joseph (1964)
(See also article in '*British Journal of Criminology*' Vol. 3, No. 4 by A. A. Walters challenging Wilkins' hypothesis).

Later evidence of adverse effects of early deprivation of stimulus, often arising from maternal deprivation, is discussed by R. McV. Hunt in '*Intelligence and Experience*' – references to work of Dennis, W. being particularly relevant.

3. *Immigration:*

C.A.C.E. (Plowden Report) *Children and their Primary Schools* (ch. 6) H.M.S.O.
Yudkin, S. *The Health & Welfare of the Immigrant Child*

Chapter 13

School, Parents and Other Agencies

It would be unwise and unscientific in the extreme to assume direct casual connections between children's early experience and their later behaviour, or between remedial action taken in school and the disappearance of adverse symptoms. The truth is that in none of the 'cases' discussed in foregoing chapters is it possible to demonstrate that this or that course of action led to this or that outcome. It is within the bounds of possibility that without any remedial action being taken some, or all, of the children discussed would have resolved their difficulties spontaneously. The experiment has not yet been devised – and would probably be regarded by most teachers as highly unethical if it were – that applies two or three different 'remedies' to the same or to genetically identical, children. Until or unless it is, the contention that one course of action is better, wiser or more useful than another remains very largely a matter of faith. Brian might have stopped pilfering had he been smacked harder and more often; Eleanor might have 'grown out of' having nightmares without the help of a psychotherapist; Billy might, after all, have coped with the demands of the Junior school. The reader who makes such contentions has every right to do so – but is under the same necessity as the writer to acknowledge that these contentions, also, are incapable of proof.

Common-sense, and what evidence there is from the experience of teachers in 'progressive' schools, from psychotherapy, and from the behavioural sciences, suggests that some approaches to children in difficulties, and some courses of action in regard to organization in school seem more fruitful, in terms of improved behaviour and performance in 'school' skills, than others. Some of these can, perhaps, be summarized here as an indication of what have already been called *principles of approach* to children with special needs. So long as it is remembered that for such principles no scientific validation is possible, and that they are intended for discussion and consideration rather than for 'wholesale' application, they may be useful.

School

It has already been stated at some length that no extra-ordinary organization, or very unorthodox timetabling or other circumstances, were characteristic of the school from which the foregoing 'cases' were selected for discussion. The belief that children are more important than timetables, and that routine, while of great importance, should be planned initially with children's *normal* needs in mind is axiomatic in most Infants' and an increasing number of Junior schools. Flexibility in regard to children's disposal of their time makes it possible for children not yet able to cope with the normal demands made on more fortunate or more stable class-mates to be allowed active, outdoor play while others read, write and engage themselves in the mathematical and scien-tific discovery and experiment that is such a feature of most Infants' schools. It is true that this course to help children like Paul, Sean, Padraic or Bobby involves a 'safe' playing-space, under the eye of a teacher or welfare assistant; but the teacher does not necessarily have to be the child's own, the schoolkeeper can sometimes play a very important rôle here, and the head teacher can often keep an eye on outdoor play while the class-teacher copes with the rest of the class. There is sometimes a corridor, or small hall, or even empty class-room which is 'safe' and within viewing and hearing distance of head or class-teacher where children still in need of 'nursery' play may be allowed to have some time each day. Often the organization of the Reception class makes such allowance possible within or just outside the reception classroom itself. As the practice of employing welfare assistants spreads, and if the attachment of nursery nurses to Infants' schools becomes widely practised, the normal 'flow' of children between class-room and outdoor playing space will be even more possible. Children from more privileged homes will not need to 'grow through' the experiences with other children, and with exercise of large motor skills, so needed by some others – indeed, they may even be bored by continuance of such opportunities and routines as they experienced in their Nursery schools, play-groups or own homes.[1] Yet there are many children, as the

[1] R. McV. Hunt, '*Intelligence and Experience*', p. 279.

foregoing chapters have shown, who are simply not ready for the work so eagerly undertaken by the more privileged. There are children whose 'encounters with experience' have been so minimal, whether from disturbance at a personal-emotional level, or from cultural or physical handicap, that they still need the time in which to develop skills normally achieved much earlier. Flexibility in regard to time is of great use here.

Nevertheless, as has already been intimated, a routine is also valuable for children with any of the difficulties mentioned above. That this need not preclude flexibility is demonstrated by the organization of the Nursery school day. The regular recurrence of 'milk time', mealtime and story-time gives to a child like Tim a sense of security, of the adult being in charge; to a child like Roy it provides, perhaps, his first lesson in orderliness and method. Children soon look for these recurrent events, and are rarely pleased about a break in this basic routine. At the same time, it should be remembered that there is nothing sacred about a particular event in relation to a particular child on a particular day. If Bobby could not settle to listen to a story, as was often the case early in his school career, he was allowed to continue his other occupation. The sanction that other children, who do want to listen, should not be disturbed, is one that should, however, be laid down and, if necessary enforced. Sometimes, a child did not want to drink his milk, or eat his dinner – and again, there was no exaggerated pressure on him to do so. He was required however, to leave other children to behave sensibly and as they wished, on these occasions. A tussle with a child over such matters as listening to a story, drinking his milk or eating his dinner not only disrupts the occasion for other children – it breaks the very routine the teacher in such case is ostensibly trying to maintain.

Thoughtful attention to the real needs for learning of normal and less fortunate children, which will include the organizing of the school day in such a manner as seems most helpful in a particular school, is an important matter. So is generous provision of opportunity, and allowing every child to take advantage of it. The theme of Hunt's book, 'Intelligence and Experience', from which much has been quoted, is that to 'maximise' a child's intellectual potential, schools need to provide situations, materials, tools and language-opportunities in abundance. Piaget's work has demonstrated

224

clearly how valuable is early sensory experience, and the attachment of 'names' to 'things' (and, later, to phenomena) in active encounter with as many experiences as possible. The dictum of Froebel that the child will, through play, effect his own growth in every direction open to him receives massive support from the work of modern investigators into learning processes. The child with emotional difficulties can use materials for another, and very necessary, sort of learning, as seems indicated by Padraic's play with the 'small world' toys, Sean's with the dolls and Teddy-bears, Paul's with paint and Martin's with a football. Whether they 'play out' fears, express longings, or develop a sense of adequacy in their play it is surely sensible to assume (even if not demonstrable) that generous provision of materials and a generous view of the uses to which they may be put, short of destruction, is a help to children's learning at all levels.

As children grow older and more skilled, especially for those without special difficulties or needs, the provision will change. More and more books, scientific and mathematical apparatus, writing materials, tools and sophisticated media for the visual and plastic arts will take the place of trains, dolls and trucks. But no child should be forbidden the use of 'younger' materials because he is seven; and no five-year-old denied the use of reference books or experiments with the apparatus in the 'top' class because he is too young. Throughout the Infants' school such materials as wet and dry sand, clay, water, clothes in which to dress up and small toys which represent the 'real world' in miniature should be available, as should many books and all the materials which make graphic representation of the world – whether in writing or drawing or painting – possible. The use to which such 'basic' materials are put will vary enormously according to the age and need of the child using them. A disturbed child like Sean may use the 'dressing-up' clothes to practise some rôle unguessed-at by the watching adult; seven-year-olds with no emotional difficulties may well use the same clothes in presenting one of their spontaneous, if highly derivative, plays for which they have written the script. Whereas Padraic used small model animals and tiny dolls to express (as it seemed) some considerable aggressive feelings, a 'bright' and well-adjusted child in the same class used them to furnish the elaborate and patiently constructed model town that took him three days to make from cardboard waste. It would seem unwise for teachers to set limits on the type and kind of materials they provide, on the age or 'kind' of child who may play with them, or on the kinds of uses (always within limits of safety and respect for the materials) to which they may be put. Materials may have a cathartic function to fulfil for children with special needs – but this is not a matter for the teacher's interpretations. The same materials may well have an educative function, in an intellectual sense, for the same children, as well as for those who appear to have no special needs. The provision of varied, plentiful and easily available materials certainly seemed to be a help to teachers dealing with the children discussed in previous chapters.

While flexibility and routine, in a nice balance, and the provision of maximum opportunity of all kinds are obvious aids to peaceful, busy work in the Infants' school, and while the introduction of a 'fluid day' certainly makes teaching a more purposeful, if very exacting, matter for most teachers prepared to give it a trial, there may be a case sometimes for special organization for very difficult children. The policy of withdrawing a child who is being a great nuisance to his fellows in the classroom, in order that he may work in peace in the head teacher's room, has been discussed in regard to Jimmy, Greg and Ingrid. It was used for other children, also, and found effective from several points of view. It is important, however, that any such 'work alone' sanction shall be applied in a non-punitive manner, and used to the constructive ends that the 'offender' derives satisfaction from the work he is thus enabled to complete, and enjoys personal relationship with an adult. To banish a child from his classroom for a 'punishment' session with the head teacher would seem to be a miserable experience for them both, and hardly consonant with a head teacher's function as the person ultimately responsible for relationships in the school. The danger that the child may view the class-teacher as too 'weak' to control him is very largely obviated if the non-punitive course is taken, and the situation demonstrated to the child as being one which *primarily* protects his classmates from interference and allows him to derive satisfaction from work of the kind they are pursuing. If the 'treatment' is sensibly applied such a child as Jimmy is more likely to see the two adults concerned as being united and equal partners than as stronger and weaker members of a hierarchy – which, in any case, should not be true of the staff relations in an Infants' school.

Only in certain circumstances, and then with reservations, would most teachers feel that a 'special' class was permissible, or even possible, in an Infants' school. For two years there was a 'small class' in the school under discussion, into which some very disturbed children – almost all boys – could be placed. Its organization was even more 'fluid' than in the normal Reception class, and it resembled a Nursery school in its routine and equipment. It was started because there were, at the time, a number of very difficult children in the school, and the work of several classes was being gravely disrupted by them. This high incidence of disruptive children seemed to be coincidental, but when the class was set up to receive them many requests were received from other head teachers, from the Nursery school and from the D.E.O., as well as from the psyhiatric unit referred to in connection with Tim, to take children who were proving too disruptive in other situations, or who needed a 'bridge' between one type of school and another. For this reason the class was about twenty in number for two years. There is no doubt that there were some advantages in this venture. The teacher was able to concentrate on the elementary social training some children had never had; she had time to deal placidly with Tim, and to give Branwell opportunities he could hardly have had in a normal class, and of which he was patently in need. For such boys as Sean and Padriac, as well as the grossly deprived George, relationship with a teacher over a prolonged period was probably a valuable experience which they could not have had in a larger class.

Such provision, however, may well have drawbacks. It is arguable that children already deviant in behaviour, or retarded in learning, or both, would be better able to approximate to the 'norm' if they were in contact with ordinary children who had no such handicaps. In contact all day with children as disturbed as themselves, might they not become worse instead of better? There was, in fact, no evidence of this – rather the reverse – but the experience of only two years and a total, in that time, of twenty-eight children, some of whom stayed only a term in the class, is not evidence from which it would be safe to draw conclusions, and it must be left to the discretion, and opportunities, of individual head teachers to decide the merits or otherwise of such provision.

Parents may be perturbed at the placing of their children in what appears to be a rather unusual class, although the particular class under discussion aroused little comment, since it was very similar to the Reception class. Only the presence of older children made some parents uneasy, and understandably enough. Explanations about Tim, Branwell and Roderick could not be made without breach of confidence, and they certainly appeared 'odd' compared with other children. On the whole, however, parents were appreciative rather than otherwise of the provision for children with special needs – as, for example, Bobby, whose mother realized that his early admission to school was made possible because there was a small class in which to put him. Padraic's mother was also glad of the chance her son had, in a small group, to come to terms with some of his difficulties.

The matter of a teacher's qualifications for dealing with a group of children with such needs as those described is one which merits careful consideration if a 'special' class is to be set up. It is true that many teachers are now able to take advantage of courses at university Institutes of Education, and thereafter specialize in the teaching of backward or maladjusted children. It has been the intention of this book, however, to describe a situation in a normal school, *in which no member of staff had specialist qualifications*. The teacher of the small class had had many years of experience in the Infants' school, and had brought up a large family of her own. She was a person of considerable stability and warmth, and these qualities, rather than specialized knowledge of disturbed children, must have been responsible for the success she had with a very difficult group. It would probably be unwise, even dangerous from the point of view of the teacher's own emotional stability, to expect a young, inexperienced or less stable person to cope with a special class of any kind. In the absence of specialist help, or of a teacher both stable and experienced, it would seem most inadvisable to attempt the setting-up of such a class, even if there were room for it, and enough children to form it.

The Parents
The attitude of the school to the parents has already been discussed in the first chapter, and the importance of good relations between a child's parents and his teachers reiterated

228

in Chapter 12. It is, perhaps, easier for teachers in Nursery and Infants' schools to build and maintain helpful relationships with parents than it is for teachers of older children – but it is probably possible to bridge the gap between home and school more effectively than has sometimes been the case, even when children are in the secondary schools. The means of forming good and helpful relations are not, as a rule, difficult or complicated. The willingness of a head to talk to parents without their having made a prior appointment is – despite its occasional inconvenience – common practice in Nursery and most Infants' schools. Informal discussion groups for parents, especially when some new venture is to be made in the school, are among the most fruitful means of drawing not only mothers but also fathers, and even aunts and grandparents, into the child's life at school. The more formal 'open day', although giving an opportunity for children to display work and, under some circumstances, to show parents round the school, probably offers less opportunity than does the informal evening discussion group for teachers to talk to parents easily. Occasional entertainments, although the effect on the children can sometimes be deplorable, certainly draw into a school many parents who would otherwise be too ill-at-ease or even indifferent to visit. All these means are simple, and all were customary in the school from which the 'cases' have been drawn. They combined to give parents in the neighbourhood the impression that the school was 'easy' to visit, and therefore made it more likely that a parent worried about a child would call and discuss him.[2]

No matter how many opportunities are given, however, there are bound to be some parents – and in some areas the majority – who will never visit their child's school. Uneasiness in the face of people viewed as 'authority', memories of forbidding teachers of their own schooldays, erroneous ideas about the school and its staff gathered from gossip, or even slight shame at their lack of knowledge, may singly or in combination make a barrier that the parents cannot surmount. In such cases the onus is on the teachers to take the first steps, if they believe that it is in the best interests of children for home and school

[2] See 'Children and their Primary Schools' ch. 4, which gives considerable weight to the argument that parent-teacher relations are crucial to learning-success.

to have some common ground. (If there are Infants' teachers who do not believe this, it is unlikely that the principles of approach here suggested will be of use, in any case.) As has been described, visits to the homes of some children can be a grim experience – but after such a visit a teacher has some evidence on which to judge a child's possible needs, if nothing else. At best, as in the case of Robert, visits to the home may be a means of keeping not only a particular child but a whole family in touch with agencies able to help them. To take tea with a woman whose husband has left her with the burden of small children to care for on a very limited income is to give her opportunity of discussing her own as well as the children's difficulties – to the ultimate benefit of the children. After a visit from class-teacher or head even parents previously unwilling to visit the school seemed able to do so; perhaps they felt that having seen the person in their own kitchen they could greet her as familiar in the 'unknown' world of school.[s]

Whether the parents come to the school or whether the teachers visit the homes, it is certainly easier for people who know each other, even on an undemanding and professional level, to discuss problems of a really difficult nature if these arise. It is possible that due to the extreme compression of material in the foregoing chapters the reader may be left with the impression that a considerable amount of 'probing' for information took place. *This was certainly not the case.* In every instance, the confidence of parents was given spontaneously, often over a long period to the head teacher or to the school doctor in the presence of both the school nurse and the head teacher. In almost every case such confidences were given in response to straightforward and ordinary questions about a child's interests or health or past illnesses. What is probably significant is that normally friendly relations, established by means already outlined, already existed between these parents and the school.

Troubles of a non-educational nature, and sometimes having nothing directly to do with a child, were occasionally brought to the school by a parent worried about finances, housing or marital troubles. Again, this may have been due to the fact that previous good relations existed, and that the head teacher of a school is the 'nearest' professional help available – and,

[s] *'Children and their Primary Schools'* ch. 4 esp. paragraph 113.

moreover, is not likely to apply what is still seen by some as a Means Test, or to dispense charity with conditions. As will be mentioned later, teachers are often in a better position than the less well-informed and less efficient parents to deal with some agencies, advise on the filling-in of forms, or indicate to an unknowledgeable parent a simple course of action in regard to some practical difficulty. Not even in visits to the homes of such parents, however, was it necessary (even if it was permissible) to 'probe' for information.

There were a few occasions on which contact with the parents was not made on the basis of previous, normally friendly relations, nor on the basis of practical worries and needs, but in response to personal needs of the parent. Such cases as Gareth's and Paul's are illustrations of the kind of demand that may suddenly be made on a head teacher. There can be no general principles of approach laid down for such contacts. Every such incident has to be dealt with as the good sense of the teacher suggests may be most helpful, and as the apparent need of the moment dictates. A lack of commitment to *definite* courses of action at the time of the first 'outburst', allied with ordinary sympathy, seems the most reasonable course for teachers to take in such cases. In every case of confidence given to head or class-teacher it is important for the listener to convey, by whatever means seem suitable, courteous and understandable to the parent, that the confidences are not, at any future time, going to be 'held against' the confider. There are few people with whom most of us feel, subsequently, so ill-at-ease as those to whom, in an unguarded or stressful movement, we have made confidences of an intimate nature. To confide is to give the confidant hostages; it is necessary for teachers, in particular, to convey that these are not going to be used except with the permission of the confider and to the good of parent and child.

Finally, it must be remembered that as this book is about children with special needs, so it necessarily deals in many cases with parents in special need. A sense of proportion needs to be kept. Only a small percentage of all the parents of all the children passing through the school in the years of the study, expected, or needed, teachers to be advisers or confessors. Most were on normally friendly terms, chatting easily to their child's class-teacher and to the head, visiting the school for 'special' occasions, supporting it in its aims, and giving most generous help towards parties, extra facilities and children of parents less well-off or fortunate than themselves. Discussion groups, or talks about new innovations, could be expected to be attended by up to 90 per cent of the parents, and never less than 50 per cent. It is true that in some neighbourhoods the task of thus integrating the school into the life and interests of the community at large is much more difficult than in others. Yet, as efforts in some very 'difficult' areas have shown, the attempt is well worthwhile in educational as well as personal terms, and is to the ultimate benefit of the children.

Other Agencies

In many of the 'cases' discussed in this work it must be apparent to the reader that teachers would have been unable to help children without the co-operation, support and treatment of various kinds administered by agencies on the fringe of, or right outside, the educational system. The work of the Health Visitor, who is also the school nurse, has already been mentioned, and attention drawn to the recommendations of the Underwood Report (p. 28). It is impossible to imagine how teachers, however well-intentioned, could have known what the Health Visitor, legitimately, knew about such families as Mary's, for example; or how they could have gained access to some homes at all. Since the Health Visitor has been, for most mothers, a familiar figure since the first pregnancy and birth, she is more likely to be trusted than the 'stranger' at school, who is not met until the oldest child is five. Yet, after the children are at school, the Health Visitor must hand over the responsibility for the well-being of her most 'difficult' families to the school – at least, in large measure. It is at this point, usually during routine school medical examination, that *explicit* good relations between school nurse and head teacher can convey to a mother that, if she wishes, she may now rely on the head as she may have done on the nurse. The importance of good relations between these two has already been stressed, and cannot be too firmly reiterated. In the same way, the school doctor, who may have been previously known to the mother at the clinic, is now seen in the context of school, often a familiar face, and seemingly as 'at home' there as he seemed in the clinic. Even if he is new to the mother, the fact

232

that he apparently knows and trusts the school nurse, makes him seem less of a stranger than he might otherwise do. That all these people, previously known or not, take an equal interest in her child, and manifestly 'get on' with each other, can be immensely comforting to some mothers. Any professional rivalries there may be between doctor, nurse and teacher, any reluctance to pool medical, social and educational information in regard to a child are much to be deplored. Such attitudes are not in the best interests of children in school – and it is with these that all three are primarily concerned.

The Child Guidance service has been frequently mentioned. It is perhaps one of the most imaginative provisions any country has ever made for its children, and a third of the children discussed in this book were treated by psychotherapy. Whether one accepts the validity of psychoanalytic theory or not, it is indisputable that in many cases, of which Bobby, Arthur and Eleanor are only three, children were greatly improved in adjustment, ability to work, and in apparent happiness after treatment at the Child Guidance clinic. It would seem a pointless argument that they might have made spontaneous recovery; so they might, and, as has been said previously, there is no proof one way or the other. It is true, also, that in cases like that of James and Ingrid improvement of behaviour or attitude seemed slow; and in the case of Sean the release apparently given by clinic personnel to this inhibited little boy may have been a factor in his ultimate rejection by his foster-mother. Nevertheless, it would be an arbitrary and bigoted teacher indeed who would not use the Child Guidance service in an attempt to help children so deviant as some of those described in previous chapters, and with whom other courses of action seemed unsuccessful.

Not only the children, however, but many a harassed mother can be helped by the visits of a psychiatric social worker, whose job (for which she has the training few head teachers can have had), is to elicit the facts of a child's previous history, the problems of the family, and the needs of the parents as well as of the child. In the case of Jonathan's mother such help was not available – and it is a matter of speculation only as to whether such help would have averted the tragedy of her suicide or not. While there is even the

233

slight chance of such skilled help being efficacious, however, it is surely part of a school's responsibility to obtain it if this is possible.

As in the case of school medical services and the nursing service, there has sometimes been more of a gulf between the schools, psychological services and the schools themselves than is professionally acceptable or in the best interests of children and their parents. In several previous chapters the matter of the interdependence of teacher and therapist, teacher and doctor, teacher and nurse has been stressed. Perhaps misunderstanding about each other's aims and limits has, in the past, made co-operation difficult. There would seem no need, now, however, for such misunderstandings to continue. It is possible to gain insight into the work of other disciplines through reading as well as through direct contact – and there seems no reason why co-operation should not be initiated by the schools if, for any reason, it did not previously exist.

The educational psychologist, as another part of the schools' psychological service, may be consulted without reference to the child's parents if this seems necessary. There are some cases where expert administration of intelligence tests, application of social maturity scales and/or assessment of reading difficulties are best left to the psychologist. Amanda's case is an example of the kind that is very usefully 'handed over'; and children like Roy, about whom there may be uncertainty as to the need for special schooling, can often be helped by early diagnosis of learning difficulty. As far as possible parents should be asked about this step, and given what information is considered wise and helpful after the child has been seen by the psychologist. There is considerable confusion in the minds of some people between the functions of psychologist and psychiatrist, and as full information as possible about the work of both is a help to parents. Nevertheless, it is allowable, if no co-operation with the parent is possible for any reason, for teachers to take the professional advice of the educational psychologist in regard to a child's *learning* difficulties without the prior consent of the parent – and it may be that this somewhat regrettable step is occasionally necessary.

The Children's Department of the local authority is another agency easily accessible to teachers. Many children in the school under discussion were in the care of the local authority, and contact with the Children's Officer was essential to children's effective learning. The cases of George and Gavin are only two of many in this school. It is true that contact with the Children's Officer ultimately responsible for the latter was not as satisfactory as might have been hoped – probably because another authority was involved, and previous contacts had not been made as they had been with local officers. As with nurses, doctors and Child Guidance personnel, however, as much co-operation as possible between those responsible, in law, for the child, and his school is in the child's best interests. It is not necessary for teachers to know every detail of the circumstances which bring a child into the care of a local authority. On the other hand, a teacher who is completely ignorant of, for example, the background of children such as George, Sean or Gavin might unwittingly hurt the child very deeply. It is dreadful to contemplate the effect of quite normal comments about 'taking it home to show mummy' on George, for example; or the well-meant question about 'your daddy having one of those' on Tim.

In connection with families such as Tessie's and Martin's, Robert's or Roy's the Children's Department has useful work to do. Sending the children on holiday, providing some essential items of clothing, supporting the deserted mother with advice and, often, practical help are all functions of that department. Such work, while not directly the concern of the teacher, can be both forwarded by her and followed-up in school. The provision of free meals, for example, can often be initiated from the school; and thereafter teachers can find simple, and tactful, means of making this provision unnoticeable to other children. In other cases, such as those of fostering and adoption, it is the responsibility of the teacher to ensure that distress and embarrassment are not caused to either child or parents by tactless questions or too-free comment. The information supplied by the Children's Officer can often prevent both.

Beyond the agencies which are officially 'linked' to the educational service are those of social welfare in general. As has been seen in the case of Grenville even the police can play a part; and their common function of calling at schools to give road-safety talks, talks about their work, and even advice in regard to the parking of cars or burglar-proof devices, can bring the local policemen into warm and valuable contact with both teachers and young children. In the case of a child with a violent father, not discussed in this book, the help of the police was invaluable in restraining him from doing further harm to a child. On another occasion in the years of this study the police escorted groups of children home after the escape from a local mental hospital of a patient believed to be dangerous. It was sometimes policewomen, too, who called at the school to take children to neighbours or relatives on the several occasions when parental accident or sudden illness made it impossible for them to return home. The once-terrifying image of the police can be erased by the sort of contacts mentioned in connection with road-safety talks, thus making their help in emergency more acceptable and friendly-seeming to a child.

There were a few occasions on which the help of the N.S.P.C.C. was enlisted to deal with suspected neglect or cruelty which had proved intractable to Health Visitor, Children's Officer and the school staff. Relations with the local inspector, (still called 'the cruelty man' by some parents), were friendly and at no point in the relevant years were court actions against parents initiated by the school, even when information was given to the inspector by the head teacher. A visit to the home by the uniformed inspector was, as it happens, all that was necessary in these few cases to bring about an improvement in unpleasant situations. Although it may be thought undesirable for teachers to initiate 'cruelty' actions there is no doubt that in some cases this may be a course preferable to allowing prolonged suffering of the child. The tact and training, as well as the experience of inspectors of the N.S.P.C.C., are always at the disposal of teachers perturbed by apparent evidence of neglect and ill-treatment; and whereas neighbours will often inform teachers of such cases, they are less likely to inform the inspector. It must, of course, be left to the sense and judgement of individual teachers to call in the N.S.P.C.C., but a talk with the local inspector does not commit the school to anything; and the advice of an official more experienced in such cases than is the average teacher can be very valuable. There are enough cases reported in the press, not to mention the numbers there must be that are not reported, to suggest to teachers that strong measures are needed to protect some children from their own parents. As we said at the beginning of this book, all children sooner or later go to school; schools must therefore expect, much as it is to be deplored, that now and again one of these many 'cruelty cases' will be found in their classrooms. If no other means has previously been found to deal with cruelty and ill-usage it may be that a head teacher is well-advised to make use of the services of the N.S.P.C.C.

A Divisional Welfare Officer able to cope with some of the problems presented to a family by an elderly relative; a Probation Officer ready to discuss the implications for the family of a delinquent father or older brother; a National Assistance Board official willing to listen to the case put by the head teacher for a mother too distressed or ignorant to put it for herself; members of the local council prepared to reconsider an eviction order; and local priests, vicars and pastors offering various kinds of support – to all these, by reason of appeal from their teachers, children owed some improvement in conditions which, in turn, could not but improve their chances of effective learning. Teachers are in a favoured position to make contact with all such agencies. They know the families, they are literate, familiar with the range of social services, and talk to workers in other services as to equals. It is not so easy for some parents to enlist the most appropriate help; often they do not even know that they are entitled to some forms of assistance and guidance. When dealing with 'officials' they can be tongue-tied, apparently truculent or seem more stupid than they are. If the school is on good terms with such parents teachers are in a strong position to help. Even well-educated and normally capable parents can be so upset by events, or so unfamiliar with social services, having not previously required to use them, that they are more in need of timely advice than might appear. So long as the need is expressed spontaneously to the teacher the advice will be welcome.

When the need is denied or concealed the only criterion a teacher can apply is the well-being of the child. If, by the normal, friendly means indicated at the beginning of this chapter, or by any other acceptable one that occurs to her, she can make contact with the parent, in the hope that the latter will acknowledge a need, it is surely her responsibility to do so. If all attempts fail, and the child seems ill, neglected, or abused in any way the Health Visitor may be able to help; or, failing this, the other agencies mentioned. Certainly, there are enough, and varied, ways to help children overcome the adverse circumstances of their lives if the schools, *which are the common ground of all children*, are prepared to call them into action. Having done so, and in as professional manner as possible, there remains the professional requirement to co-operate generously with other 'experts' for the good of the child.

Suggestions for Further Reading

C.A.C.E. (Plowden Report) *Children and their Primary Schools* ch. 4 *'Participation by Parents'* H.M.S.O. (1967)

Bradburn, E. *Friendliness in Schools* Educational Review Vol. XII p. 112

Mays, J. B. *Education and the Urban Child* Liverpool U.P. (1962)

Ministry of Education *The Health of the Schoolchild* H.M.S.O. (1960)

Parents and the Primary School: A Survey of Parental Opinion (by a Primary School Headmaster) Educational Research Vol. VII No. 3 (1965)

Chapter 14

Final Considerations

The theme of this book has been that of ordinary teachers dealing day by day, and largely in their own classrooms and about their own school with difficult children. At risk of being repetitive it must be stressed that these teachers managed to teach full classes of 'normal' children at the same time, and were not specialist teachers in any of the recognized categories. Both head and staff realized that, despite all their efforts, they failed with some children – and had to accept this as they accepted success, without *undue* feelings of a personal nature. To feel that one is a failure, that one has 'lost face' by having failed to effect much improvement in a particular child, to be unable to accept advice and help from others, and to be affronted by the failure of a child to respond to one's over-tures are alike useless and energy-sapping reactions. When relationships within a school are spontaneous and warm in quality, where a head teacher is both supportive and able to acknowledge that she is not always right, where teaching skills are conscientiously forwarded by discussion, reading and being open-minded to new findings and methods, and where the help of those other agencies previously mentioned can be appropriately sought and generously accepted – there disappointment and difficulties can be most readily borne and, in many cases, avoided and overcome eventually.

Despite the number of children who were helped by the skill of the Child Guidance team there were at least two-thirds of children with special needs for whom such help was not, for one reason and another, obtained or obtainable. For the majority of the children discussed in this book, and for nearly sixty of the eighty of whose difficulties they are representative, it was the teachers' skills that were paramount in effecting improvement at best, or at least in preventing deterioration. Something has been said in the previous chapter, and many references made throughout the work, to the sort of skills involved: generous and appropriate provision; systematic teaching of language and number skills in order to give children a sense of adequacy; orderly classrooms, and flexible timetables; good record-keeping; consistency of behaviour; a lack of haste; and ability to question cherished educational habits, for example. Without such skills a teacher is unlikely to have a great deal of educational success with 'normal' children of good intelligence, much less with 'problem' children of any kind. Yet none of these skills are beyond the ordinary teacher, and are, indeed, the matter of much of her college course. It would be a sad, and certainly unintended, outcome if teachers felt, after reading this book, that they were unable to deal with children in special need as they have been dealth-with in this particular school. Certainly, a high degree of insight into the needs for growth of all children is an essential ingredient in most of the 'cases' discussed. But this came by way of that spontaneity of feeling, exercise of the teaching skills outlined above, and readiness to discuss, read and listen in the staffroom, rather than by way of special instruction. Indeed, it is difficult to think of any kind of instruction that *can* give insight, for it has a lot to do with empathy, as well as with experience and personal maturity, and in these sheer knowledge, although important, has a relatively minor part.

It is hoped that it will have been apparent from the cases discussed, and the manner of discussion, that no special access to medical records, or any highly specialized knowledge of psychiatric or other non-teaching disciplines, is necessary to good relations with doctors and others, or to intelligent appreciation of the kind of approach used by these other specialists. Perhaps this school was fortunate in being served by doctors and psychotherapists willing to explain their findings in a manner helpful to the teaching staff, and to suggest ways in which the school could help. Yet there must be many such doctors and Child Guidance teams, as well as educational psychologists, and many other teachers who are able to appreciate work in fields other than their own. It is neither necessary nor desirable for teachers to feel that they must, or ought to, know everything about a child on the medical or psychiatric side – any more than it is necessary for doctors to know the details of the teacher's systematic teaching of language skills, or how she organizes her classroom and day. It is important for each to respect the work of the other, however; and this is surely possible even to young teachers and newly-qualified doctors. Co-operation with other specialists in regard to the well-being of a particular child is likely to teach both doctor and teacher more about each other's disciplines, and in a legitimate and acceptable context, than is the reading of the test-books or attempts on the part of either to do the other's job. This latter, in fact, would be most undersirable, and the point cannot be too often stressed.

This book could be called a specialist one – but it is concerned with the specialism of teaching, including that of being able to draw a 'difficult' child into the life of his school in order that he may become a more adequate person. It therefore deals with things as they are – large classes, ordinary teachers with no specialist training, normal equipment and no extra help. It may well be that a teacher using all those skills mentioned, and which are not beyond most, is better able to give something of value to each child in a class of forty than inadequate teachers could ever give to two classes of twenty. From the spontaneous, well-organized, open-minded and generous teacher something 'rubs off', no matter how many children have to share her; from a teacher whose heart is not in her job, who is idle, or close-minded, or ill-supported by her head teacher and colleagues, nothing of value can, whether she has a class of fifteen or fifty. The teachers whose work is described in this book were certainly in no advtantageous position, and their achievements can be accepted as those possible to almost any teacher.

Once more, and for the last time, it must be reiterated that a course of action found effiacious with one child will not transfer to another, and an attempt to use courses described here as 'ready-made' remedies to apparently similar cases will end in failure. It is even possible that real harm could be done to children by such doctrinaire practice, and it must be appreciated that while principles of approach can be indicated, detailed advice about someone else's 'problem children' cannot possibly be given in any book.

It is a Herculean task to meet the everyday needs of normal children in the ordinary classroom situation, demanding skills and dedication required of few. Yet many teachers not only rise to this demand but go further – in helping children whose needs are greater than and different from the normal. If we wish to reduce the number of retarded, delinquent, neurotic and simply inadequate people in our society it might be worthwhile to rethink our principles of approach to children in special need in the Infants' school. There is no proof that our efforts will be successful; but it is surely part of a teacher's faith that they are worth making.

Bibliography

Aichorn, A. *Wayword Youth* Hogarth Press (1957)
  Delinquency and Child Guidance Hogarth Press (1964)
Allport, G. *Pattern and Growth in Personality* Holt, Rine-
  hart and Winston (1963)
Barton Hall, M. *Psychiatric Examination of the Schoolchild*
  Edward Arnold (1947)
Benedict, R. *Patterns of Culture* (1935) Routledge P'back
  (1961)
Bettelheim, B. *Truants from Life* The Free Press: Illinois
  (1955)
Birch, H. G. *Brain Damage in Children: the biological and
  social aspects* Williams and Wilkins, Co. (1964)
Blyth, W. A. L. *English Primary Education* (2 vols.) Rout-
  ledge (1965)
Bowley, A. *The Natural Development of the Child* (4th
  Edition) E. and S. Livingstone (1963)
Boyce, E. R. *Play in the Infant School* Methuen (4th Ed.
  1951)
Buhler, C. *Childhood Problems and the Teacher* Routledge
  (1953)
  From Birth to Maturity Routledge (1935)
Burn, M. *Mr. Lyward's Answer* Hamish Hamilton (1956)
Carmichael, L. (Ed.) *Manual of Child Psychology* (2nd Edi-
  tion) John Wiley (1963)
Carthy, J. D. and Ebling, F. J. (Eds.) *The Natural History of
  Aggression* Academic Press (1964)
Cattell, R. *The Scientific Analysis of Personality* Penguin
  Books (1965)
Central Advisory Council for Education *Children and their
  Primary Schools* H.M.S.O. (1967)
Cleugh, M. F. *The Slow Learner* Methuen (1957)
  Teaching the Slow Learner Methuen (1964)
Comfort, A. *Sex in Society* (1950) pub. in Pelican Books
  (1964)

Authority and Delinquency in the Modern State Routledge (1950)

Dollard, J. et al *Frustration and Aggression* Yale U.P. (1939)

Douglas, J. W. B. *The Home and the School* Macgibbon & Kee (1964)

Erikson, E. *Childhood and Society* Hogarth Press (1965)

Ewing, Sir A. *Educational Guidance and the Deaf Child* Manchester U.P. (1957)

Fenichel, O. *The Psychoanalytic Theory of Neurosis* Routledge (1946)

Floud, J., Halsey, A. H. and Anderson, C. A. *Education, Economy and Society* Free Press of Glencoe (1963)

Floud, J., Halsey, A. H. and Martin, F. M. *Social Class and Educational Opportunity* Heinemann (1957)

Freeman, H. E. and Simmons, O. G. *The Mental Patient Comes Home* John Wiley (1963)

Freud, A. *The Psycho-Analytical Treatment of Children* Imago (1946)

Freud, S. *Introductory Lectures* (10th Impression) Geo. Allen and Unwin (1961)

New Introductory Lectures on Psycho-Analysis (4th Impression) Hogarth Press (1949)

Three Essays on the Theory of Sexuality (1st English Edition) Alcuin Press (1949)

An Outline of Psycho-Analysis (4th Impression) Hogarth Press (1949)

The Problem of Anxiety Norton, N. Y. (1936)

Gabriel, J. *Children Growing Up* U.L.P. (1964)

Gardner, D. E. M. *The Education of Young Children* Methuen (1956)

The Rôle of the Teacher in the Infants' and Nursery School Pergamon Press (1966)

Gesell, A. *The First Five Years of Life* Methuen (Reprint 1954)

Gesell, A. and Ilg, F. L. *The Child from Five to Ten* Hamish Hamilton (1946)

Glueck, S. and E. T. *Unraveling Juvenile Delinquency* Commonwealth Fund (1950)

Glueck, S. (Ed.) *The Problem of Delinquency* Houghton Mifflin (1959)

Glueck, S. and E. T. *Family Environment and Delinquency* Routledge (1962)

Goldman, J. *Selected at Six* Hodder and Stoughton (1963)

Griffiths, R. *The Abilities of Babies* U.L.P. (1954)

Hebb, D. O. *A Textbook of Psychology* W. B. Saunders (1958)

Hilgard, E. *Introduction to Psychology* Methuen (1957)

Horney, K. *Our Inner Conflicts* N. Y. Norton (1945)

Hunt, R. McV. *Intelligence and Experience* Ronald Press (1964)

Illingworth, R. S. *The Normal Schoolchild* Heinemann (1964)

Isaacs, S. *The Educational Guidance of the Schoolchild* Evans Bros. (1937)

   Intellectual Growth in Young Children (1930) Routledge (7th Impress. 1960)

   Social Development in Young Children (1933) Routledge (7th Impress. 1952)

Jackson, B. *Streaming: An Education System in Miniature* Routledge (1964)

Jackson, B. and Marsden, D. *Education and the Working Class* Routledge (1962)

Jackson, L. *Aggression and Its Interpretation* Methuen (1954)

Jackson, L. and Todd, A.M. *Child Ttreatment and the Therapy of Play* Methuen (1948)

Jersild, A. T. et al *Children's Fears, Dreams, Likes, etc.* Child Dev. Monograph No. 12 (1933)

Jersild, A. T. and Holmes, F. B. *Children's Fears* Child Dev. Monograph No. 20 (1935)

Kaplan, L. *Mental Health and Human Relations in Education* Harper and Row (1959)

Kennedy, M. V. and Somerset, H. C. D. *Bringing up Crippled Children* New Zealand Council for Ed. Research (1951)

Lewis, H. *Deprived Children* Oxford U.P. (1954)

Lewis, M. M. *Language, Thought and Personality in Infancy and Childhood* Geo. Harrap (1963)

Lorenz, K. *On Aggression* Methuen (1966)

Lowenfeld, M. *Play in Childhood* Gollancz (1938)

Malinowski, B. *Sex and Repression in Savage Society* (1927) Routledge (1960)

May, D. *Children in the Nursery School* Bristol Inst. of Ed. (1963)

Mays, J. B. *Education and the Urban Child* Liverpool U. P. (1962)

Mead, M. *Male and Female* Pelican (1964)

Mellor, E. *Education through Experience in the Infant School Years* Blackwell (1963 Ed.)

Neill, A. S. *Summerhill: a Radical Approach to Child Rearing* Gollancz (1962)

Newson, J. and E. *Patterns of Infant Care in an Urban Community* (1963) Penguin Books (1965)

Packard, V. *The Hidden Persuaders* (1957) Penguin Special (1960)
The Status Seekers (1959) Pelican Books (1961)

Peters, R. *Ethics and Education* Geo. Allen and Unwin (1966)

Piaget, J. *The Language and Thought of the Child* (1923) Routledge (3rd Ed. 1959)
The Moral Judgment of the Child (1932) Routledge (4th Imp. 1965)
The Origin of Intelligence in the Child Routledge (1953)
The Child's Conception of Number (1941) Routledge (1952)

Plowden Report *See under C.A.C.E.*

Robertson, J. *Young Children in Hospital* Tavistock (1958)

Rutter, M. *Children of Sick Parents: an environmental and psychiatric study* Oxford U. P. (1966)

Schonell, F. E. *Educating Spastic Children* Oliver and Boyd (1956)

Smith, W. C. *The Stepchild* Univ. of Chicago Press (1953)

Storr, A. *The Integrity of the Personality* Heinemann (1960)

Stott, D. H. *Studies of Troublesome Children* Tavistock (1966)
Delinquency and Human Nature Carnegie U.K. Trust (1962)
The Bristol Social Adjustment Guides U.L.P. (1956)

Suttie, I. *The Origins of Love and Hate* Kegan Paul (1948)

Tanner, J. *Education and Physical Growth* U.L.P. (1961)

U.N.E.S.C.O. *Education and Mental Health* Harrap (1953)

Vernon, M. D. *Backwardness in Reading* Cambridge U.P. (1957)

Watson, T. J. *The Education of Hearing-Handicapped Children* U.L.P. (1967)

Wilkins, L. T. *Delinquent Generations* H.M.S.O. (1961)

Willmot, P. and Young, M. *Family and Kinship in East London* (1957) Penguin Books (1962)
Family and Class in a London Suburb Routledge (1960)

Wills, W. D. *Common Sense about Young Offenders* Gollancz (1962)
Throw Away Thy Rod Gollancz (1960)

Wilson, H. *Delinquency and Child Neglect* Geo. Allen and Unwin (1962)

Winnicott, D. W. *The Child and the Family* Tavistock (1957)
The Child and the Outside World Tavistock (1957)
The Family and Individual Development Tavistock (1965)

Wootton, B. *Social Science and Social Pathology* Ward (1959)

Wynn, W. *Fatherless Families* Michael Joseph (1964)

Journals and Periodicals:

British Journal of Educational Psychology; British Journal of Sociology; Education; Educational Research; Educational Review; Maternal and Child Care; New Society; Special Education

Index

Also available in Fount Paperbacks

Something Beautiful for God
MALCOLM MUGGERIDGE

'For me, Mother Teresa of Calcutta embodies Christian love in action. Her face shines with the love of Christ on which her whole life is centred. *Something Beautiful for God* is about her and the religious order she has instituted.'   *Malcolm Muggeridge*

Instrument of Thy Peace
ALAN PATON

'Worthy of a permanent place on the short shelf of enduring classics of the life of the Spirit.'
Henry P. van Dusen, Union Theological Seminary

Sing a New Song
THE PSALMS IN TODAY'S ENGLISH VERSION

These religious poems are of many kinds: there are hymns of praise and worship of God; prayers for help, protection, and salvation; pleas for forgiveness; songs of thanksgiving for God's blessings; and petitions for the punishment of enemies. This translation of the *Psalms in Today's English Version* has the same freshness and clarity of language, the same accuracy of scholarship based on the very best originals available as *Good News for Modern Man* and *The New Testament in Today's English Version*.

The Gospel According to Peanuts
ROBERT L. SHORT

This book has made a lasting appeal to people of all denominations and none. It has been read and enjoyed by literally millions of people. A wonderfully imaginative experiment in Christian communication.

Also available in Fount Paperbacks

Bible Stories
DAVID KOSSOFF

'To my mind there is no doubt that these stories make the Bible come alive. Mr Kossoff is a born story-teller. He has the gift of making the old stories new.'   *William Barclay*

The Book of Witnesses
DAVID KOSSOFF

'The little stories are fascinating in the warm humanity they reveal. Right from the first one, the reader is enthralled . . . Bringing the drama of the New Testament into our daily lives with truly shattering impact.'   *Religious Book News*

The Bible Story
WILLIAM NEIL

'Like all his work it is hardly to be faulted, and I have never read so splendid a conspectus of the whole Bible. It will help a great many people to get their ideas sorted out. William Neil writes with such authority and lucidity that it can hardly fail.'   *J. B. Phillips*

The Plain Man Looks at the Bible
WILLIAM NEIL

This book is meant for the plain man who would like to know what to think about the Bible today. The first part deals with what the Bible is and what it is not. The second part shows that the Bible is also a record of certain things that happened.